POSTMODERNISM AND THE SOC

Postmodernism and the Social Sciences

Edited by

Joe Doherty
Lecturer in Geography, University of St Andrews

Elspeth Graham
Lecturer in Geography, University of St Andrews

and

Mo Malek
Lecturer in Management, University of St Andrews

MACMILLAN

First published 1992 by
MACMILLAN ACADEMIC AND PROFESSIONAL LTD
Houndmills, Basingstoke, Hampshire RG21 2XS
and London
Companies and representatives
throughout the world

ISBN 0-333-53452-2 (hc)
ISBN 0-333-53453-0 (pbk)

A catalogue record for this book is
available from the British Library.

Typeset by Typeset Gallery, Malaysia
Printed in Hong Kong

Contents

Preface

In August 1989, 70 or so scholars gathered at the University of St Andrews for a conference entitled 'Postmodernism and the Social Sciences'. The conference was designed to provide an interdisciplinary forum at which researchers interested in the impact of postmodernism in their own disciplinary traditions would have the opportunity to share their findings and speculations with other social scientists to mutual benefit and in the interests of furthering understanding of the 'post' phenomenon. The chapters of this book – with the exception of Chapter 1 which was specially commissioned – are drawn from the papers presented at the conference. Unfortunately, space limitations have prevented the inclusion of all the conference papers; difficult choices had to be made and we hope that the papers not included will see publication elsewhere. The contributions which are included here cover all the social sciences represented at the conference and, we think, convey the breadth and diversity of the views expressed. They also encapsulate the spirit of the conference, identified by several participants as 'critical postmodernism', a characterisation which we are happy to endorse. This is certainly the theme which we, as editors, have stressed and attempted to elaborate in our Introduction and concluding contribution.

Our thanks are due especially to the contributors for their prompt responses to our requests for revisions and rewrites; we hope the final product does justice to their efforts. In addition, whether represented here or not, we would like to take this opportunity to express our thanks and appreciation to all the conference participants for a stimulating and instructive three days of discussion and debate. The conference was made possible by the provision of financial support from the British Academy, the Institute of British Geographers and the Research Committee of the Faculty of Arts, St Andrews University, and ran as smoothly as it did due to the secretarial and administrative expertise of Pam Lee. We need finally to record our thanks to David Riches, an initiator and co-organiser of the conference who decided reluctantly, because of other demands on his time, not to participate in the editing of this book; his early hard work and his continuing support for the project have been much appreciated.

Notes on the Contributors

John Bowers is a lecturer in psychology at the University of Nottingham. In addition to postmodernism, his research interests include the foundations of cognitivism in the psychological/social sciences, the relations between humans and machines, theories of discourse, and the role of formalism and quantification in science. With BAMN, he also composes and performs electronic dance music – *The Deep Joy E.P.* (Simulation Records) is their latest contribution to postmodern culture.

Erica Burman teaches developmental and educational psychology at Manchester Polytechnic. Her research interests are in the areas of discourse analysis, feminism and subjectivity. She has published articles and chapters on feminist critiques of deconstruction, discourse analysis and developmental psychology, edited *Feminists and Psychological Practice* (1990), and is currently preparing a textbook, *Deconstructing Developmental Psychology*.

Joe Doherty is a lecturer in the Department of Geography at the University of St Andrews. His research interests include the process of urbanisation in developed and underdeveloped countries and the operation of the Scottish housing market. He is currently co-editor of the international geographical journal *Antipode* and co-director of the Dundee-based Joint Centre of Scottish Housing Research.

Sheila Dow is a Reader in economics at the University of Stirling. Her research interests include methodology, history of thought, post-Keynesian economics, monetary economics and regional economics. Relevant publications include *Macroeconomic Thought: A Methodological Approach* (1985) and 'Beyond Dualism', *Cambridge Journal of Economics* (1990).

Richard Fardon is Lecturer in West African and Caribbean anthropology at the School of Oriental and African Studies in the University of London. His interests include the ethnography of West Africa and contemporary anthropological theory. He has published two ethnographies on the Chamba peoples, *Raiders and Refugees* (1988) and *Between God, the Dead and the Wild* (1990), and edited collections on anthropological theory, including *Power and Knowledge* (1985) and *Localizing Strategies* (1990).

Elspeth Graham is a lecturer in the Department of Geography at the University of St Andrews. She is the author of several articles on conceptual and philosophical issues in geography and is currently Chair of the History and Philosophy Study Group of the Institute of British Geographers. She is also Director of the St Andrews Centre for the Social Sciences.

John Haldane is Reader in Moral Philosophy and Director of the Centre for Philosophy and Public Affairs in the University of St Andrews. He is also a Visiting Lecturer in the School of Architecture, Polytechnic of Central London. He has published widely in such journals as *Analysis, British Journal of Aesthetics, Philosophy, Philosophical Review* and *Philosophy and Phenomenological Research*.

Mark Hoffman is a lecturer in international relations at the London School of Economics. His research interests include international relations theory, and conflict and peace studies. He is co-editor (with Nick Rengger) of *Beyond the Inter-Paradigm Debate: Critical Theory and International Relations* and co-editor (with Ian Forbes) of *International Relations, Political Theory and the Ethics of Intervention*.

Scott Lash is Reader in Sociology at Lancaster University. He is co-author (with John Urry) of *The End of Organised Capitalism*. His most recent publication is *Sociology and Postmodernism* (1990).

Mo Malek graduated from London University and lectured at Queen Mary College before moving to St Andrews in 1981 where he has been a lecturer in economics. His area of interest includes political economy of development and methodology of social sciences and his most recent publications are: *Overseas Aid* (1989, with D. Schumacher and R. S. May) and (as editor) *European Development Aid* (1991).

Ian Parker is a lecturer in social and abnormal psychology at Manchester Polytechnic. His teaching and research interests are in discourse analysis and psychoanalysis. He is co-editor, with John Shotter, of *Deconstructing Social Psychology* (1990), and author of two books on critical psychology: *The Crisis in Modern Social Psychology, and How to End It* (1989) and *Discourse Dynamics: Critical Analysis for Social and Individual Psychology* (1991).

Nick Rengger is a lecturer in politics at the University of Bristol. His main research and teaching interests are in international political theory, political theory and intellectual history. He has just finished a book, *Tradition and Transition in International Theory*, and has edited a book with Mark Hoffman, *Beyond the Inter-Paradigm Debate: Critical Theory and International Relations* (to be published in 1991).

Robert Shields is the author of *Places on the Margin: Alternate Geographies of Modernity* (1990), and is researching and editing *Life Style Shopping: The Subject of Consumption*, a book on the individual, the public sphere and shopping centres as sites of changing culture. He is a research associate of the Centre d'Etudes sur l'Actuel et le Quotidien, Université de Paris V – Sorbonne, and holds a postdoctoral research fellowship at Carleton University, Ottawa.

Neil Smith is Professor and Chair of the Department of Geography at Rutgers University. His research interests include space and social theory, history of geography, and urbanisation. Author of *Uneven Development* (2nd edn, 1991) and co-editor of *Gentrification and the City* (1986), he is completing a biographical treatment of the imperial geographer, Isaiah Bowman.

Introduction: The Context and Language of Postmodernism
Elspeth Graham, Joe Doherty and Mo Malek

*No matter how troubling it may be,
the landscape of the postmodern
surrounds us. It simultaneously
delimits and opens our horizons. It's
our problem and our hope.*

(Huyssen, 1988: 221)

THE RECENT BEGINNINGS OF POSTMODERNISM

In any collection of essays on the topic of postmodernism, it is tempting to dispense with an editorial introduction and not only because it is a difficult topic to introduce. The collection in this volume is based on a conference held at the University of St Andrews in August 1989. The aim of that meeting was to bring together social scientists from different disciplinary backgrounds to explore the common 'problem' of postmodernism. What does it mean? What are the individual social sciences making of it? Can they talk to each other about it? The results were both interesting and exhilarating with many voices saying different things and probably generating more controversy than agreement. What follows is a selection of essays covering all the major social sciences. They display a wide variety of responses to postmodernism. Herein lies the temptation to let the reader loose immediately to experience the variety, the fragmentation, the differences and perhaps the confusions which have become as much features of the literature on postmodernism as they are said to be of postmodernism itself. Such an editorial approach would certainly be in tune with the mood of postmodern writings. Yet we have decided not to take this course for two reasons. First, although the volume is not intended to be a celebration of postmodernism, neither is it intended to be a sustained critique. Its task is rather to contribute to an important debate within the social sciences by examining the impact of postmodernist ideas in their (modernist) academic locales. It is still the case that postmodernism has not captured the imaginations of the majority of social scientists and that the concern of the

1

authors in this volume with the issues it raises may be unfamiliar to many, certainly within the disciplinary mainstreams of psychology and economics. The struggle with new ways of thinking is always difficult to chart and some preliminary guidance hardly seems out of place.

Secondly, the literature of postmodernism is both confusing and confused. That is to say, for those unfamiliar with this literature, its understanding requires the learning of a new language. Notions of *'différance'*, 'intertextuality', 'reflexivity' or even 'discourse' (in its postmodern usage) are not self-explanatory to the modern mind. Not only are their meanings frequently opaque but even those who use them least self-consciously often leave their meanings vague. When the author of a recent article describes this as a 'particularly confused part of the contemporary intellectual landscape' (Hudson, 1989: 142), it would be difficult to show that he was exaggerating. Meanings are not only altered as part of the switch to postmodernism but in the process adopt an apparent fluidity which taxes clear thinking. The literature is full of conundrums with plenty scope for sorting out or tidying up. Thus if, in what follows, the editors' lingering modernist preconceptions come to the surface, this is peculiarly appropriate, for it will only reflect the current state of affairs in the social sciences at large. To completely discard the language and preconceptions of modernism, should it be deemed desirable or unavoidable, is likely to be a painful business.

Perhaps the first question we should pose in laying the groundwork is: 'What is postmodernism?', though it will arguably remain unanswered at the end of the book. Jean-François Lyotard (1984a), a major voice in contemporary postmodern writing, devoted an essay to 'Answering the Question' but hardly resolved the matter. One of the reasons for such difficulty is the chameleon-like nature of 'the postmodern', popping up in different habitats displaying subtle shifts in what is presented to public gaze. Further, the compass of postmodernism is daunting. The literature requires a heady journey through continental philosophies, literary theory, architecture, aesthetics and poetry, as well as social theory. The feeling of drowning can be difficult to dispel. Even the atmosphere conveyed by such writings can be unsettling for it is an atmosphere of celebration and play underpinned by a fundamental suspicion of any all-encompassing rationality. Indeed it might be (and often is) taken as an identifying characteristic of postmodernism that it challenges and rejects the very basis of modernist rationalism. In many of its manifestations postmodernism is seen as a response to the 'crisis' of the Enlightenment Project, a project with its roots in the writings of the pre-Enlightenment philosopher Descartes. The Enlightenment had advanced rationalism, universalism and transcendental forms of thinking. Postmodernism challenges such totalising discourses. The enormity of this challenge is difficult to comprehend partly because its success would remove so much that is familiar in our (modernist) ways of thinking and partly because the transformation in practice could not be as dramatic as the stark contrast between the two -isms might have us believe. In the social sciences, as in the arts, postmodernism is seeping into the collective consciousness bit by bit. Its transmutations en route mean that common threads, just as you think you have grasped them, often disappear. Searching for a clear answer to the question: 'What is postmodernism?' may turn out to be somewhat like hunting the dodo but it is far too early to abandon the attempt. Besides, there is still much to be learned from taking a closer look at what passes for postmodernism in the literature.

We shall start with architecture, not only because it provides one of the earliest uses of the term in 1949 in a reference to 'the post-modern house' (Hudnut, 1949: ix, 108) but also because architecture provides us with one of the most substantial expressions of postmodernism in the built environment. If postmodernism is all around us as some authors claim, then we can see it best in the concrete productions of the architectural imagination. In architecture, the term 'postmodern' is used to describe a new architecture of the 1970s and 1980s which broke with the tenets of the previously dominant architectural style, modernism. In this sense postmodernism replaces that which went before and derives its identity from what it rejects. This relational definition of the postmodern introduces a common thread in the wider literature where the emphasis on its being a *post*-phenomenon and a break with the immediate past is both explicit and implicit. In architecture the modernist Utopias of Mies van der Rohe or Charles-Edouard Jeanneret (pseudonym Le Corbusier) are replaced by the mixed imagery of Philip Johnson's AT&T highrise in New York with its neoclassical references, its Roman colonnades and its Chippendale pediment. It is important to note here that the change from the modern to the postmodern is not one of superficial decoration or even of built form, for the change involves a reaction to and an overthrowing of a complex conception of the architect's task. When the prize-winning modern architecture of the Pruitt-Igoe flats in St Louis was deliberately destroyed in July 1972 because no one wanted to live there, it was not a mere design fault that was blamed. It was the modernists' dream of architecture as a pure art in which form is paramount that had failed the litmus test of practical living. The dramatic destruction is taken by many to symbolise the end of modernism in architecture with its hostility to mass culture. The postmodernists seek to replace the élitism of modernism with a new philosophy of architecture, one more in sympathy with pop culture.

It is always easier to say what postmodernism is not than what it is, and postmodernism in architecture is no exception. It is emphatically *not* modernism. But whereas there is a style of building in which form and materials are identifiably modern, the question of a postmodern style is a good deal more contentious. Some would argue that in the return to the vernacular which is characteristic of the reaction against the modern and in the borrowing of older, classical references, the so-called postmodern architects are merely harking back to a premodern era. Modernism may simply have been a detour which has left architecture where it was, albeit facing in the opposite direction. In this sense it is the old which replaces the recently new and *post*modernism is equally *pre*modernism. This, of course, is not the whole story. Nor is it our intention to pursue that story here. Our interest is in the lessons for the social scientist of which there are two. First, we should expect postmodernism to be a rejection and replacement of whatever we characterise as modernism. Secondly, the prefix 'after' inevitably requires some sort of periodisation. It is this periodisation that is likely to prove highly problematic most especially because of the ease with which the conceptual is confused with the historical. It is all too easy to conflate the superseding of one set of ideas by another (a conceptual matter) and a sequence of events (who actually believed what when) in historical time. The built environment provides us with the best metaphor here for what we can see, when we look around a city, is a mixture of the pre-modern, the modern and the postmodern with one or other being dominant depending upon our viewpoint. Taken as a whole, most cities remain a jumble of architectural styles. Yet the task of unravelling the chronology of building remains distinct from the task of identifying the schools of architecture represented in the built form.

The problems of defining postmodernism are certainly not confined to architecture. Indeed the elaboration of postmodernist ideas in architecture has been, in part, an inherited venture. Discussions of postmodernism began in earnest in the circles of literary criticism in the 1960s when a small group of critics began penning obituaries to modernism. Postmodern fiction grew into a literary movement and with it a new understanding of literary works began to alter the previously accepted conception of literary analysis and criticism. This new understanding owed much to Jacques Derrida's reading of the nineteenth-century philologist Ferdinand de Saussure. Derrida, whose name has become synonymous with the postmodern in many circles, put forward a view of intertextuality which rejected the modernist grounding of language. In Derrida's conception, every literary text is penetrated with traces of other texts so that neither is the single text itself the ultimate locus of meaning, nor does the author determine the meaning of the text. Thus language, the language of the text, becomes the focal concern; and postmodern literary theorists turn to the philosophies of Ludwig Wittgenstein and Martin Heidegger who, in different ways, underline the primacy of language and its essential groundlessness. For example, Heidegger's view of language is that it leaves us with the world exactly as we find it, given in language, once we rid language of the metaphysics which has falsified our understanding of it. This is the attack on the Enlightenment Project again (or at least a retreat from its attempts to ground understanding in certainty) which Lyotard (1984a) expresses as an incredulity towards metanarratives. It leaves literary 'criticism' in what has been called 'the self-enclosed play space of language' (Thiher, 1984) to deconstruct the text. How this deconstruction is achieved is less important in the present context than the recognition that postmodernism in literary theory involves a radical break with modernism both in terms of how the task of literary analysis proceeds and the object of that analysis. The text has become the object and the task becomes the disentangling, or deconstruction, of the free play of *différance* in the discourses that inhabit the writing. No one discourse is given privilege over another and analysis becomes celebration as the old assumptions of categorical priorities fall away. This, it seems, is where postmodernism becomes associated with fragmentation and 'other voices', an association carried over into the social sciences. A parallel is evident in Jacques Lacan's rewriting of Freud, for example, which seeks to replace classical Freudian ego psychology and interprets the Unconscious as 'the discourse of the other'. Here Lacan is concerned both with the determination of the subject by language and with the role played by the analyst's interventions during psychoanalysis. Again we do not need the full story here to gain an insight into the tremendous shift that postmodernism requires in ways of thinking about language, discourse and text.

If the text becomes the object of study and the text is a tissue of all other texts, then the ultimate locus of meaning becomes the culture itself as encoded in language (Thiher, 1984). There is nothing beyond language to confer meaning on the text. Even the author has no privileged position in the matter. This in turn has abundant implications for the social sciences, especially those in which discourse might become (or has become) the object of study. Postmodern anthropology, on this account, becomes 'the study of man – "talking" ' (Tyler, 1987: 171). But, more importantly still, the postmodern becomes much more than the description of a literary movement or an architectural school. It becomes a cultural condition of Western societies.

a condition in which the intelligibilities of western historical experience are subverted, in which traditional meanings and values are destroyed, in which referentiality fails and all finalities appear suspect and exhausted.   (Hudson, 1989)

Since Western culture must lie somewhere near the heart of Western social science any such transformation from the modern to the postmodern cannot be ignored. Further, its association with other transformations, though contested, must be understood if social science is to comprehend its own object and task. Post-structuralism, post-industrialism and even post-history appear to inform postmodernism in some of its various guises. To understand why this is we need to take a closer look at the languages of modernism and postmodernism and their uses in contemporary social science.

FROM MODERNISM TO POSTMODERNISM

The problems associated with defining postmodernism are compounded by the fact that its definition is predicated on the meaning of modernism. Modernism is not so much disputed territory, though there are disputes, as it is a complex phenomenon with interweaving phases, trajectories and tendencies. If postmodernism is 'after' modernism, then an understanding of the latter is a prerequisite for understanding the former. Yet the social science literature is, arguably, a poor basis for providing such an understanding, for in the lexicons of social science the language of modernism is poorly and only selectively represented. Those areas of modernism cultivated in and emanating from the worlds of literature and art are little known or studied. The terms modernism, modernity and – especially – modernisation, when employed by social scientists, invariably emphasise the social, the economic and the technological with, at best, occasional genuflexions in the direction of culture (Berman, 1982; Hebdige, 1989). Modernisation, for social science, refers principally to the economic, social (including political) and technological innovations and developments associated with Western society over the past 400 years, and thus with the rise of capitalism. Modernity is used to refer to the transformed nature of life under capitalism, studied most intensely in relation to the processes of nineteenth- and twentieth-century urbanisation which gave rise to the major cities and metropolitan centres of Europe and North America. Modernism, until recently the least frequently referenced of these terms, refers to the wave of experimental movements in the arts, culture and philosophy associated with modernisation and modernity. To fully comprehend the nature of modernism (and hence postmodernism) we need to move beyond the purely social and economic processes associated with modernisation and explore their relationship with what is, for many in the social sciences, the relatively unfamiliar territory of culture. In a brief but insightful paper presented in 1987 at Bristol University Raymond Williams did just that.

In this paper Williams posed the question: 'When was modernism?' (Williams, 1989). He suggested that the term 'modern' first appeared and began to be used more or less simultaneously with 'now' in the late sixteenth century to mark off that period from both mediaeval and ancient times. By the eighteenth century the term and its derivatives – 'modernist', 'modernise' and 'modernism' – were being used widely to suggest a dynamic, changing and updating process. They continued to be used throughout the nineteenth century to imply, favourably, a process of improvement and progress. By the middle of the twentieth century, how-ever, the term modernism had, according to Williams, very clearly taken on a retrospective meaning, referencing a far-from-homogeneous cultural movement which flourished between 1890 and the 1940s. However, to complicate matters, as Williams himself observed, a new phase of modernism emerged after the Second World War with features quite distinct from preceding phases. Williams in suggesting such a periodisation, in common with many others who have dissected modernism (e.g. Berman, 1982 and Harvey, 1989), displays an implicit assumption, contra some postmodernists, that it is possible to identify a 'period style'; that political, economic, social and cultural phenomena congeal at various times in a distinctive manner to form an identifiable historical 'phase'. Such periodisations have their problems for they introduce a simplicity and neatness which, while useful didatically, have also the potential for distortion and misrepresentation of a complex history. Modernism, to use Wittengenstein's metaphor, is like a spun thread which gains its strength, not from a continuous strand that runs its entire length, but from the overlapping and entwining of many separate fibres (quoted in Thiher, 1984: 201).

Notwithstanding such issues, an unravelling of the skein of modernism has more often than not required the imposition by commentators of an analytical structure as an aid to understanding. Both Berman and Harvey, for instance, employ a fourfold periodisation which they claim captures the main trends and currents of modernism: the Enlightenment; a post-1848, aesthetic phase; the heroic interwar period; and the high modernism of the post-1945 period. The Enlightenment, a name attached specifically to an eighteenth-century philosophical movement, is more generally associated with the so called 'Age of Reason' which has its beginning in the seventeenth century. With the advancement of scientific knowledge which characterised this period, hitherto accepted beliefs were questioned and the traditional spiritual and religious authority of the state and, especially, the church undermined. In the hands of such scholars as Newton, Locke, Pascal and Descartes, reason, rationality and science came to be seen as the basis of human progress and advancement; progress and advancement closely identified, especially in the work of Rousseau, not only with an increase in knowledge but also with individual liberty and equality. The fundamental philosophical notion introduced at this time, which in many ways can be regarded as the hallmark of modernism throughout its succeeding phases, was a belief in the essential order of things; that under the seeming surface chaos of the world, of society, there exists a rationality, a basic truth that can be identified and harnessed for human good. The Enlightenment was a period of overt and extravagant optimism that such truth could be identified and such progress achieved.

The post-1848, aesthetic phase of modernism issued a challenge to the monolithic enlightenment concept of rationality and science as the route to understanding and truth. In its place the notion that there are many ways of discovering eternal truths was proposed; a trend sometimes referred to as 'relativism' or 'perspectivism' (multiple perspectives). Harvey suggests that such a challenge was implicit much earlier in, for example, Rousseau's rephrasing of Descartes famous aphorism as 'I feel therefore I am'. This, Harvey (1989: 19) argues, signalled a shift 'from a rationalist and instrumentalist to a more consciously aesthethic strategy for realising enlightenment aims'. In this post-1848 period, across a range of scientific and, especially, cultural endeavour, experimentation and innovation gave rise throughout Western Europe and North America to a flowering of artistic, literary, philosophical and political output which faltered only with the outbreak of the First World War. The names of the contributors to these developments are among the stars of modernism: Nietzsche, Marx, Lenin, Weber, Baudelaire, Joyce, Pound, Manet, Picasso, Saussure and Einstein. A common thread running through much of this work is a sense of scepticism and indeed pessimism, contrasting with the optimism of the preceding Enlightenment. This thread is closely associated with a loss of faith in the ability of science and reason, particularly in the form of industrial capitalism, to realise those ideals of individual liberty and equality embedded in the Enlightenment project. The political upheavals and trends of the time, from the revolutions of 1848 and the Paris Commune to the struggles for trade union recognition, were the active politics of resistance and protest which paralleled the outpouring of philosophical, cultural and political insights and analysis. The maelstrom of activity that Berman (1982) identifies as characteristic of the *fin de siècle* provided an exciting intellectual ferment, but left the nature of the eternal truth as illusory as ever.

The so-called heroic period of modernism followed the traumas of the First World War. This period is represented by the search for a 'hero', a 'myth' which would harness again human endeavour towards Enlightenment goals, transcending the barbarism of the 'war to end all wars'; a myth which would cauterise the wounds of war and place again the concepts of progress and achievement on the agenda of human history. The myth took on various forms. For some artists (such as Picasso, Eliot) it remained nebulous and insubstantial, an eclectic amalgam striving for universal expression which shunned concrete social form. For others, such as the Bauhaus movement of the 1920s, it crystallised in the concept of the 'aesthetic in the machine'; the cojoining of 'beauty' and 'rationality' in the attempt to harness the order and efficiency of technology to socially useful ends. Le Corbusier's characterisation of housing as 'machines for living in' similarly encapsulated some of this mythology. Elsewhere these concepts of order and rationality took on a darker hue. In the hands of the Italian Futurists the 'myth' moved on from a mere categorisation of a set of desired objectives to emerge, under the authoritarianism of Mussolini's Fascism, as a 'hero' intent on imposing itself on society at whatever destructive cost to the old order or alternative scenarios. A comparable 'hero' was to be found in the concept of socialist realism which underpinned many of the cultural and artistic endeavours of the Soviet Union and East Europe during these interwar years and, under the brutally destructive tutelage of Stalin, was harnessed to totalitarian ends.

The years following the Second World War ushered in the fourth, high modernist phase; a phase which coincided with the world-wide dominance of the USA and the international penetration of capitalism. In a mood emulating that which succeeded the First World War, Enlightenment optimism was revived and combined with a form of authoritarianism in which progress and advancement become the concerns of an élite of planners, artists, architects and intellectuals. The preceding phases of modernism, and especially *fin de siècle* modernism of the aesthetic period, had been characterised by a high degree of experimentation, innovation and challenge to the existing order. In its high phase, modernism relinquished this avant garde role and was employed in the service of the status quo. The establishment, in the form of international corporate enterprises, the state and other forms of institutionalised power, embraced and took over modernism. As Williams (1989: 51) observed, the avant garde texts of yesteryear became established readings; marginalised artists became the classics of organised teaching; modernism was 'cannonised'. Modernism, quintessentially the search for the new, for alternatives, is turned against itself; in establishment hands modernism, no longer challenging the established order, negates itself, becomes anti-modernist.

Such is one version of the periodisation of modernism. It is clear even from this brief account that modernism is far from homogeneous; it has many strands. But one feature, shared by all 'modernisms', has been identified by Harvey (after Baudelaire). Modernism through its various phases, has been characterised by tension; a tension between the reality of change and of mobility on the one hand and the search for and belief in the immutable and the eternal on the other – an ordered reality behind the chaos. The search for a resolution of this tension in large measure explains much of the dynamism and experimentation which characterised the various modernist trends and tendencies. However, with the establishment takeover in the high modernist phase, it was claimed that eternal truth, the nature of ordered reality, had been identified and achieved, the myth had become real in the form of the 'American Dream', in the triumph of Western liberal democracy. The search for progress, ideological and material – and in this sense history – was at an end; the tension relieved; stasis achieved.

As Berman (1982: 29–36) vividly shows, such claims did not go uncontested. Though relatively unsubtle in reaction, as many voices were raised in opposition to as in support for high modernist conceptions. Social science, post-1945, echoes these developments. The various trajectories and trends of modernism have left their mark, the modernist heritage of social science is a methodological diversity. Postivism is the favoured methodology of high modernism; the 'objective' application of scientific method untrammelled by concern for ideology, harnessed to the value systems of Western democracies. The dissenting voices take on a variety of forms, ranging from structuralism and realism to behaviourism and humanism. What all these methodologies share, however, and what makes them 'modern', is a commitment to the search for the underlying order in society; an implicit acceptance of the desirability of identifying a 'master' narrative, a totalising discourse which will embrace a universalistic understanding of society.

From among these strands of opposition to the stultifying conceptions of high modernism emerged another and rather different voice of opposition – postmodernism. In one sense and in some versions postmodernism revives something of the 'spirit' of modernism; the avant garde/subversive, populist, anti-establishment spirit. In this account postmodernism is portrayed as another phase in the development of modernism, of modernity. But in another sense, and in other, perhaps stronger versions, it rejects modernism, challenging the search for truth, denying progress, recognising only mutability, change and fragmentation. Postmodernism by accepting change and rejecting truth appears also to offer a resolution of the tension implicit in the modernist project and thus, by rejection of its fundamental premise, seems finally to bring modernism to an end. It also offers a fundamental challenge to all modernist versions of social science.

THE DISCOURSE OF POSTMODERNITY

Social science was born of modernism and shares many of the fundamental premises of the modernist project. In so far as postmodernism challenges modernism, it thus also challenges deep routed conceptions in the social sciences. For the social scientist trying to understand this challenge, the temptation to preserve vestiges of the modern and thus fail to appreciate the depth of the challenge is always present. Postmodernism, it seems, requires a new language, a new way of thinking but a way of thinking which still has a few established signposts in the social sciences. A relative inattention to the worlds of art and literature where postmodernism is better established has tended to shelter social science from the full impact of a postmodern movement. Even with the recent upsurge of interest in postmodernism, the social sciences still have some way to go in working out new discourses of postmodernity for the various social science disciplines. The artistic and literary spheres do not always provide easy analogies in this respect and the apparent conflicts in even their better-worked-out discourses provide an array of potentially confusing possibilities for the social sciences.

The first step in learning a new language must be to master some of its basic usages. In the case of the postmodern this can constitute a major hurdle. For instance, many writers (for example, Featherstone, 1988) have drawn a distinction between postmodernity and postmodernism similar to that between modernity and modernism sketched in the preceding section. Thus postmoder*nity* is said to describe a pervasive cultural condition marking a new epoch in human affairs. Our experience is now of a *post*-industrial order and, in academia, *post*-structuralism and even *post*-history are becoming part of our contemporary conceptual baggage. Postmoder*nism*, on the other hand, is often used to label an artistic style or movement and its translation into social science discourse in this guise is more problematic. The translation is clouded by the number of different uses to which the term 'postmodernism' is put in the wider literature and the blurring of the distinction between postmodernity and postmodernism which some of these involve. Hudson (1989), for example, identifies 14 distinctively different ways in which postmodern*ity* is characterised in the international literature; while Jameson (1984) suggests that postmodern*ism* can be interpreted as the cultural logic of the consumer stage of capitalism, a 'mode of production' in which cultural production performs a very specific function and takes a specific form. Here Jameson is using the term postmodern*ism* in an epochal sense although he is careful to emphasise that his periodisation does not imply that postmodernism is homogeneous nor that it is simply another stage in the evolution of society. For the social scientist such uncertainties of meaning can be disconcerting, but it is clear that 'postmodernity' as a condition of contemporary culture (whatever account of it we give) is an important phenomenon to be investigated and understood.

In contrast, the importance of 'postmodernism' as a style or way of doing things in the social sciences is still far from clear. In art or architecture the notion of a style of practice is well accepted and modernist art and architecture are certainly characterised by a number of avant-gardes introducing 'new' styles and new techniques. Even postmodernist art and architecture are generally identifiable, if not in terms of a homogeneous style. A parallel in the social sciences is not immediately obvious, although the schools of thought surrounding the various reaction to positivism and the methodologies founded on it are perhaps closest to the aesthetic avant-gardes. 'Postmodernism' could thus be thought to stand for a style of theorising, for particular modes of understanding (methodologies) based upon 'postmodern' assumptions, for, in effect, a way (or set of ways) of *doing* social science. The nature of these 'ways of doing' is still poorly worked out so that, because of the absence of a clear referent, *new* ways of doing are sometimes characterised as postmodern mainly because they are new. The challenge for the social sciences must be to determine what postmodern ways of doing social science would be and what implications they hold for our understandings of the social world.

In no small part the ambiguities of postmodern discourse are due to the fact that postmodernism refers to a contemporary phenomenon (here and now) which, if not ephemeral, by its very definition is still fluid and as yet not final. Modernism in its various phases stretches back over some 400 years with all the philosophical grounding that that implies. The term 'postmodernism' has only been used in intellectual circles since the early 1950s. As a description of society, 'the postmodern' refers to a pattern of life (cultural, political, economic) which is recent, being said to have dominated industrialised societies in the postwar period and especially since the 1960s. The notion of the 'post-industrial society' became familiar, if not commonplace, only in the last decade and postmodernism in the sense of a way of doing social science is still a 'style' under negotiation. Part of that negotiation must be the resolution of ambiguity and an attempt to move beyond the negative definitions of the term which see a postmodern style as being *not modern*.

Even here we arrive at a contested meaning. In the last section we identified two versions of the postmodern (a weaker and a stronger version). It is precisely this issue of the relationship between modernism and postmodernism that allows the identification of different versions for it is this that they contest. In the weaker and perhaps more accommodating version, postmodernism *cannot* be given the simple negative definition which excludes the modern. Rather, it is portrayed as overlaping with and returning to a lost modernism which promoted the 'avant garde' and the anti-establishment in intellectual life. Thus postmodernism becomes another mutation of modernism, of modernity, which, given modernist assumptions of progressive social change, would constitute a further stage of social development. However, critics are quick to point out that there is nothing much in this version of postmodernism that was not present in the earlier stages of modernism (Callinicos, 1990). In contrast, radical or stronger versions of postmodernism take as their point of departure *opposition* to the idea of Enlightenment rationality in what is defined as modernity. Here postmodernism is conceived as a rejection of the most fundamental aspects of modernism. In this sense postmodernism and modernism become mutually exclusive categories and postmodernism rejects both the feasability and the desirability of the modernist project. Some resolution of these contested meanings is required within the social sciences before the language of postmodernism can be widely understood.

Whether we favour the milder or the stronger version will inevitably depend upon how we read 'the modern' and thus 'the postmodern', though neither can be considered homogeneous. As we have seen, a number of periods or stages have been identified as constituting the modern. It is not clear whether postmodern society will also evolve in this way. Those who elaborate the nature of postmodern society often choose to emphasise different characteristics and relationships, portraying a fluidity which leaves questions of evolution or orderly change in doubt. Some would reject all talk of 'phases' or 'stages', arguing that such modernist notions are simply inapplicable under conditions of postmodernity. Others employ a kind of periodisation but apply it to the analyses of 'the postmodern' rather than to any evolution of postmodern society itself. Rée (1990), for example, identifies two generations of writings on postmodernism: an earlier generation represented by Lacan, Foucault, Derrida and Deleuze starting in early 1970s, which he labels 'neostructuralist', and a second generation, pioneered by Lyotard, which is more overtly radical or political than the first. The differences between these two generations are illustrative of the variety of writings which have been dubbed 'postmodern'. The first generation, based around a small number of Parisian intellectuals, was concerned with a centrally philosophical project in, for example, its struggle against Hegelian historicism. It was (and is) concerned to question the Enlightenment account of the nature of knowledge. In this it reshaped contemporary debate in epistemology. The second generation is not only more self-consciously postmodernist than the first, and has intellectual roots in Marxism, but its work tends to be less abstract and more easily related to the traditional concerns of the social sciences. Jameson (1984), for example, through his reading of the postmodern movement in the arts, draws conclusions about postmodernist space in the city. His tour of the Bonaventura Hotel in Los Angeles emphasises the *rejection* of the Utopianism of high modernism and its replacement with the popular image and respect for the vernacular. His attempts to revitalise notions of cognitive mapping long familiar to geographers and planners extend a direct challenge to the mainstream of urban studies to rethink their conceptions of urban space. Rée accuses the later postmodernists of introducing a banality to the debate which encourages some to dismiss the earlier writings out of hand. However this may be, his warning against becoming slavish followers of fashion may be timely for the social sciences where there is a danger of neglecting the early roots of postmodernism in favour of its more recent candy coating.

Whilst recognising the uncertainties of meaning which undoubtedly surround the term, it is, nevertheless, possible to say something about the character of postmodernism as it might relate to the social sciences. The stronger version is the more interesting in this context, for its challenge to mainstream thinking in many of the social sciences promises a revolution in our conceptions of how social science is to be done. There are three facets of modernist social science which come under particular attack: the assumption of a sovereign subject or actor; the acceptance of a correspondence theory of truth; and the formulation of the idea of progress. We shall examine these in turn and ask what the implications of their rejection would be.

The assumption of an independent actor as the basic component of society underlies many of the modernist social sciences including anthropology, geography, sociology and economics. In economics this assumption assumes a particularly abstract character in 'economic man', the perfectly rational know-all who always acts to protect and promote his own interests. Of course, there is a well established critique of such an assumption even within the modernist tradition, but a much more sweeping critique is suggested by postmodernism. Those who favour the ending of the modernist project support their stance with a critique of the strong Kantian–Cartesian conception of reason and all its rules, criteria and by-products of rational speech and action. It is from this critique of the very heart of the Enlightenment Project that the postmodern rejection of the sovereign subject arisies. As Baynes *et al.* observe:

> Interwoven with this critique of reason is a critique of the *sovereign rational subject* – atomistic and autonomous, disengaged and disembodied, and at least on some views potentially and ideally self-transparent. (Baynes *et al.*, 1987: 4)

The implications of such a critique for the social sciences are fundamental. Much of modern sociology was founded upon a conception of 'the pre-social actor' as a rational and autonomous subject pursuing his own self-interest. Even a very recent textbook on the *Foundations of Social Theory* (Coleman, 1990) takes such a conception as one of its basic assumptions. For this reason it is roundly criticised by a sociologist who has written extensively on postmodernism and who claims that what Coleman offers is 'a good example of sociology as it used almost universally to be in its not-all-that-distant pre-critical stage' (Bauman, 1990a: 24). Bauman finds a lack of engagement with both the contemporary discourses of modernity and of postmodernity. Thus the more recent critical stage or stages of sociology embrace new discourses which must alter the basic assumptions of the discipline and give rise to new ways of thinking about the social.

Closely related to the idea of the sovereign rational subject is a second facet of modernism which postmodernism rejects: the acceptance of a correspondence theory of truth. Accepting a correspondence theory of truth means accepting the idea that knowledge is a representation of reality. According to Baynes *et al.* (1987: 4–5), the theory of knowledge as representation assumes that 'the subject stands over against an independent world of objects that it can more or less accurately represent'. There are many well-known criticisms of this theory from those of Wittgenstein and Heidegger to those, more recently, of Richard Rorty. One, initiated by Wittgenstein but taken up by many others, focuses on the role of language in our understanding of the world. Wittgenstein rejected the notion that language has a representational function, that language mirrors some external world. Instead he emphasised the *activity* of speaking a language and participating in what he called a 'language game'. Language in this sense does not represent but rather *gives* us our world. The idea, as it has been enthusiastically incorporated in postmodernist writings, is that any representation of the world expressed through the medium of language cannot be objective or disinterested in any ultimate sense for, if Derrida and the deconstructionists are right, it is culture and not some independent world of objects which is encoded in language. Thus there is no one true account but only many voices, perhaps using different languages. This critique goes way beyond a rejection of naïve empiricism with its assumption that the perception of reality is unproblematic, and it elevates language and text to a key position in any discipline which aspires to study social phenomena.

The postmodern critique, in its strongest versions, is even more far-reaching than has so far been suggested. Postmodernism, as we have seen, is critical of many of the major constituents of the Enlightenment Project. A third facet of this project which postmodernism rejects is the modernist formulation of the idea of progress with its undercurrent of historicim. Implicit in the Enlightenment Project is the concept of an ideal configuration of society towards which civilisation might progress. Although the nature of this ideal state is conceived differently by each of the major political ideologies, their accounts all presuppose its existence. Whatever its characteristics, it becomes the standard against which each can measure social progress and without which the notion of progress itself ceases to hold any meaning. Further, under modernism this notion of an ideal state of society is often linked with some kind of stage theory of development, a development of civilisation which is linear and progressive despite periodical setbacks. Under postmodernism's many voices, with no discourse privileged over another, the notion of any ultimate ideal state must be rejected and with it the modernist notion of progress. This is why many postmodernists are adamant that postmodernism must not be seen as simply another *stage* of modernist social development. Jameson, for example, stresses that

> it is essential to grasp 'postmodernism' not as a style, but rather as a cultural dominant: a conception which allows for the presence and coexistence of a range of very different, yet subordinate features. (Jameson, 1984: 56)

Postmodernism thus undermines the whole idea of stages of development and progress through them, of what is often called a linear history. If we hear 'many voices', we also open ourselves to different interpretations of what might count as 'progress' or, more radically, we may even give up all talk of progress in the constant celebration of the here and now. Such a critique of progress and historicism holds a further implication which many find unpalatable. This is the rejection of the idea of emancipation, whether in its bourgeois liberal guise or its Marxist alternative, towards which humanity could converge. The abandonment of any conception of an ideal form of society can thus be represented as politically disenabling, an implication which worries many, particularly on the political left.

These rejections of the sovereign subject, of representational knowledge and of the notion of progress all hold profound implications for the social sciences. Some of these implications are extensions of a critical modernism. To abandon economic man as a building block of economic theory, for example, would be consistent with both the critiques of critical modernism and of postmodernism. Two of the most far-reaching implications, however, have a particular flavour under postmodernism and their brief consideration will help to illustrate the scope of the postmodern challenge. These are the implications of relativism and of a radical alteration in our conceptions of knowledge and enquiry. Both constitute major challenges to modernist social sciences.

Relativism has for the most part been alien to modernist thinking. If knowledge is the representation of some independent world, then only its extent and not its content can vary between cultures, social groups or individuals. To the postmodernist, however, 'reality' is not something waiting to be discovered. Rather, what we have called knowledge is itself a social or cultural construction. Thus there are many realities, each with its own claims to coherence or acceptance. This relativism is often introduced in the notion of Wittgenstein's 'language games'. To deny that there is an independent world of objects (or reality) of which we can have knowledge is to accept that words in a language do not describe such a world. This knowledge is a social construction and the use of language is reduced to a game with its own internal rules. Further, there is not just one such game but many, none of which can claim to come nearer to an independent 'reality' than another, for the notion of an independent reality has itself been rejected. To advocates of postmodernist thinking, the lesson to be learned is that no one language (or one voice) can be privileged over another – hence the association of postmodernism with many voices. Critics of postmodernism declare themselves suspicious of the triumph of nihilism this seems to imply.

It is important to appreciate that this postmodernist relativism is different from the perspectivism of the post-1848 era, the so-called 'aesthetic phase' of modernism. The acceptance of multiple perspectives was a far less radical relativism than the stronger versions of postmodernism are committed to. Although critical of the idea of a single path to the truth, the aesthetic modernists still believed that there were eternal truths to be discovered.Thus they were still well within the boundaries of modernist thought and did not challenge the more fundamental assumption that there is an order in society, a truth to be discovered. In contrast, the postmodernist rejection of the universality of reason and an independent world of objects which we may come to know holds the altogether more radical and disturbing implication that there is no such thing as *the* truth. In so far as it may be meaningful to talk about truth at all, we must speak of multiple truths which are neither absolute nor universal. This not only changes our conception of what might constitute knowledge but suggests that we may need new ways of arriving at or negotiating 'knowledge' within particular language games.

If we, as social scientists, take the postmodernist turn, not only does a whole suite of concepts require revision (concepts like progress, liberty, equality, justice, reason and rationality all closely interlinked in a systematic and mutually reinforcing network of relations in the Enlightenment Project), but we are also committed to a reinterpretation of knowledge itself. This is illustrated by Lyotard's celebrated study of the postmodern condition which has as its object 'the condition of knowledge in the most highly developed societies'. According to Lyotard, knowledge (*savoir*) cannot be reduced to science, nor even to learning (*connaissance*):

> what is meant by the term knowledge is not only a set of denotative statements, far from it. It also includes notions of 'know-how', 'knowing how to live', 'how to listen' (*savoir-fair, savoir-vivre, savoir-ecouter*) etc. Knowledge, then, is a question of competence that goes beyond the simple determination and application of the criterion of truth, extending to the determination and application of criteria of efficiency (technical qualification), of justice and/or happiness (ethical wisdom), of the beauty of a sound or colour (auditory and visual sensibility), etc.   (Lyotard, 1984a: 26)

Thus knowledge under the postmodern condition is redefined and, combined with the postmodernist rejection of a concept of 'truth' waiting to be discovered, marks the end of 'enquiry' and its replacement by 'conversation'. In enquiry the 'end' is all that matters and a map can guide the seekers to the predetermined destination of 'truth'. Paths to this truth may be many but all the best paths in academic endeavour must lead in that direction. Conversation is quite different. In conversation the ultimate goal disappears and travelling becomes important simply for its own sake. The object and subject of conversation mix and mingle to become a unified body *not* in search of truth but participating in a language game. In this game there is no correspondence with an independent reality and no universal rules. The conversation does not head in any particular direction nor does any one conversation take precedence over any other. This shift from enquiry to conversation radically alters the notion of intellectual endeavour and thus fundamentally changes the conception of that set of intellectual enterprise we call social science.

What we have sketched are only some of the features of a postmodernism which challenge many of the previously settled notions underpinning social science. By rejecting the rational sovereign subject, its associated idea of knowledge as representation and the historicism of modernist notions of progress, postmodernism attempts to provide a new outlook which is radically different from those of past critiques to modernist methodology. However, this new outlook is still not in clear focus within the social sciences. Even amongst those most sympathetic to postmodernism, the meaning of the term continues to be the subject of dispute and debate. To many postmodernists the very question: 'What is postmodernism?' is both misconceived and irrelevant. The appropriate question, they argue, must be: 'What does postmodernism do?' and not 'What does it mean?' (Fish, 1980). Whether this adaptation legitimately avoids the question of meaning is a moot point. Callinicos (1990), for example, introduces an overt political perspective when he argues that postmodernism is essentially an assault on the left. He joins others like Lovibond (1989) in arguing that, by rejecting the agenda of modernism (of which liberation, emancipation and ideas of progress are an integral part), postmodernism inevitably leads to a paralysis of social movements which rely on modernist notions for the identification of a common purpose and focus for action. Thus postmodernism, they conclude, implicitly supports the status quo. This might be a candidate for something that postmodernism does but, since postmodernism would not be alone in any assault on the political left, the matter of doing cannot by itself help us to understand the nature of postmodernism. The debate about what postmodernism does would be no less complex than the debate about what postmodernism means, nor are the two debates distinctive enough to be pursued separately.

Postmodernism offers a resolution of the tension (between the notion of a stable order to be gained and the constant flux of the social world) implicit in the modernist project by dispensing with the notion of an ideal or stable order. The implications of this resolution pose a major challenge to the modernist domination of mainstream social science. The assessment of this challenge in the different disciplines of social science has only just begun but its impact is likely to be of a different magnitude depending upon the nature of each of the modern disciplines. Some have already opened up their doors and lively debate has reached the columns of national newspapers as well as the library shelves. For others, like economics, postmodernism has hardly yet arrived. For such a thoroughly modernist discipline, postmodernism not only promises a radical rethink of its most fundamental premises but may force a renegotiation of the boundaries of the social science disciplines in which the continued existence of economics is under threat. The danger of closing ears to those bent on undermining the status quo is as great as the danger of being seduced into a thoughtless acceptance of the new discourse of postmodernity.

POSTMODERNISM AND THE SOCIAL SCIENCES

The papers which follow are written by authors representing a number of social sciences. To some extent each tackles the topic from the standpoint of their own discipline. This was their brief. It should therefore be of no surprise to find that the discussions vary both in terms of the particular aspects of postmodernism they tackle and in terms of the attitudes of the authors towards the phenomenon of postmodernism itself. That the geographer is concerned with 'spatial difference', for example, is a reflection of the way in which one element of the postmodern closely touches a traditional geographical interest. The chapters thus adopt different starting points and reach quite disparate, though not necessarily incompatible, conclusions. Indeed, there are several important shared themes which emerge.

The first of these concerns the relationship between modernism and postmodernism. Several of the authors stress that there is no clear break between the two such that it would make sense to claim that postmodernism has replaced modernism. Fardon (Chapter 1) sees postmodernism as attempting to deconstruct or decentralise modernism rather than replace it. And Shields (Chapter 2) interprets postmodernism as a complex moment of change which continues and extends a modernist inheritance. Burman (Chapter 5) claims that postmodernism coexists with modernist accounts and she uses examples from developmental psychology to show that, far from transcending modernism, postmodernism is deeply implicated in modernist structures. Each of these authors begins to erode any simple notion of postmodernism coming after modernism. The sense in which one follows the other is clearly not the sense in which one television programme follows another. To complicate this matter further, Bowers's discussion of technoscience (Chapter 6) has as its central theme the claim that science has been misrepresented as quintessentially modern. To the extent that narrative has played an essential part in maintaining the position of science and the power of scientists, Bowers argues, an element now regarded as postmodern has always been a crucial component of scientific practice. And Lash (Chapter 9) adds to both complexity and perplexity by suggesting that those features (such as the rejection of humanism, of history and of avant gardes) frequently associated with postmodernism are in fact not features of postmodernism at all but of modernism. The implication is clearly that many are still confused when they speak of *post*modernism and that basic conceptions of both modernism and postmodernism, as well as the relationship between them, require further careful analysis. As with other complex terms, the only certainty appears to be that a simple interpretation of the 'post-' prefix can be rejected. Different authors portray the relationship between the two -isms in different ways (or perhaps focus on different aspects of it). None of the authors in the volume represents that relationship as implying a straightforward choice for the social sciences – *either* adopt modernist notions and methods *or* embrace the postmodern. Most suggest, however, that postmodern social science would look rather different from modern social science. Rengger and Hoffman (Chapter 7), for example, *contrast* two schools of thought (one a modified modernism and one postmodern) in international relations, although they also want to marry the two in a 'postmodern project of deconstruction, conversation and reconstruction'. The relationship between modernism and postmodernism is clearly a topic of continuing interest and concern.

The second theme evident in a number of the chapters is related to the first and was mentioned briefly earlier in the Introduction. This is the notion that postmodernism as a cultural phenomenon is not yet all-pervasive. This is represented in rather different ways in different chapters and can be linked to the shared conviction that the social sciences are still predominantly modern. Fardon (Chapter 1) somewhat grudgingly admits that postmodernism does exist and that the concept has some limited use for analysing certain aspects of contemporary culture. He is concerned, however, to retain the notion of cultural heterogeneity which has become central to contemporary anthropology and emphasises that the impact of postmodernity will be different in different places. Although he embraces the idea of an anthropology of postmodernism (as a limited cultural phenomenon), he comes close to rejecting the notion of a postmodern anthropology. Social science, or at least this particular social science,

Fardon implies, is still a haven of modernism. Both Parker (Chapter 4) and Rengger and Hoffman (Chapter 7) admit the intrusion of postmodernism into the social sciences (social psychology and international relations respectively) but conceive its introduction in terms of a label for some 'new' approaches or theories which incorporate some aspect of postmodernism. In social psychology, for example, the 'new' approaches are characterised by a turn to discourse analysis and deconstruction. This, however, remains peripheral in what has been, since the beginning of the century, a thoroughly modern discipline. Likewise in international relations, new schools of thought have developed recently which offer critiques of mainstream modernist approaches. Most of the social sciences are in a similar position with a more or less powerful modernist mainstream. At the extreme, the critical periphery is least developed in economics and conversely modernist notions have their firmest hold there. Dow (Chapter 8) maintains that postmodernism has not been well articulated in economics and that the modernist mainstream is so powerful that debates over its central concepts like 'economic man' are contained well within modernist assumptions. Even 'new' schools of thought, like Neo-Austrian, Post-Keynesian and Marxian economics, could not be labelled postmodern because they rely on general theories and universal rules which are the trappings of modernism. Despite this, or perhaps because of the weight of the mainstream, Dow concludes that the methodological pluralism of postmodernism is both desirable and long overdue. Such a conclusion is not shared by Haldane (Chapter 10) who argues the philosophical point that the idea of a postmodern social science is incoherent. If he is right, the failure to allow the intrusion of the postmodern into many of the social science mainstreams may be connected with self-preservation. This ups the stakes in the present discussion for, according to Haldane, if we have postmodernism we do not have social science and if we wish to retain social science we must reject postmodernism. Other authors do not see themselves as faced with such a stark choice. Their concern is rather to explore the elements of postmodernism as they might impinge upon the various social sciences and to enquire into the differences these elements might make.

This brings us to the third and final common theme of the following chapters, a question which concerns many of the authors. What difference would postmodernism make to the various social sciences? Fardon (Chapter 1) restricts his vision to postmodern culture as a phenomenon to be studied, remaining much more sceptical about the potential of postmodernism to furnish new methods or approaches by which it may be studied. Both Shields (Chapter 2) and Smith (Chapter 3) see promise in the renewed attention to the spatial which postmodernism encourages, with its accompanying removal of time from its privileged position in social analysis. Their conclusions are similar although the emphasis is different. Shields, coming from sociology, argues for a social theory of space, whereas Smith, coming from geography, argues for a spatialised social theory. Both see postmodernism as championing the local over the global and thus as challenging the great structural theories of modernist social science. In this way, postmodernism within the social sciences promises not only a revival of space, but also a reduction in the scale of theorising and analysis. Bowers (Chapter 6) adds another dimension to the concern with the spatial in his discussion of the globalisation of technoscience. Like Shields and Smith, he takes up and develops Jameson's (1984) ideas on cognitive mapping and argues that social science must turn its attention to mapping the networks of association of technoscience, for these, he argues, are the lines of power in postmodern societies. Again this suggest new subject matter and new questions for the social sciences. Both Burman (Chapter 5) and Rengger and Hoffman (Chapter 7) envisage similar extensions of concern to, for example, the social construction of desires and hidden social relationships. And both argue that modernist methods are not adequate to the task of tackling such issues. By impli-cation, new methods must be sought to provide answers to new questions.

The nature of these new methods is still very much a topic of debate, as are their implications for the future of the social sciences. That a multi-plicity of voices is present in this debate is both exciting and, at times, bewildering. Fragmentation and uncertainty prevail on the periphery but not as negative features of a collection of minority points of view. They are celebrated as a challenge to what postmodernism would call the unfounded universals and certainties of modernism. Whether this challenge will rock the mainstream in social psychology or in economics is a matter of speculation, as is its effect if it does. Whether we suppose (or hope) that the influence of postmodernism in the social sciences will be conservative or radical, its challenge should not be ignored. Just as postmodernity describes the condition of pockets of culture, so postmodernism describes certain 'new' approaches and questions in the social sciences. Until the common nature of these 'new' approaches is further explored by dialogue between the various social sciences, and until the complexities of the postmodern challenge to modernist social science are unravelled, there can be no understanding of the importance or significance of postmodernism. It is the aim of the chapters which follow to add to this understanding. Whatever the conclusions to be drawn, there is little doubt that on them depends the future direction of the social sciences.

1 Postmodern Anthropology? Or, an Anthropology of Postmodernity?

Richard Fardon

PREAMBLE

Postmodernism's 'populist priorities' are reputedly one of its distinctive characteristics (Jameson, 1988b: 112); no apologies, therefore, for beginning with a quotation from a review of the last decade in the weekend supplement of the *Guardian* newspaper,

> Few -isms have provoked as much perplexity and exasperation as postmodernism, no doubt because of the way in which the word 'modern' is squeezed in between both a prefix and a suffix, each as dubious as the other.   (Adair, 1989: 40)

Yet, as Gilbert Adair goes on to say, 'the phenomenon exists and, even if its definition is ambiguous it's handy to have a word for it' (ibid.). I share this sentiment, as I do Iris Zavala's opinion, reviewing Hispanic literature, that the

> programmatic concept of post-modernism ... could be retained as a transitional concept to be applied to some projects and to some analyses of contemporary culture, *but one which cannot be valid, however, as a pan-global denomination.*   (Zavala, 1988: 83; my emphasis)

Other than coming after whatever is counted as modern – in whatever area of activity we happen to be talking about – it seems impossible to define postmodernism. Since most postmodernisms are self-consciously anti-essentialist, the lack of short definition is symptomatic of the movement's character. This makes postmodernism an irritant to anyone who thinks that movements claiming '-ismatic' status should know themselves better. It is, however, possible to point towards features that are ascribed

24

to postmodernism during the various intellectual language games in which the term takes part. Zavala captures the breathlessness of the moment in a passage worth quoting at length:

> the inventory of features assigned to post-modernism includes: self-referential discourse, heterodoxy, eclecticism, marginality, death of utopia (read: communism), death of the author, deformation, disfunction, deconstruction, disintegration, displacement, discontinuity, non-lineal view of history, dispersion, fragmentation, dissemination, rupture, otherness, decentering of the subject, chaos, rhizoma, rebellion, the subject as power, gender/difference/power (probably the most positive as a revision of patriarchy), dissolution of semiotics into energetics, auto-proliferation of signifiers, infinite semiosis, cybernetics, pluralism (read: freedom versus 'totalitarianism'), critique of reason, procession of simulacra and representations, dissolution of legitimizing 'narratives' (hermeneutics, emancipation of the proletariat, epic of progress, dialectics of the spirit), a new episteme or sign-system　(Zavala, 1988: 85)

This confounding, comprehensive and contradictory list derives whatever coherence it has from numerous implicit engagements with different modernist projects. Since modernism is also heterodox when examined closely, issues of continuity and discontinuity between postmodernism and modernism are insoluble in essentialist terms. A more helpful approach may be to characterise the relations *between* particular modernisms and postmodernisms. While it is a truism that ideas speak to precedent ideas, in postmodernism's case this dialogue takes a particular form. Rather than encompassing or displacing previous knowledge, postmodernism deconstructs, decentres, juxtaposes – in short, fragments the coherence of pre-existing schemes. Because of this attack on the foundations and presences of modernism (Laclau, 1989), postmodernism continues to be dependent on modern forms for its existence. Whether postmodernism is modernism's bad conscience or psychotic twin is – fortunately – not something I have to resolve here. However, the dependent, sometimes parasitic, involvement of particular postmodernisms with particular modernisms is germane to what I shall have to say about anthropology. Somewhat amending an analogy of Jameson's (commenting on Manfredo Tafuri's apocalyptic vision of the Seagram's Building, see Jameson 1988b: 42–4), we also could liken the landscape of postmodernism to those glass-shelled office blocks that acquire character only in reflecting fractured and partial images of the vernacular architectures that surround them. A forest of such parasitic forms, reflecting only one another, could be the imaginary and vertiginous shape of a wholly postmodern cityscape.

If postmodernism, following Lyotard (1979b, 1989), is a condition of the possibility of knowledge (and self-knowledge) within western societies – or at least in certain sectors of them – what is it useful to understand by postmodernity? Drawing upon a number of writers (Harvey, 1989; Jameson, 1984; Laclau, 1989; Soja, 1989), I imagine postmodernity to describe a global state of political and economic conditions with features that include: post-imperial centres and post-colonial states, partial trans-formations of capitalist manufacturing (including predominantly post-(heavy) industrial societies, new industrialising centres and de-developing peripheries), flexible strategies of global accumulation that transect national autonomies, changing technologies that reinforce international disparities based on access to knowledge and the means to extend it, and a wholly revolutionised communications technology that enables all the foregoing to occur at all. Harvey (1989) notes a feature common to this in the speed of turnover presently achieved. Capital throughputs yield rapid dividends, otherwise they are shifted elsewhere. Within this global situation, the culture of simulation or the society of the spectacle – in short, the culture of postmodernism – is a largely Euro-American phenomenon. Even in the 'West', the parodic awareness of alternatives does not yet describe a general condition but most typifies sectors of the society for whom consumption appears relatively unconstrained (yuppies, dinkies and their fellow acronymboids – as well as the members of various (often short-lived) sub-cultures). Postmodernism is, on this analysis, a local symptom of postmodernity – albeit one susceptible to export. And this export may provoke quite contradictory responses (from the avid con-sumption of idealised American images to a revulsion against all things western).

An evident complication follows: if postmodernism is a local symptom of postmodernity, ought analyses of the condition be postmodern? Is postmodernism the only way to understand postmodernity? Would this not represent another extension of regional concerns to global relevance? Is there in fact any choice in this matter: given a close relation between postmodernity and postmodernism in the West, and given also the relations between metropolitan centres and peripheries that characterise knowledge about non-western societies, is it not inevitable that western interests routinely displace the interests the peripheral (in these terms) entertain about themselves? My scene-setting has brought me to the subject of anthropology.

THE INCEPTION OF ANTHROPOLOGICAL MODERNISM

There is no consensus among anthropologists for which I could try to be a mouthpiece. As a contribution to a collection of views of social scientists, my ideas must be treated as idiosyncratic.[1] My overall argument is that anthropologists are well advised to recognise a dialectical character in the entailments of several postmodern projects and the various modernist paradigms of anthropology. Beyond this, postmodernism can be eschewed neither as a topic of anthropological interest nor as a condition of metropolitan anthropological knowledge. Numerous developments (rightly or wrongly; necessarily or merely expeditiously) attached to the post-modernism label have well-established precedents in reactions to modernisms in anthropological theory.

To simplify what follows I shall assume that anthropology (both social and cultural, but not physical) is concerned paradigmatically with the study of cultures and societies other than those of western Europe and North America – that is, its brief refers to the societies of Africa, Asia, Melanesia and South America plus a few others. This is an increasingly problematic assumption: although it can be argued, I think with justifi-cation, that anthropology 'at home' has borrowed the model of estrange-ment typical of cross-cultural research. However, this is merely to beg the nature of the places from which anthropologists are estranged in (or by?) their researches. Anthropology is the study of unfamiliarised or estranged ways of life (and I use the verbal form to emphasise the active, ongoing and reiterative fashion in which past and present exercises in compre-hension of the unfamiliar are connected). There can be no avoiding the significance of developments in the contemporary sensibilities of an anthropologist's own milieu upon the possibilities of ethnographic knowledge.

Anthropological modernism is conventionally dated from the first two decades of the twentieth century when evolutionary models of society – especially typical of the second half of the nineteenth century (but with their genealogies to eighteenth-century notions of progress and beyond; and fortified but not initiated by Darwinian ideas) – were replaced by a new set of methodological imperatives. This development coincided with revolutionary changes in representation before and after the First World War (Einstein, Picasso, Saussure and Joyce were among the scientists and artists changing the conventions of temporal and spatial difference in western culture more generally: see Harvey, 1989). The terms to describe this break in anthropology vary (functionalism, particularism, cultural relativism, the discovery of fieldwork, the invention of the anthropological fieldworker/writer) and they are best grasped in their interrelation and by contrast to evolutionism. Many theoretical notions weather the transition (thus the important role in anthropological modernism of Durkheim, Spencer, Tylor, Morgan, Marx and various other evolutionary thinkers) although their significance is changed in a fresh context. Conventionally (and with simplification), the modernist shift in anthropology is associated with the names of Boas in America and Malinowski in Britain. One upshot of their influence was the invention of the ethnographic text as a scientific term within a broader discourse of cultural difference. The contemporary sense of 'culture' (and the problems this idea still poses) is a key residue of early anthropological modernism.

FOUR MODERNIST SCENARIOS IN ANTHROPOLOGY

Postmodern anthropology does not form in reaction to early anthropological modernism.[2] Instead modernism in anthropology diverges into at least four varieties. This growth might be envisaged as a reassertion of older philosophical differences temporarily sidelined by the Malinowskian and Boasian syntheses. The four modernisms I shall recognise are: structuralism, utilitarianism, neo-Marxism and hermeneutics. Further positions (ethnomethodology, neo-Durkheimianism and so on) could be specified; however, my interest is in modernisms that became the bridgeheads to anthropological postmodernism, and I would argue that the four named do so in a way that others have not.[3] I do not treat feminism as a modernist paradigm; this is because each of the four positions is logically available to a feminism, as is postmodernism.[4] Each modernism is reflected (of course in reverse) within the glassy edifice of postmodernism to which I referred earlier. This helps explain not just the variety of postmodernisms but also the observation (for which I claim no originality: see Hobart, 1990) that American and French postmodernisms are rather different and suffer on translation of their ideas between France and the USA.

Structuralism

Edwin Ardener (1985) suggested that structuralism represented the high point of modernism in anthropology. He thought his view would be at variance with reflections on disciplines within which structuralism would seem to break with modernism. I am less sure that the view is controversial and certainly accept that structuralism is one anthropological modernism.

However, I suggest that only early Lévi-Strauss (the Lévi-Strauss of *The Elementary Structure of Kinship* (1969) and of the early writings on myth) be accepted as high anthropological modernism and that contending voices within his works become more dominant from *La pensée sauvage* (1962; trans. 1966) onwards.[5] The prominence of Lévi-Strauss within the structuralist movement propelled anthropology to one of its irregular assignations with the wider universe of intellectual affairs. Lévi-Strauss's development paralleled that of Barthes in ways that are less often remarked. The inception of one anthropological postmodernism is to be found in Lévi-Strauss's *jouissance* (à la Barthes) at the inventiveness of *bricolage* and concrete thought. He gradually lets go the assumption that myths speak of the societies in which they arise, or even of the overt philosophical concerns of these societies, to embrace the idea that myths instantiate the ingenuities of mythical thought – through the medium of whoever's mind. Despite such parallels between the 'pleasures of the text' and Lévi-Strauss's later writings, in French anthropology, as Merquior noted: 'However speculative it may seem by the more empirical criteria of Anglo-Saxon theories of knowledge, in French academe during the sixties structuralism meant "rigour"' (Merquior, 1986: 5). By and large, structuralism still does mean rigour to French anthropologists. Post-structuralism, by virtue of its attacks on Saussurean dualisms of signifier and signified, and *langue* and *parole* (Giddens, 1979; Parkin, 1982), can be defined as a postmodernism in relation to the high modernism of structuralism.

Hermeneutics

Concern with symbolic form in American cultural anthropology has a different history and inspiration from structuralism, although the two occasionally cross over. As significantly, it has a different tone. Where Lévi-Strauss is typically scientific and aloof, anthropologists like Clifford Geertz or James Fernandez prefer a homespun, superficially discursive style in which we seem almost to stumble on the insight that interpretative anthropology is about the way people make meanings. Interpretative anthropology is a 'rough and ready' discipline in which results are achieved by wryly observant travellers who 'waddle' into the fray to peek 'over the shoulders' of the natives. These visitors decry explicit or detailed techniques to solve the conundra of other folks; their chameleon-like capacity to blend into the surroundings and fit into another culture is what gets them results (Geertz, 1983, 1988; Fernandez, 1986). Despite the importation of Ricoeur's hermeneutics, most of the immediate inspiration of American interpretative anthropology is domestic: in a particular amendment of philosophical pragmatism, in Boas's relativism and cultural particularism – as well as the culture and personality theories of his pupils, and in Kenneth Burke's explorations of rhetoric. Interpretative anthropology is part of the same academic culture that gives us Stanley Fish's reception theory or Nelson Goodman's ways of worldmaking. At the beginning of the 1980s, Clifford Geertz – doyen of American anthropologists – noted the new prominence of analogies of game, drama and text in writings by American anthropologists (Geertz, 1980).

Of Geertz's three analogies, game and drama remain squarely within modernist parameters: the first points towards utilitarianism (see below) and the second to the hermeneuto-utilitarian hybrid of symbolic interactionism. The analogy of the text is more elusive. If American anthropology has had a postmodernism in the 1980s, then it has concerned textual analysis. Of the various themes explored in the literature of this movement, most attention has been attracted by problems of the authoritative status of ethnographic reporting (for example, Clifford, 1988; Clifford and Marcus, 1986) and the related question of the position of the ethnographer in the creation of the account. For better or worse, the term reflexivity has become established as the banner under which such discussions go. Analyses of authorial status have varied from the psychologistic bias of Nash and Wintrob's (1972) early account, to more strictly textual accounts of narrative voice. It is not difficult to detect vacillation between large claims about the dissolution of the author and just as large claims about the dissolution of the author and just as large claims about the essential honesty of a prominent authorial voice within a genre of naïve realism (for example, Peacock, 1986; Stoller, 1986; Stoller and Olkes, 1987; Tyler, 1987). Claims of the first type often aver to post-structuralist French inspiration; however, American anthropological postmodernism remains typically a reaction against the American tradition. Since, unlike high structuralism, the late modernism of this tradition was not represented to be methodologically akin to scientific enquiry (one genealogy traces interpretive anthropology's ancestry to the German distinction between knowledge of nature and knowledge of the spirit (*geist*) of a people, time or culture), its postmodernism has a less determinate framework of enquiry to engage with than does its French counterpart. Thus, ideas migrating between American and French postmodernism seem to change character. It becomes difficult to decide what is the modern and what is the postmodern in recent American anthropology: various of Geertz's ideas have been claimed for both (Jameson, 1988a; Gunn, 1987: 111). The muddle is acute in relation to the crucial idea of culture (see below).

Utilitarianism

My third and fourth modernisms must be treated briefly. Utilitarianism is meant to cover a variety of models of human behaviour that draw inspiration from economistic exemplars. Pre-eminent among these are explicit scenarios in which 'rational', maximising individuals are assumed to negotiate social interactions as if making so many market transactions in a state of perfect competition (Barth, 1966). Games analogies (Bailey 1969) and various types of social drama analysis (from Gluckman, 1940, to Turner, 1968, and Goffman, 1970) represent diluted and slightly hybridised versions of the market model. This tradition of thought has been popular in Britain over a long period (Durkheim (1893) presented himself as the scourge of Spencer's individualism); ripostes to the idea are as longstanding. Simplifying grossly (as I am having to do throughout), we could detect a counter to utilitarianism in Oxford anthropology's (and particularly Evans-Pritchard's) concern with translation and pre-suppositional analysis. The deconstructive turn of Needham on kinship (1971) or emotions and much else (1981), or Southwold on religion (1978), or Ardener on ethnicity and peripheral places (1974, 1987), can be seen to fall into an established counter-tradition within British anthropology. Thanks to the prominence of ideas of the individual and of individual interest in the market model, deconstructive thrusts aimed at ideas of the person or of understandings of motivation cut to the heart of the utilitarian model.[6]

Neo-Marxism

The inspiration for neo-Marxism in anthropology was predominantly French. A philosophical concern largely inspired by readings of Althusser became available to anthropologists writing in English via the published disagreements between Godelier, Terray, Meillassoux, Rey and others (for example, Seddon, 1978). Significant American figures include Mintz and Wolf (see, for example, Mintz and Wolf 1989). In Britain, the journal *Critique of Anthropology* and the group of teachers and students around University College London during the 1970s were important influences and/or manifestations of these developments. Some strands of neo-Marxism had particular problems with the peculiarities of anthropological practice. To the extent that world system theory located agency in global articulations of trade, production and consumption, the anthropological speciality of intensive research in (often remote) small localities began to appear less germane to problems on any pressing theoretical agenda. A further problem of agency was posed by the consistent failure of Third World events to fall into an appropriate class mould. Again, the local investigation of people's expressed views (a large part of the ethnographer's trade) was liable to be devalued by reference to the superior insights of the observer's analysis. I am unsure what shape an anthropological post-Marxism might take;[7] the journal *Critique* is undergoing a period of editorial revisionism with the publication of articles on culture and writing that would have been considered in-admissable ten years ago. Outside anthropology, precedents might be the work of the early Baudrillard on the consuming society, and of Laclau and Mouffe (1985) on theories of hegemony. Foucault is as much a post-Marxist as a post-structuralist and, for the present writer, was a salutory lesson on the problems of agency involved in all the modernist theories I have enumerated. Post-Marxism will generally, it seems, have to get by without the (universal) labour theory of value and without the simplifications of (universal) class defined by reference to labour value. Both of these outcomes seem potentially conducive to anthropologists.

My summary of four modernisms is contentious, necessarily crude given constraints of space, and omits many hybrid and genuinely variant positions that have been taken during the complicated and intriguing development of anthropological thought between (roughly) 1950 and 1980. My intention – given the argument I proposed about the continuing dependence of postmodern upon modern theories – has been only to underline the diversity of modernisms (and by implication potential and actual postmodernisms) in anthropology.

POSTMODERN ANTHROPOLOGIES

More ink has been spilled in denunciation than promotion of postmodern anthropology; books explicitly about anthropological postmodernism are rare.[8] However, in the more diffuse sense that tension with established modernisms necessarily creates postmodern anthropologies, contemporary anthropology is either postmodern or anachronistic. Laclau (1989) points to an anti-foundational imperative in postmodernism (noting also that a foundational account of anti-foundationalism risks being a contradiction in terms); some objects present to modernism (modernist anthropology in this case) have become unavailable to postmodernism. Anthropologists could list numerous of these (with disagreements on each candidature): *langue*, individual, society, sign, exchange, religion, ethnicity. I suggested at the beginning of this essay that the master concept of modern anthropology has been culture. In spite of attempts to deconstruct it, the image of cultures as discrete, coherent, singular and self-sustaining may be the greatest bulwark of modernism (Kahn, 1989). This shows most clearly in the contrived ways that anthropologists deal with 'culture contact', 'creolisation', 'cultural pluralism' and so forth. In this light, where might anthropological attention next be tending?

To predict after the example of the statistician (extrapolation of present trends into the future) is dangerous because intellectual trends are dialectical rather than secular processes. Two current trends now seem liable to be turned around under the pressure of their own success. To the degree that very general conceptions of writing and of power have received wide acceptance, they may be felt to be indiscriminate in their detailed engagement with instances. However, the deconstructive scrutiny of concepts closely tied to western traditions of knowledge cannot be abandoned in favour of a return to naïvety. In this spirit, I would anticipate continuing critical concern with the culture concept as the crucial organising term in much anthropology.

On Anthropological Writing

Concern to delineate fact from fiction – a preoccupation of positivistic anthropology in its engagement of an independent world of social relations – was superseded during the 1980s by an awareness of the made-up characteristics of all writing.[9] Unfortunately – at least if we wish to continue to use these two terms – the turn to fiction is about as bad as the turn to fact. Shorn of its partner neither term makes much sense, even if we are orientated rather differently by marching under one rather than the other banner. Fact and fiction are relational terms – but in no simple sense. Something already done (*factum*) requires a subject to (*fingo*) suppose, imagine or fabricate it. One of the senses of *fictor* was sculptor, which immediately begs a history of supposition, imagination and fabrication in the work of representation. To further complicate matters, some of the facts that interest us may concern facts about past imaginings. Judgements about facts and fictions constantly presuppose one another; and these judgements, if we now speak of anthropologists' writings, involve comparison between texts as much as between texts and the world. Texts are facts or fictions, or particular alloys of both, in terms of suppositions made for a purpose. The same text can be a factual guide in some respect and fictional in another; moreover, judgements are liable to change over time. Collapsing fact into fiction is disabling because it threatens to curtail the plurality of anthropological texts by denying their potential factuality. In fact (or my supposition), the variety of anthropological texts looks set to increase by dint of further blurring the distinction between academic and popular anthropology. This is what a postmodernist perspective might suggest. Confessional forms of reflexivity are likely to find a popular niche but to be eclipsed in professional anthropology by virtue of their high modernist conception of reflexivity and (oddly enough given that reflexivity and the first person account have been conflated by some anthropological commentators) because of their naïvety about fact.

On Anthropological Postmodernism

To the extent that postmodern culture remains an issue for at least certain sections of western populations, the variety of response to postmodernity is likely to become pressing. The impact of postmodernity on the sort of places anthropologists study has been extremely diverse: from the enrichment of Japan and the Pacific rim to impoverishment in Africa and Latin America where mounting debt and IMF/World Bank intervention may have set the course for de-development. Yet Latin American and African novels and music are as conspicuous features of contemporary culture as the simulation of American presidency under Ronald Reagan, Japanese computers, or, for that matter, the Islamic fundamentalism of Iran under the ayatollahs. Even the most radical of postmodern theorists seem concerned with very partial prospectuses of contemporary lives – and it is incumbent upon an anthropologist to underline this point in a collection of pontifications on the state of social science. Postmodernism is largely preoccupied with the life-styles of an indeterminate proportion of about a quarter the world's population. This ought give us pause to think.

The Argument from Power

It is true in a banal way that all anthropology is prey to western ethnocentrism. Given disparities in the way that academic disciplines have been created and become productive of knowledge, it could scarcely have been otherwise. However, as I have tried to show in small compass, anthropology is highly diverse, and it is not clear that several traditions and their critiques are helpfully considered equally ethnocentric and in quite the same way. Moreover, while anthropology may lack disciplinary essence, its institutional manifestations do not seem about to go away. The less-banal point about the power implications of a discipline as both entrenched and productive (in a Foucauldian sense) involves the ways in which contestation can be promoted. A more fully reflexive anthropology might be the vehicle for a searching evaluation of the scales of knowledge involved in postmodernity: of the way that time, space, expertise – and correlatively ignorance – structure global relations. This necessarily involves facing the circumstances of people on the cusp of the shift to postmodernity (rather like the eighteenth-century Scottish intellectuals who looked south to urbanisation and industrialisation and north to the clan-based, agro-pastoral economies of the Highlands: see Jameson, 1984, 1989). The most innovative (broadly anthropological) writing may well come from the societies of contrast. If postmodernism is the condition of contrast, then greatest dissonance may occur where television from the West beams into shanty towns, where modernist architecture springs up alongside earth-and-sheet-zinc dwellings, where commodities appear magically but are tantalisingly out of reach, and where scientific and religious certainties – and their authoritative truth-clans – conflict. Whether irony, allegory, pastiche, collage and so forth are appropriate to describe such experience can be guessed only from the evidence of how people feel persuaded to act. The life and death immediacy of their engagements seems to require description as more than mere appearance. There is, moreover, severe danger in essentialising form. Irony and pastiche of, say, Latin American dictatorship is an engaged subversion (Martin, 1989).

A Deconstruction of Culture?

A hypothetical projection of current trends suggests an extension to culture of the deconstructive critique already made of the idea of society (Strathern, 1988). Culture is liable to be a tougher nut to crack. Society has an older sense, without the necessary connotations of boundary and essence, that is close to what is now termed sociality. No term I know of can do for culture the work that sociality can do for society: evoke society as a necessary state of human existence without denoting a bounded entity. If we ask what society is made up of, the most common and influential answer is: of individuals. This formulation can be neatly compromised by demonstrating that the two terms partake of one another (societies are peopled by definition, people are social by definition – feral children apart). One upshot of this exercise may to substitute explicitly overlapping conceptions: agency and sociality are instances of this line of thought.

A similar set of moves is impossible in the case of culture. To the best of my knowledge, there is no counterpart for society to Kroeber and Kluckhon's (1952) compendium of definitions of culture. However, culture has been the key term or the informing idea of a number of anthropological modernisms: notably of anthropology as translation – in the Oxford tradition – and of anthropology as hermeneutic study – in variants of American cultural anthropology. The constituents of culture are debatable: the components of Edward Tylor's classic definition are the ragbag assortment of beliefs, knowledge and practices which constitute a people's learnt aptitudes; for Clifford Geertz, who treats culture as a model of and model for people's lives, its components are less easy to distinguish. Writers in the Geertzian hermeneutic vein liken culture to a text into which the investigator penetrates in order to grasp the design of entailment between its parts. Cultures are either conceived as unintegrated and with indistinct boundaries or integrated with strong boundaries. Problems stem from the logic of this situation: cultural integration and cultural boundary are directly related; moreover, culture is a powerful theoretical tool only under an integrated definition. The democratic impulse that persuades cultural anthropologists to steady pluralisation of cultures (to accommodate different places, or different ways of life pursued by sections of the population of the same place) necessarily complicates boundary problems at the same rate.

The upshot is a multiplication of the essences, or genii, of cultures. Human cultures are understood, like human beings, through their characters and careers. By direct analogy, culture may be susceptible to reconceptualisation just as the individual biography has been relativised and recentred thanks to ethnobiography. Ethnobiography has been a label for the attempt to retell non-western lives in their own conceptions of person and biography. An ethnocultural approach would, analogously, try to explicate local notions akin to knowledge, truth, fiction and fact. Knowledge, rather than culture, might be a more biddable concept with which to apprehend these issues.

Whatever the fate of my prognosis, the growth of transnational organisations, opinions and belief (from regional organisations, to religious fundamentalism and the ecological movement) cannot help but challenge the boundedness of culture. Models of culture may be borrowed from the not-always-verbally-articulate cross-fertilisations of world music and world dance rather than from language and nation.

CONCLUSION

Although announced as the end of metanarratives (or even history), postmodernism – the sandwich of past era between prefix and suffix – is necessarily a periodising device. As such, it is part of some big story. A rupture (modernism/postmodernism) clearly deserves some kind of explanation. So far, only analyses from the perspective of political economy have seemed capable of articulating a big story. This is predictable in the case of the Marxist narrative tradition, which has always gained purchase on the analysis of ruptures in the histories of social orders. However, even in this case, analysis has usually been so Euro-American centred as to preclude asking what postmodernity may mean to Nigerians, Japanese or Filipinos. Postmodernism is an interesting condition of postmodernity, it may even be a feature of life in the countries in which a majority of anthropologists make their living by teaching and writing. It is less obvious that postmodernism is the global reflex of postmodernity or that cultural postmodernism – as opposed to numerous other reactions to modernisms – can particularly help anthropologists understand the lives of the people among whom they research.

Acknowledgement
I have profited from detailed comments made by Catherine Davies and Mark Hobart on an earlier draft of this paper. But my debt to them both, and to Marilyn Strathern, is diffuse and longstanding. The earlier version was also circulated as a discussion paper in the seminar of the Centre of Religion and Philosophy at the School of Oriental and African Studies. I am grateful to Gerald Hawting for the invitation and to David Parkin and John Peel for provocative responses.

NOTES

1. I shall try to face problems raised but unresolved in essays in which I have lately argued that postmodern anthropology so far lacks a project (Fardon, 1990a), and that the appearance of having one is produced by some rather sharp historical practices (Fardon, 1990b). These pieces have been written in response to recent initiatives. Seen dialectically, they are thus indebted (as am I) to authors who have put these matters on a current agenda.
2. The notion that postmodernism responds to problems in early modernism has been encouraged (among other ways) by the attention paid to re-reading the ethnographic classics of Malinowski, Evans-Pritchard and Bateson (Strathern, 1987; Fardon, 1990b).
3. Ronald Inden has composed four abstract-logical ideal types (derived from the permutations of individualistic and holistic, and culture and society)

which cover similar ground. I prefer historical ideal types in this context to simplify the description of postmodern reactions (Inden, n.d.).

4.   I am treating feminism, like socialism or Christianity, as the label for an aspiration that must constantly be renewed in terms of theory. Although it is not a distinction I would defend to the death, it seems to me that these aspirations are always reconstructed rather than deconstructed. The point is clear in extreme cases – think of structural functionalism, for instance – but blurred in others – such as Marxism (see note 7).

5.   Were this paper devoted to utilitarian approaches, I should need to distinguish between utilitarianism, transactionalism, individualism, economism and so forth. For present purposes their kinship is more to the point. Recent American anthropology has typically conjoined a holistic approach to culture and motivation (my second modernism) to a voluntaristic view of the individual (my second modernism) – on the authority of a particular reading of Weber.

6.   This account is indebted to Pace (1983) and particularly to Geertz's reading of the different books contained between the covers of *Tristes Tropiques* (Geertz, 1988).

7.   As explained in note 4, I am uneasy about prefixing 'post' to terms like feminism, socialism, Christianity, Marxism – or, for that matter, Fascism. Terms like these imply (at least for me) commitment to contestation: that is to the renovation (thus neo-Marxism, new feminism, and so on) or abandonment of the labels themselves.

8.   For exceptions to this generalisation see the collected essays of Stephen Tyler (1987) and James Clifford (1988). The essay seems a favoured postmodern vehicle. Perhaps the scale and ambition of the essay answers the requirements of what cultural postmodernism has to say. Book-length works by the two named authors read differently.

9.   The extent of anthropological interest in writing is disputed. Yet the 1989 Association of Social Anthropologists' annual conference addressed the subject of *Anthropology and Autobiography*; and the 1987 conference witnessed a debate between two senior retired anthropologists on ethnography and fiction (Firth, 1989; Leach, 1989). It seems incumbent on those who dispute the centrality of concern with representation to define for us what they now understand by fact!

2 Social Science and Postmodern Spatialisations: Jameson's Aesthetic of Cognitive Mapping

Robert Shields

MAPPING POSTMODERN SPACE[1]

At the end of Frederic Jameson's widely disseminated 1984 article 'Postmodernism or the Cultural Logic of Late Capitalism' there is a sudden and remarkable change in the tenor of his narrative. After a lengthy synthesis which celebrates social upheaval, fragmentation and relativism in the culture of urban America, he shifts to the spatial terminology of cognitive maps and proxemics favoured by an older generation of behaviouristic urban planners. Adopting the term of Kevin Lynch (1956), Jameson calls for a 'new social mapping' which will restore to wholeness our '*cognitive maps*' of social reality:[2] 'The political form of postmodernism, if there ever is any, will have as its vocation the invention and projection of a global cognitive mapping, on a social as well as a spatial scale' (Jameson, 1984: 92).

Lynch's alienated, anomic city was, above all, a space in which people are unable either to map mentally the urban totality or locate their own positions and relationship to social and economic forces. The term 'cognitive map' is thus consonant with functionalist concepts of a systemic social structure used by Parsons and Merton. Jameson's proposed project for the disalienation of individuals in the face of a fragmented structureless postmodern culture of multi-ethnic, global cities, 'involves the practical reconquest of a sense of place, and the construction or reconstruction of an articulated ensemble which can be retained in memory and which the individual subject can map and remap along the moments of mobile, alternative trajectories' (Jameson, 1984: 90).

While it is unclear what sense of individual and what notion of place Jameson has in mind, this article begins from the premise that Jameson's reworking of one of the terms which underpinned so many of the designs for urban renewal in the 1960s is a significant development in the discourse on postmodernism and is indicative of other partially unstated spatial claims made in such theories of the contemporary moment. This article examines the 'stakes' in postmodernists' claims about a changing spatiality and goes on to argue the need for a social theory of the spatial. From a taxonomy of social uses of spatial divisions and concepts a hypothesis emerges: changes are taking place in certain spatial categories of Presence and Absence but not in those of Differentiation and Social Division by Separation which continue to support a more Modernist regime of spaces and zonings facilitating the status quo in most western societies (see Shields, 1990). Postmodernism, at least when defined by spatial changes, emerges not as a revolution or watershed but as a complex moment of change which none the less continues and extends a modernist inheritance.

Jameson's explanation of postmodernism is that changes are taking place in the spatio-temporal balance of the categories underlying popular classifications and peoples' conceptions of the world and their relationship to this totality. Presumably this thesis and Jameson's narrative concerns only the western societies of the 'developed nations.' The element common to the contemporary cultural changes the catalogues as 'postmodern' is that they present the breakdown of foundational categories by which the world is understood through spatial and temporal metaphors. These two axes of intuition (Kant, 1968) appear in everyday expression as 'metaphors we live by' (Lakoff and Johnson, 1979) – for example, spatial metaphors of indistinctness, where analytical distinctions are 'flattened out' as if in one plane; or temporal metaphors of distinction and definition, 'drawing boundaries' around categories. Time and concepts based on temporal metaphors focus on division, differentiation and hierarchies; space and concepts based on spatial metaphors ground the conceptualisation of co-ordinated events, simultaneity and expansions of trends across previously separate and exclusive categories. Jean-François Lyotard has argued that the 'Postmodern Condition' (Lyotard, 1984a) is symptomatically found in growing anomalies between everyday 'reality' and the 'common sense' categories and forms of intuition inherited from the Enlightenment even if this same disjunction is paradoxically also a feature of early twentieth-century modernism (most notably driven to an extreme in the surrealist movement).

Jameson argues that the spatial side of this equation has gained new importance in the context of global telecommunications and travel, world economies of interdependence and a loss of authority on the part of the linear narratives legitimising the structures of modernity and those ideals which originated with the European Enlightenment thinkers. Hence the relevance of the non-linear metaphor of a postmodern 'cognitive mapping' which suggests the co-ordination of existential understandings and abstract conceptions of geographical and social totality and brings into focus 'those very difficulties in mapping which are posed in heightened and original ways by that very global space of the postmodernist or multinational moment' (Jameson, 1984: 91). To use a simple example, this schism is most evident in those moments when one realises with a start that the world is not conforming to one's expectations. Having to rearrange one's spontaneous and intuitive ordering of the world and daily problems adds to a sense of confusion, a loss of bearings. Everyday life becomes increasingly counter-intuitive. 'Things aren't what they used to be' is a more banal phrasing of this complaint.

I do not want to debate the 'reality' of a postmodern condition here. For my purposes it is a candy-coated word in which a growing number express their experience of *contemporaneity*. But *claims about 'space' and a spatialised discourse are central to assertions of a postmodern condition*. The notion of postmodernity involves arguing that disparate cultural and economic trends have unifying tendencies and are mutually reinforcing. That is, events previously theorised as being in separate conceptual hierarchies or reducible 'in the last instance' to an economic determinism, are now, it is argued, being co-ordinated in newly spatialised manners. The focus is therefore more often on contiguity and interdependence than on causal determination; on local variation as general trends take on contingent manifestations in the context of historically and spatially rooted localities.

COGNITIVE MAPS

Under the label of 'cognitive maps', Lynch collected graphic descriptions of peoples' conception of their neighbourhoods and social worlds by interpreting the exaggerations and inaccuracies of respondents' sketch-maps. The ideal environment for Lynch was one which was clearly 'legible', in which sites and boundaries designated as important by planners would be recognised as such and reflected in the impressionistic cognitive maps/sketch-maps of inhabitants.[3] Crude though the theory was, it has enjoyed remarkable popularity in the social sciences, despite its inherent behavioural determinism, mentalistic stress on the supposed rationality of perception, unsophisticated conception of semiosis and ignorance of the social context of the mental construction of such 'cognitive maps' (Guelke, 1978). For these reasons it is now rarely used uncritically by geographers. Missing from Lynch's cognitive maps is any sense of the emotional or 'affective' content of images of places and spaces. Lash (forthcoming) notes that the figures of the city are also missing: those nineteenth-century Parisian *flâneurs* beloved of Benjamin (1978), Neapolitan street-sellers or the bowler-hatted London businessmen who add so much to urban mythology. And these figures are not just objects of a touristic gaze: they all possess legitimate interpretations, images of the city, 'cognitive mappings' which are contested, class- and neighbourhood-based images of totality, not just blandly hegemonic narratives. The notion of communal 'cognitive maps' occludes this diversity of thought and person. In brief, 'cognitive mapping' summarises a monological vision of the popular imagination and the cultural role of myth from the authoritative viewpoint of *modernist* regimes of bureaucratic urban planning and administration which is difficult to simply 'cleanse' from the phrase. So why, within the upbeat rhetorical play of his article, does Jameson adopt the apparently anachronistic terminology of cognitive mapping? How strange to find a celebrant of the postmodern calling for new, *authoritative* cognitive maps.

Despite the collage of disparate terms and sources for which it has been criticised (Davis, 1985), the article is more than its surface celebration of the eruption of the Dionysian, legitimised as 'postmodern pastiche' (Jameson, 1983). The call for a new sententiousness reveals Jameson's Marxian roots even in the midst of his disillusionment at the possibility of a redemptive moment within the patriarchal economies of late capitalism. Ironically, it also returns us to the functionalistic projects for social integration promoted by sociologists in the 1950s (Halbwachs, 1964). None the less, he argues that he is not seeking a return to the categories and qualities and values of modernity which are epitomised by the rational, bureaucratic planning of the postwar era. Jameson targets his pedagogical project at the level of individuals who now have to cope with the complex, multi-cultural and thus discordant set of representations which have replaced the old univocal and Eurocentric categories developed by the Enlightenment thinkers. The simpler, nationalistic understandings of the world no longer hold for a world-space dominated by multinational capital. Rather than just a change of degree or scale, what is needed is a qualitatively different notion of the relationship between the individual and totality – 'not . . . some more traditional and reassuring perspectival or mimetic enclave', but an as yet unimaginable mode of representation, 'in which we may again begin to grasp our positioning as individual and collective subjects and regain a capacity to act and struggle which is at present neutralized by our spatial as well as our social confusion' (Jameson, 1984: 94).

Soja concludes that Jameson's 'aesthetic of cognitive mapping' is only a provisional model for understanding postmodernity as an instrumental cartography of power and social control; in other words, a more acute way of seeing how space hides consequences from us by exceeding the local and national scale on which capital has been regulated:

> Foucault's carceral city of cells, ranks, and enclosures . . . is transposed by Jameson on to the landscape of perhaps the quintessential post-modern place, Los Angeles, the production site for some of the most pervasive and persuasive cognitive imagery in the world today. Jameson maps out from Los Angeles and other postmodern landscapes, material and literary, a hidden and insidious human geography that must become the target for a radical and postmodern politics of resistance, a means of tearing off the gratuitous veils that have been drawn over the instru-mentality of contemporary restructuring processes.   (Soja, 1989: 63)

'Space', rendered as a neutral void by the Cartesian, rational empiricism of modernity, was never so replete with symbolic importance as in debates on postmodernity. But in them it appears unexplained with almost mystical overtones, a metaphor rather than a definite concept. What is lacking in these debates is a more systematic command of the role and mechanics of the spatial. An adequate theorisation of the spatial would exceed the usual scope of geography to take in the tendency to use 'space' as a metaphoric device by which social distinctions are defined. What one would imagine to be the research topic of human geography is con-sequently obfuscated by a lack of any social theory which relates classes, the discursive sphere of meaning, and the non-discursive sphere of sites and spaces of action. A *social* theory of the spatial is needed. This will then allow a discussion of what is at stake in the apparently scholastic debate over the renewed importance of the spatial over the temporal, and the role of spatiality in providing the basis on which relationships between individuals and social totalities can be imagined.

A SOCIAL THEORY OF SPACE: SOCIAL SPATIALISATION

An argument that the spatialisation of consciousness derives from the social relations of capitalism can be found in Lukács's 1923 book *History and Class Consciousness.* He argued that the relations of production under capitalism, with its introduction of quantified and commodified clock time, cause peoples' sense of time to loose its 'qualitative, variable, flowing nature' with the result that it 'freezes into an exactly delimited, quantifiable continuum filled with quantifiable "things" . . . in short, it becomes space' (Lukacs, 1971: 90). However, the history of sociology includes a number of mostly forgotten investigations of the social construction of spatiality and the cultural relationships between spatial and temporal cognition in the work of Sorokin (1943) and Kolaja (1969), not to mention the urban ecologists of the Chicago School and the work of Tönnies and Simmel on which they drew. More recently, the spatial contexts of social action have been foregrounded by Anthony Giddens (1984) and taken on a higher degree of importance through British studies of localities and economic restructuring (Cooke, 1989).

The social significance of spatiality is that properly social divisions and cultural classifications are typically spatialised, that is, expressed using spatial metaphors or descriptive spatial divisions. In this form, they appear 'natural' and immutable, and alternatives are occluded. As an ensemble, these form what might be called 'imaginary geographies', recodings of geographic space where sites become associated with particular values, historical events and feelings. Sites become symbols (of good, evil or nationalistic events), and in tandem with other sites can be taken up in metaphors to express the opposition of different value positions. Places and spaces are hypostatised from the world of real space relations to the symbolic realm of cultural significations. Bachelard (1958) and Tuan (1974) call this 'topophilia': humans' affective ties with their environment which couples sentiment with place (Shields, 1990).

This social context of 'topophilia' has been less commented upon than the apparently subjective and emotional experience of meaning in the landscape. 'Imaginary geographies' are not merely idiosyncratic but are regularised across classes and local, inter-class coalitions and reference groups. Furthermore, the tying together of social and geographic divisions interpenetrates and is contiguous with the operation of more general spatial dichotomies and concepts. For example, such spatialised divisions as 'insiders' and 'outsiders' ground the sense of even non-propinquitous community (Cohen, 1986). Beyond merely imaginary geographies one can identify '*social spatialisations*' where the discursive sphere of meaning and imagination has a causative influence on the non-discursive realm of spatial practices and the physical environment where sites present the sedimented traces of successive historical modernisations. These spatialisations vary across classes and localities but share common elements which provide the basis on which different groups may be co-ordinated. Spatialisation is perhaps most visible in spatial practices and the connotations people associate with places and regions in everyday talk. When people attribute certain characteristics to a place and then make a decision on this basis, talk becomes deed; ideas, reality. As such, there are empirical traces of this formation left in the landscape. For example, one can follow the rise and fall of not only the popularity of a place as a tourism destination through the record of attendance figures but also of specific leisure activities, modes of the carnivalesque and regimes of pleasure (Shields, 1990; Stallybrass and White, 1986).

While this acculturated space is usually described just as 'space', this has introduced numerous linguistic difficulties (see Soja, 1980; Sack, 1980; Lefebvre, 1974). As Soja has pointed out, 'space' is a difficult term because of its broad meanings and wide semantic field (1980; see also Sorokin, 1943; Kolaja, 1969). The 'space' of physical geography is differ-ent from social 'space' (Bourdieu, 1977: 82) but much misunderstanding arises because of the lack of clarity about how these are coterminous, that is, the manner in which spaces and places become overlaid with meaning and do 'double service' as guiding metaphors incorporated into a social spatialisation.

The conventions of social spatialisation represent one side of a 'binding of time and space' (Giddens, 1984), the fundamental co-ordination of perceptions which allows for the sociality of everyday interaction and the creation of durable social forms and institutions. Social spatialisations represent an often-overlooked part of hegemonic systems of thought and supposition because spatialisation sets in motion more an 'ideological geomancy' than an imaginary geography. As a fundamental system of spatial divisions (for example, subject–object, inclusion–exclusion) and distinctions (such as near–far, present–absent, civilised–natural, right and wrong side of the tracks, East–West, North–South), spatialisation provides part of the necessary social co-ordination of perceptions to ground hegemonic systems of ideology and practice. These far exceed any 'natural' experience of spatiality such as the experience of gravity and the consequent differentiation of up and down (Needham, 1973: 11). Such basic 'forms of intuition' are necessarily a priori bases for ideology (Foucault, 1975: 10). Geographers such as Sack (1980) have also shown convincingly how spatiality underwrites western rational causality. Be-cause people often think laterally, exploiting puns, 'popular etymologies' and suggestive metaphors, a discursive, conceptual spatialisation formed in the crucible of everyday practices becomes influential in legitimising and naturalising further practices. In this manner, myths become directive images (Ricoeur, 1973) and 'metaphors we live by' (Lacoff and Johnson, 1979). Jameson's comments on cognitive mapping relate to the importance of social spatialisation as a form of intuition which grounds modes of representation.

THE CHANGING SOCIAL SPATIALISATIONS OF WESTERN MODERNITY

Jameson condenses the ideas of Henri Lefebvre (1974) that a modernist stance toward spatialisation underwrites western cultures' general de-valuation of the ephemeral connotations and social significance of places and *genus loci*, or the unique emotional meanings and attachments of places. The affective 'space' filled with myth, sacred sites, enchanted forests of earlier societies is recoded as 'property'. In place of a symbolic economy which differentiates places based on their affect and *genus loci*, a system of exchange values engulfs not only the physical aspect of space as 'land' but also the emotional attachments and 'topophilia' of place. Its homogenising effect inhibits the growth of attachment and community sentiment as an alternative system of *sociality* or emotional community (Weber's *Gemeinde*) outside the system of legitimated, structured and policed grid-group relations of *society* (Lefebvre, 1974, 1981; see also the work of Maffesoli (1988) on the *quartier* and see Shields (1989) on shopping malls). This reductionistic view, which Lefebvre calls an Abstract Spatialisation, has passed into the discourse of western social science and administration and conceals from view the fragmentation of the elements of spatialisation (for example, a divorce between represen-tations, at the level of the imaginary, and practices in the context of built sites) in the interest of founding a sociotechnology[4] of control in the service of power (Lefebvre, 1974, 1981). For example, the strong em-phasis on the interpretative component of individual understandings of the world implicit in geographic research (Pocock and Hudson, 1978) de-emphasised the formative and compelling nature of spatialisations as part and parcel of social surveillance and 'discipline' (cf. Foucault, 1973a).[5] Meanwhile, the spatial appeared irrelevant to sociologists, despite the lip-service paid to the idea that a society might vary over its various 'locales' (Giddens, 1984; for a more focused study see Cooke, 1989; for a critique see Duncan, 1985).

What makes spatialisation interesting is the paradox that, in spite of the commonsensical veneer of empirical rationality (space is a void), in everyday life people still treat the spatial as charged with emotional

content, mythical meanings, community symbolism and historical significance. It is the latter repressed emotions, not the former rationalism, that
one finds built into the framework of intuitions, perceptions and biases
which characterise the everyday life (the old Weberian perspective on
Veralltaaglichung) of otherwise rational institutions. One result is the
growing professional interest in the sociology of everyday life with its
transitory arrangements and fleeting alliances which none the less are *the*
common elements in any comparative sociology. Anthony Gidden's im-
pressive reintroduction of geographic variation into sociology unfortunately leaves the impression that the lack of 'space' in twentieth-century
sociology is merely a methodological issue (Gross, 1981–2). Its absence
from sociological theory is never fully accounted for. At most, Giddens
follows Lukács and other such as Thompson (1967), acknowledging a
transformation of time and space as a consequence of capitalism.

Despite its continuity in everyday life, missing from the perception and
understanding of 'space' under the official culture and social sciences of
western modernity is the sense of the spatial as a materially produced
form, a *concrete abstraction* which is both the material ground of labour
and the result of the operations and inscriptions of capital in the form of
land value and the property regime. At first glance this crucial claim
apparently says little. However, discounting the spatial as a matter of
immaterial and neutral voids removes any possibility of conceiving
of places as supports for the social interactions of communities, or of
understanding the affect of place, the attachment to locality and sites
'sanctified' in everyday life which motivates so much of local socio-
political action. Commonly missing in mainstream social science has been
just such a grasp of the importance of sites and localities in culture and in
the organisation of daily life. Locality, the social nature of the urban, the
meaning of a term such as 'community' – all these become paradoxes.
Thus, against the Realist theory of Andrew Sayer (currently popular
amongst British geographers and urban theorists) which 'throws the baby
out with the bath water', spatialisation is not merely a contingent
'contentless abstraction' (Sayer, 1985: 60) but must be understood as a
complex combinatory which crosses the line between abstractions and
realities. As a concrete abstraction it is only empirically tangible when
'embodied' as properties in practices or objects, hence the difficulty that
has been encountered in describing it as an abstract 'thing'.

Realist dismissals of the spatial as a mere contingency reinforce the
commonsense empiricism of western modernity. While spatialisation is
indeed *not* the locus of causal forces which are attributed to sites and
spaces, its *causative* nature must be recognised. It is a mediator of

causality so powerful that people may discount anomalies or indications of danger. Entire societies may refuse to recognise indicators of risk (social, environmental) which do not fit into this spatial 'imaginary'. Spatialisation has a mediating effect because it represents the contingent juxtaposition of social and economic forces, forms of social organisation and constraints of the natural world and so on. But as a 'cause', in and of itself, it plays no role for it is not a locus of causal forces. Human agents have causal power; the spatial merely has a channelling effect. But particular things may have specific causal forces only because they are divided or aligned in a certain manner; that is, because they are 'spatialised' in a certain arrangement, a certain formation, which allows them to actualise their powers. Spatialisation is 'causative' in the sense that it expresses or channels causation like that class of verbs such as 'persuade' which might express causal relationships in language: someone's words might be 'persuasive' but it is the person who is 'doing' the persuading, not the words themselves (even if one might sometimes say, 'That person's words were persuasive'). Again, spatialisation is not just a matter of realism's contingent arrangements of objects-in-space, it includes normative perceptions (this should go with that) and designs which pre-exist the actual arrangement of objects.

The peculiar modernist denials of the spatial are in marked contrast to the radical importance of the spatial as social relations were extended across the world, as the nineteenth-century colonial empires were consolidated as social totalities rather than merely far-flung economic blocs. Edward Soja argues that the

> rise of despatialising historicism, only now beginning to be recognized ... coincided with the second modernization of capitalism and the onset of an age of empire and corporate oligopoly. It so successfully occluded, devalued, and depoliticized space as an object of critical social discourse that even the possibility of an emancipatory spatial praxis disappeared from view for almost a century.   (Soja, 1989: 4)

Technological changes in the area of communications (telephone), transportation (railways, then air travel) and information (television) have also been widely discussed as having significant impacts on the spatial imagination (Kern, 1983; Meyrowitz, 1985). This was also a time of the missionary spread of Christianity which legitimated imperialism in the name of the salvation through conquest of a barbarian world (Saïd, 1978). Europe became a type of centring *axis mundi* in a morally barren global space, as the missionaries coming out from Europe 're-enacted' on a global scale Moses' carrying down of celestial wisdom and morals to the Israelite tribes from Mount Sinai. Gross, updating Bergson's critique, argues that there has been a

> growing tendency to think in terms of the similarities and identities between things along the spatial horizon, as opposed to the differences within the same things over a span of time; the increasing loss of a sense of continuity ... due to an inability to grasp durée; and an inclination, attributable to a flawed durational perspective, to accept the existing pattern of social and political life as permanent. The given is less and less seen as part of a continuously unfolding temporal life process. Rather, it now tends to be viewed as something which expands only laterally across a spatial field. This makes 'what is' seem unalterable to many, since an exclusively horizontal proliferation makes the given appear impervious to the normal permutations of growth and decay inherent in temporality. (Gross, 1981–2: 84–5)

This brings us back to Jameson's predicament; the problem of how to orientate oneself as an active agent within a postmodern culture which places a premium on the spatial but appears to be losing track of the temporal and historical. As Jameson suggests, the recent re-emergence of space in social theory is not merely methodological but a reflection of changing problematics and an operational indicator of postmodernisation. Similarly, established concerns have appeared recorded in spatial terms such as *locality*, '*world* system' and the restructuring of *multinational* capital. A new primacy needs to be given to spatial divisions which conceal the linkages between production (for example, in the developing world) and consumption (for example, in the developed nations), the use of products and technologies (nuclear, non-biodegradable and toxic wastes) and their disposal elsewhere (the 'not-in-my-backyard' phenomenon), to give only two cases (Soja, 1980). It is time to suggest that the return of the spatial is correlated with socio-cultural changes in the culture of western modernism which repressed spatialised thought and changes in the administrative techniques of modern bureaucracies that masked the importance of spatial variation and locally specific resistance through the practices of town-planning bureaucracies which made the urban public places of communities subsidiary to transportation systems (Sennett, 1976: 12–14).

Following Jameson, it is possible to advance the hypothesis that this lacuna, the absence of the spatial, occurred partly because of the epistemic role of spatial understandings which have underwritten modernist ideologies by allowing only certain allegorical comparisons and metaphors to appear to be 'rational'. It is possible, then, to account for both the absence and re-emergence of the spatial if a specific, modernist social spatialisation, now undergoing change, could be shown to have under-written both social and theoretical practice. An example of these changes is the changing division of labour between geography and sociology, one institutional arrangement (having a social dimension as well as being a theoretical partition) that has legitimated a modernist social science which generally looked at societies as if they existed on the head of a pin and kept those who might assert the social importance of the spatial in a separate discipline from those concerned with social theory. Current *rapprochements* between these two fields, if not accepted by professional mainstreamers, has been widely manifested both in journals and in the formation and funding of research initiatives, in the resistance to non-spatial approaches to urban sociology (see debates in *Society and Space* and Saunders, 1985). Despite critiques of grand theory-building on a part of postmodernists, no alternative explanations have been advanced to account for the correlation of such changing attitudes toward spatial variation, scale and 'distanciation' across professions, institutions and national cultures. For this reason, even if we wish to reject postmodernism in its 'strong' form, postmodernism still presents the only appropriately scaled set of theoretical tools with which to discuss contemporary social change. I should like to call this thesis 'weak' postmodernism.

A typology may be sketched out whereby three major themes are apparent in western social spatialisations: (a) inclusion–exclusion; (b) differentiation or separation; and (c) the dichotomy of presence and absence (these are discussed in more depth in Shields, 1990). Deleuze and Guattari (1976) argue that the most basic spatial divisions are those of inclusion and exclusion which make social reproduction, even civilisation, possible: the exclusion of madness, folly and chaos from a territorialised, governed, space of rationality (though not necessarily western reason) and order. Foucault (1975) gives primacy to the theme of inclusion–exclusion in his work on madness and the asylum. In its most primal form, what is excluded or is on the 'outside' is more than just absent or something abstract which is not immediately present; the excluded is tantamount to what does not exist. Elsewhere, primacy is given to the more subtle shadings of social differentiation by the use of spatial separation. Thus Lefebvre (1974), for example, argues that production is set off from consumption by spatial division: the factory is differentiated from the home; work from play and leisure. One finds all three of these 'themes' operating to differing degrees in historical spatialisations and this list or taxonomy is only a beginning. But it serves the purpose of differentiating aspects of the spatial such that change can be isolated, rather than speaking of the spatial as a unity.

The opposition of presence and absence, or more colloquially 'here and there', was made famous in Freud's work as the opposition 'Fort-Da' arguing that it underlies the differentiation of the ego from its surroundings, of the 'I' from the 'not-I', and hence lies at the centre of the development of bourgeois subjectivity which was the focus of Freud's work. The modernist ego, positioned in a subjective realm 'inside' an enclosing body separated off from a objective world is pure metaphysics. In contrast, it should be noted that Foucault radically respatialises the subject by subsuming this distinction under the rubric of 'inclusion and exclusion' and hence does not distinguish between the spatial division of near and far and the spatialised expressions of the epistemic division of culture versus nature (for example, the asylum). This undermines the status of the subject, reducing egocentric 'individuals' to mere bodies penetrated by relations of power but not separated from their environment (see Shields, 1990: ch. 6). Re-workings of the spatial metaphors and models of individual identity erode the bases on which the notion of the detached, rational, legally responsible citizen was forged from the Enlightenment on through modernity. Similarly, many writers on contemporary cultural change suggest that new communication technologies are having impacts on the conception of the world as a space of distance and difference. They speak of a sense of decentring, of an overload of information about far-off, distant, absent places and a simultaneous feeling of a virtual presence everywhere, courtesy of the televisual eye (Baudrillard, 1983; Kroker and Cook, 1988).

There is a long tradition in geography of the contrast between the known, local world of everyday life and the distant, foreign space of the world beyond which has been considered to lie outside individuals' cognitive maps (cf. Wright, 1947; Bachelard, 1958; Tuan, 1974). But due to new communications technologies which give the illusion of a sense of nearness to everywhere, '*Terra incognita*' becomes an increasingly romantic idea with less and less empirical content. In as much as this is true, it becomes difficult to distinguish the limits of the everyday, known world from the distant world. Despite being framed by the television screen and hence slightly limited in their impacts (Bauman, 1988c), television images conjoin the near at hand and the far off. Meyrowitz argues this point in his recent book *No Sense of Place* in which he notes: 'Where one is now has less to do with *who* one is because where one is now has so little to do with what one knows and experiences' (Meyrowitz,

1985: 158). In contrast to the sort of linking of site, social status and activity exposed by situationist theorists such as Goffman (1963), 'We bypass many previous generations' dependence on physical location as a prime determinant of access to people and information. Unlike tribes with special huts and sacred places ... our culture is becoming essentially placeless' (Meyrowitz, 1985: 317). Subsequently, the everyday world of locality acquires a new and problematic significance as the socio-spatial arena in which people both resist and adapt to the postmodern situation where the markers of cognitive mappings which allow us to know our place are obliterated in an exploding scale of socio-political relations.

Anthony Giddens has partially discussed this thematic in his theorisation of 'space-time distanciation', the 'stretching of social systems across time-space' (Giddens, 1984). However, he does not examine the implicit notions of the immediate and intimate and movement away from them which is harboured in the distanciation model (Hirst, 1982). Callinicos (1985) also critiques the intermingling of 'presence' and 'absence' in social life which is central to Giddens's project to construct a comparative societal model.

The telescoping of this 'world beyond' into the everyday relations of what is 'at hand' has also been widely discussed by geographers under the rubric of the 'annihilation of space' (Harvey, 1989). But I am suggesting that this 'catastrophic' vision should be replaced by a vision which isolates a postmodern 'unbinding' of one specific aspect of the established spatio-temporal relations of modernity: that of presence and absence. While Jameson suggested that a dislocation between individual itineraries and social mappings lies at the core of the experience of everyday post-modernity, we have arrived at a hypothesis which suggests finer distinctions, while supporting his 'hunch' about spatiality. A nascent 'postmodern' spatialisation is characterised by the disappearance of one class of spatialised differences of presence and absence, by a sense of 'simultaneity' and a resulting effect of cultural superimpositions. Old oppositions such as the contrasting cultures of distant places have come into new contact. In everyday life in the West one comes into contact with the as-yet personally unassimilated cultures of distant lands. This has always been an element of the experience of modernity, but has increased to an unprecedented degree as a result of the electronic media (news, documentary) and particularly television (Meyrowitz, 1985); mass tourism on a global scale (Urry, 1988: 35–55); the new economic importance of foreign ownership in the economies of once-dominant western countries; or immigrants who have brought cultures which had been constructed as distant poles of contrast by an older western cultural intelligentsia (see

Saïd, 1978) into an intimate relationship with our lives; just down the street, as it were. Finally, the political fallout of societies destabilised by colonialism and superpower competition has been brought home to the insular West in the form of terrorism and urban ethnic strife.

As opposed to the old univocal authority of western cultural 'mappings' of the world as a geographical surface of distances on which cultures were inscribed, the result of cultural superimposition is a situation of dialogism in which the authority of the cultural discourses and geomancies of each is eroded. A carnival of voices brings with it a new regime of multiple truths in which cultural beliefs about 'what is' (which of course extend far beyond 'provable' facts) are forced into an uneasy, relativistic co-existence. Such a 'dissolution of grand narratives' corresponds exactly to the postmodern diagnosis (Lyotard, 1984b).

In such conditions Jameson's analogy of a map to describe social spatialisation loses its usefulness. What kind of map is polyvocal, giving different directions depending on the corner one views it from? With any change in the difference between near and far, 'social maps' with their welter of detail concerning what activities, places and things may share the same cultural space in a Foucauldian table of classifications appear to begin to collapse into a zero-point of undifferentiated simultaneity where they become unreadable and their authoritative claims disappear. Under these conditions they are no longer 'maps' of a space (cultural, economic, geographical) but mere punctual 'instances' which do not perform their function, namely, show an *objective* relation between separate points, places and spaces.

The map with its one-to-one mimesis of topographic 'reality' and authoritative representation betrays Jameson's goal of a radically new mode of representation, giving rise to the ironic, functionalistic overtones of his description of the postmodern political project. Barnes (1989) suggests that a new mode of representation might be thought of, using the model of the hologram in which information is laid down so that every single point is a microcosm, carrying the full set of information. Broken in two, the image remains fully reproduced by the two holograms which result. Such a model removes any notion of a privileged centre, re-structures the implicit relationship between the particular and universal; between Jameson's postmodern subject and the socio-spatial totality. Rather than 'speaking' with a single, authoritative voice it presents a chorus of instances which however convey the holographic 'map' in a spectrum of colours, giving rise to the prismatic effect holograms have.

THE POSTMODERN UNBINDING OF TIME AND SPACE?

Although the focus here has been on the partial nature of any 'unbinding' of spatialisations, it is difficult to resist making a comment on its expression as a dualism of time and space. Jameson argued that the cultural changes he catalogues are *indicators* of epoch-making social changes, an ongoing, postmodern 'unbinding' of space and time with consequent changes in the bases upon which we form our judgements, place events and social facts into categories and build theoretical models. He suggests that postmodern cultural changes can only culminate in a new spatialisation – a move from the modernist 'abstract spatialisation' which foregrounded the definition of space as a neutral void. At stake is more than the sets of metaphoric divisions and separations which provide the basis for 'commonsense' divisions and 'spacings' of social institutions and their jurisdictions. Implicit in this change would be new understandings of the relationship between subject and object, ego and body – a new placement of individuals (Foucault, 1982a) within cultural 'webs of their making', to use a term of Clifford Geertz's (1973) and perhaps a radical change in just what is meant by our understanding of the 'individual'.[6]

However, Jameson implicitly deploys a dualistic model which positions a historical *Zeitgeist* on a spatial – temporal continuum. More appropriately than pitting space against time – which only reinforces the capitalist logics of an abstract and malleable spatiality unanchored in the experience of everyday life – would be a focus on the 'unbinding' and rearrangement of a modernist time–space regime, conceived of as less a continuum than a constellation. The introduction of the term 'spatialisation' has been part of an attempt to do just that, but focusing on the spatial. Bakhtin's (1984) notion of *chronotope* by which he characterised the literary time–space relations of the novel may be one alternative to a space–time dichotomy.

The opening up of the previously inconceivable question of space in the investigations of modernity and postmodernity in the 1980s (Kern, 1983; Frisby, 1985) is evidence of what I have argued to be the postmodern unbinding of some aspects of the spatial. Postmodernists such as Jameson, by questioning the status of 'space' and pulling at the threads of the binding garments of western spatialisation acquire a political relevance in fields ranging from neighbourhood interest groups through urban and regional planning and environmental management to geopolitical theory. A new legitimacy is given back to previously separated aspects of culture and politics, environment and economy. However, this political project, which eschews class divisions in favour of a radical individualism based on relations of proxemy and locality, has not been grasped by postmodernists (see Anderson, 1983; Frampton, 1983; Berman, 1983).

At the level of social spatialisations, postmodernism presents both breaks with modernity and substantial continuity. One should be cautious, then, before proclaiming a spatial 'revolution'. The need for more finely graded theorisation of spatial change and of 'postmodernism' should be clear. The new political and theoretical importance of the spatial can be linked to an unbinding of certain categories of presence and absence which characterised modernity. This radically destabilises older frameworks of analysis such as political economy which are based on the assumed universality of modernist categories. This has posed problems for many analyses of modernist categories. This has posed problems for many analyses of postmodernity (see Harvey, 1989). However, the work of postmodern theorists such as Jameson continues older dichotomies of inclusion and exclusion in its geographical focus on the West and theoretical obsession with defining what is 'postmodern' and what is not. This has had political consequences, such as a lack of recognition of the political and ethical dimensions of contemporary cultural changes. Even if one agrees with claims that there has been a loss of legitimacy of grand narratives, this chapter has endeavoured to show that the continuity and robustness of founding spatial metaphors partially counterbalances cultural change, maintaining order in the midst of painful and contradictory trends.

NOTES

1. This article develops some ideas from more in-depth case histories in Shields (1990). I should like to thank the School of Urban and Regional Planning at Queen's University, Kingston, Canada, and the Department of Sociology, Lancaster, UK, for their hospitality while I was writing this article.
2. A person's cognitive map is the 'mental image' of one's urban environment, the biases and inaccuracies of which might be revealed by comparing a sketch-map drawn from memory to an accurate city map. Key landmarks would be noted on the cognitive map and might even be exaggerated, while much detail would be forgotten, the scale and distance between points might vary depending on the perceived difficulty of travelling between the two places or the time travel takes, as opposed to the objective distance between the two places. These are illustrated in recently popular satirical cartoons of

        people's 'imaginary geographies' mapping, for example, the conservative American 'world views' according to the importance and reputation attached to various countries and regions. Nicaragua in particular looms large, threatening the small towns of Texas.

3.   'Cognitive map' is a term originally developed in gestalt psychology to describe the conceptualisation of the environment as an intricate system of spaces and routes. See Tolman (1948).

4.   'Sociotechnics' is defined as the study of rational techniques and processes of social change. See Podgorecki (1975).

5.   Harvey denounces the phenomenology of human geography as parochial (1973: 24) by arguing that it cannot comprehend the objective social forces that lead to the destruction of place. But this 'easy' critique is anticipated in Heidegger's 'phenomenology of being' which rejects the search for a priori foundations of knowledge such as 'objective social forces' for a focus on understanding human existence and experience within the context of a historically constituted social world.

6.   This involves what Deleuze and Guattari (1976) call a 'reterritorialisation': a shift in imaginary geographies and cosmologies, those spatial paradigms that coalesce notions of the world as a coherent geo-cultural space of more or less distant places, national societies and regional cultures – of the world as a diversely inhabited *space*.

3 Geography, Difference and the Politics of Scale
Neil Smith

Possibly in response to a book that subjected it to a 'postmodernist' analysis (Kaplan, 1987), Music Television (MTV) initiated a special feature entitled 'Postmodern MTV', but the differences between this and the rest of MTV are at best subtle. The postmodern version may be more artsy, European, introspective, fragmented, more dependent on pastiche and juxtaposition, more replete with graphics of space and time, perhaps even more political with distanced interjections of 1960s turmoil and a warmer embrace of *glasnost* fashions. And it may be studded with funkier adverts for 501 jeans but this hardly elevates it definitively beyond MTV's staple fare. With one exception. Postmodern MTV is *not* heavy metal; heavy metal macho would seem to be the epitome of a decayed modernism in music, and it too occupies much of MTV's airtime.

To the social sciences, meanwhile, postmodernism has played rather like a Shakespearian tragedy. There is a gay abandon to the discourse and promises of better worlds to come, while the stage is strewn with dead bodies that will assuredly revive for an encore. The apocalyptic drama of the plot is manifest: postmodernism heralds the death of the Enlightenment, the circumcision of rational thought and totalising discourse, the end of Marx, Marxism and the working class, the death of history and of narrative, the death of the subject, and so on.[1] If most of these claims are demonstrably hyperbolic, the visceral intellectual thrill of postmodernism is undeniable; there is a certain headiness in being able to proclaim the end of eras, and no minor eras either: it is modernism this time that is dead.

There is also a palpable sense of relief among some social theorists that an escape route has been found from a modernism that had become too monolithic – heavy metal. We are now to be delivered into a new world with new concepts to conquer, new ways of seeing, new conundrums of representation. Things are no longer what they seem. That which was previously conflated as a whole now explodes in fragments; homogeneity implodes as universal difference; every generalisation can be broken down into different experiences; every experience itself a generalisation to be broken down again, deconstructed and reconceptualised through the language of mirrors and motifs, signifiers and simulacra. Postmodernism promises a new intellectual terrain in which the only rule is that there are no rules. Precisely at the time when the history of the 1960s is being so imaginatively rewritten as anti-politics, postmodernism delivers a revolution without the revolution. The aspirations of two decades ago no longer require struggle but by the 1980s are benignly given: 'we are the world'.

But they are given only in part. Eastern Europe notwithstanding, the social ,economic and political rules and structures of exploitation and oppression not only remain in force but are manifestly reaffirmed from Tiananmen Square to Latin America, from the global terrorism of a decaying US hegemony to the everyday tyranny of the market. The celebration of postmodernism as an emancipatory force retains credence only by a significant distancing from such events. To some social theorists for whom the economic, political and historical grammar of social knowledge was synonymous with the constraints of modernism, the cultural language of postmodernism offers an escape, an abrogation of responsibility for very real social and material events which none the less remain an indispensible 'text' of the enterprise. Homelessness and Aids, insanity and death, even terrorism, become among the most precious objects for and of semiotic deconstruction; politics is rendered a discourse; discourse is defended as the most trenchantly political act in so far as discourse itself 'constructs' the world.[2] If to this we add the self-referential style of much postmodern discourse, then it may not be too outlandish to see a neo-Kantian idealism brought back within reach. Such egocentrism of self-absorbed western intellectuals has not gone unnoticed (Spivak, 1988). As Fitch (1988: 19) has argued:

> Under the influence of the postmodern mood, the left has generated a new political grammar. The political subject has changed. It is no longer the masses, the workers, the people. Them. Nowadays it's us. It is the left intellegentsia itself that has become the subject of political activity. Our concerns. Not theirs.

Having said this, and accepting that the advent of postmodernism in the social sciences is bound up with a broader neo-conservatism (Habermas, 1983), it would be a serious mistake – even as its lustre is already fading – to dismiss postmodernism out of hand. There may be a justified fear that postmodernism is really post-Marxism, 'simply a fashionable exit from the rigors of Marxist analysis and the wearying life of political and intellectual struggle', a belated expression 'of the yuppie individualistic ethic and the rightward political shift that we see in the population generally' (Graham,

1988: 61). But as Graham goes on to argue, the politics of postmodernism are at the same time more complex, and the critique of essentialism embodies a 'serious critical message' that Marxists can ignore only at great cost (Graham, 1988: 62). Not only postmodern but postcolonial and (to a lesser extent) poststructural theory has empowered new subaltern voices. The assumed priority of the white, male and First World voice is decisively challenged, at least in theory, but the more difficult task of reconstructing an inclusionary politics that both avoids the paralysis of ecleticism and retains a sense that political activity implies more than 'discourse' is proving more difficult (Spivak, 1988; Radhakrishnan, 1989).

In this Chapter I want to sug est that the reawakening of interest in space and geography that is 'implicit in the postmodern' (Jameson, 1989: 45) is central to a successful political renaissance; at the very least it is necessary to develop a language through which we can articulate a politics of spatial difference. For whatever other death sentences may be declared in the enthusiastic morbidity of postmodernism, two things clearly are not dead: culture and geography. Culture has been made the very essence of the enterprise, and geography, having been dead for much of this century (Smith, 1989), has experienced something of a renaissance within critical social theory (Soja, 1989).

My main fear is that without such an explicit discussion of space and spatiality, the recent flurry of spatial metaphor in social theory and literary criticism ('mapping', 'subject positionality', 'location' and so on) will actually reinforce rather than challenge the taken-for-grantedness of geographical space, and that this in turn will significantly hamper the development of an emancipatory politics. How else are we to react to Jameson's (1984: 89) admonition that 'a model of political culture appropriate for our own situation will necessarily have to raise spatial issues as its fundamental organizing concern'? Although Jameson's own mix of metaphoric and material conceptions of space is itself ambiguous, especially in the obscure equation of 'cognitive mapping' with class struggle (Jameson, 1989: 44), I think he is correct in trying to recast an integrative Marxist politics with a spatial grammar. By an 'integrative Marxist politics' I intend a politics that neither replicates the exclusive privileging of class as in various heavy-metal Marxisms, nor yet denies that specific social 'location' and relatedness *vis-à-vis* others which enables a privileged perspective on the social world. In the resulting negotiation of privilege that continually defines and redefines left politics, a spatial grammar is already employed, albeit largely as metaphor. Connecting such metaphors to the materiality of space offers a glimpse of how privilege might be negotiated.

The chapter begins with a discussion of the geographical turn – akin to Soja's (1989: 39) 'spatial turn' – in social theory and the way in which postmodern analyses have entered the geographical discourse and vice versa. Secondly, I examine two specific tendencies in the conceptualisation of spatial difference. Finally, I propose that a spatialised social theory will have to come to terms with geographical scale as a central concept around which spatial difference can be rendered coherent. The production of geographical scale is the primary means by which geographical difference is organised.

THE GEOGRAPHICAL TURN

Geographical space has emerged as a preferred language for interpreting social experience. To use Kristin Ross's phrase (1988: 76), 'history has gone spatial'. Or as Foucault (1986: 22) has suggested, 'the present epoch will perhaps be above all the epoch of space'. In a work that predates all but the foundational discussions of postmodernism in social theory, John Berger proffers the most direct argument for the priority of geographical space. Sequential narrative, he says, is rendered moot today by our vast awareness of 'the simultaneity and extension of events and possibilities'. Improved communications, the scale of power, personal responsibility for global events, and uneven economic development all underpin a new geographical sensibility such that:

> Prophesy now involves a geographical rather than historical projection; it is space not time that hides consequences from us. To prophesy today it is only necessary to know men [and women] as they are throughout the world in all their inequality. Any contemporary narrative which ignores the urgency of this dimension is incomplete and acquires the oversimplified character of a fable. (Berger, 1974: 40)

The rediscovery of space in critical social theory and the emphasis on difference come from disparate intellectual and political roots – geography is championed against the overly rigid strictures of historicism and difference against the 'totalising discourses' of modernism. Citing this work of Berger and Foucault as well as Giddens, Sartre, Althusser and numerous others, Edward Soja's *Postmodern Geographies* (1989) offers the most sustained and insightful reflection upon the 'reassertion of space in critical social theory'. For most of the twentieth century social theory and geography have pursued radically different agendas, the former largely indifferent to the spatiality of experience an the latter (most clearly in the United States) defensively isolated from the social scientific mainstream. In the last two decades, however, a rapprochement has begun, at first tentative, now increasingly vigorous. From the one side Marxists trained in geography aggressively pioneered the connection with social theory; from the other, a broad range of social theorists has rediscovered space as highly problematic in a cultural and social discourse dominated by history and, at its extreme, by historicism. The reassertion of space, for Soja, is clearly grounded in contemporary social, economic and geographical restructurings:

> there is currently a complex and conflictual dialectic developing between urgent socio-economic modernization sparked by the system-wide crises affecting contemporary capitalist societies; and a responsive cultural and political modernism aimed at making sense of the material changes taking place in the world and gaining control over their future directions.   (Soja, 1989: 26)

The geography has become a powerful language of postmodernism is indisputable. Baudrillard's *America* (1989) features the author as semiotic tourist of the American psyche. If this work recalls the traditional European (and especially the French) penchant for dissecting the American *Zeitgeist*, it also goes much further. The signs and symbols that reveal the experience of America are distilled out of a Disneyland world of landscape as mediascape. One explores the meaning of America much as one hops on an airline shuttle or rides a Greyhound bus from city to city reading the fleeting signs as the only reality. This simulacral appropriation of the cultural landscapes of *l'Amérique* enjoys an influence well beyond the intellectual cafés of Paris and New York. A revived rural regionalism in France aims its nostalgia against this construction of an urban American modernity in which meaning is conveyed as a disjointed pastiche of geographical graffiti (Karnoouh, 1986). In Britain, conservative nationalism and ruling-class heritage shape the design of new and renewed places that result from the collaboration of a revived historic preservation movement with postmodern architecture (Wright, 1985). Kenneth Frampton (1983), by contrast, calls for a 'critical regionalism' in architecture, very much in opposition to such reactionary geographies of an invented national past. Kristin Ross (1988) reads Rimbaud's verse and prose as an early marker of the emergence of a produced social space. Especially among the latter thinkers, there has been a fruitful engagement with Henri Lefebvre's (1976; forthcoming) longstanding efforts to understand the reproduction of capitalist society as the reproduction of space.

Nor has the rediscovery of space been entirely confined to intellectual circles. Anticipating the 1987 financial crash, Thomas S. Johnson, President of New York's fourth largest bank, Chemical Bank, feared openly that with financiers utterly overcommitted, 'there is the possibility of a nightmarish domino effect as every creditor ransacks the globe attempting to locate his collateral' (Nash, 1986). That such a global rampage by capital did not immediately follow the ensuing crash neither denies the power nor yet perhaps the prescience of our banker's global vision.

If the reassertion of space was already well under way, the explicit connection between postmodernism and geography as a discipline came only after Jameson's (1984) pathbreaking depiction of postmodernism as 'the cultural logic of late capitalism'. The attraction of Jameson's analysis lay in the breadth of connections he forged between a transforming economy and culture and a restructuring global capital. It was an intensely geographical politics of postmodernism that Jameson depicted, nearly seven years prior to the war with Iraq:

> this whole global, yet American, postmodern culture is the internal and superstructural expression of a whole new wave of American military and economic domination throughout the world: in this sense, as throughout class history, the underside of culture is blood, torture, death and horror.   (Jameson, 1984: 57)

Postmodernism he conceived as

> a periodizing concept whose function is to correlate the emergence of new formal features in culture with the emergence of a new type of social life and a new economic order – what is often euphemistically called modernization, postindustrial or consumer society, the society of the media or the spectacle, or multinational capitalism.   (Jameson, 1988c: 15)

Contemporary culture, he argued, is 'increasingly dominated by space and spatial logic' rather than time. In his discussion of the architecture of the Bonaventure Hotel in Los Angeles, Jameson exposes people's political and symbolic alienation from the new urban geography; the postmodern city is exposed as text to the late capitalist cultural context. A new radicalised cultural politics, then, involves 'an aesthetic of cognitive mapping': [d]isalienation in the traditional city ... involves the practical reconquest of a sense of space' (Jameson, 1984: 71; 89).

Among geographers, who since the late 1960s had sought a spatialised politics, a spectrum of responses greeted Jameson's (and others') rather

oblique rendevouz with geography and a geographical politics. In sum-
marising some of the central themes here, I cannot hope to convey the
diversity and complexity of specific contributions but at best to intimate
several directions taken under the broad rubric of the postmodern debate.
David Harvey adopted Jameson's scepticism about the historical novelty
of postmodernism but unlike Jameson, challenges the notion that modernism was, by its nature, monolithic in style and project (Harvey, 1989;
see also LeFaivre, 1987). Heavy-metal modernism is not modernism *per
se* but an historical reduction to one essence of the modern; it is too easily
forgotten that modernism itself was a deeply subversive project, and with
this is 'forgotten' the very real processes of cultural struggle and
appropriation that reproduced modernism in its monolithic postwar guise –
'commodified Modernism' for Callinicos (1990; see also Berman, 1982).
Where postmodernism offers a rich depth of insights, Harvey applies these
to nurture a still-vibrant and growing Marxism. He attempts to 'ground'
the fragmentation and eclecticism, destruction and renewal emblematic of
postmodern cultural discourse in a parallel destruction and renewal in the
emergence of new regimes of accumulation in the post-postwar economy.
'There is strong evidence', he suggests, 'that post-modernity is nothing
more than the cultural clothing of flexible accumulation' (Harvey,
1987: 279). The culture of contemporary urban restructuring becomes a
spatial text for new forms of old social and economic contradictions
inherent within capitalism. What is new, for Harvey, is the depth and
intensity of 'space–time compression' under this newly emerging regime
of accumulation.

Harvey's (1989) widely read engagement with postmodernism has
attracted a strangely bifurcated response. Among cultural critics he is
either praised for giving 'political economy its full weight as a crucial
factor in our postmodern world, overcoming the pernicious postmod
allergy to economics' (*Voice Literary Supplement*, 1989), or else accused
of reinstating a Marxist essentialism of class and economics (Deutsche,
1990). Among Marxists, his sortie into cultural criticism has been appreciated whereas his political economic analysis is more often questioned.

Soja's postmodernism is the most explicit effort to recentre geographical space. Before anything else, it represents an attack on the essentialism
of history. He seeks

a fundamental reformulation of the nature and conceptualization of
social being, an essentially ontological struggle to rebalance the interplay between history, geography, and society. Here the reassertion of
space arises against the grain of an ontological historicism that has

privileged the separate constitution of being in time for at least the past century.   (Soja, 1989: 61)

Although he is correct about the privileging of time over space, it is less clear either that this dates merely to late modernism, as Soja suggests, or that the appropriate response is philosophical. In the first place, the privileging of time over space may well have roots in social practice rather than philosophical error (Thompson, 1955; Sohn-Rethel, 1978), and in the second place, although Soja is clearly aware of the danger, the call (on *philosophical* grounds) for a 'spatialized ontology' runs the risk of indulging special disciplinary pleading, however meritorious the case may be.

A more extreme postmodernism distances itself further from any such explicit theoretical commitment derived from modernism. In its own 'oppositional rhetoric' (Graham, 1988: 60), to take the extreme case, this work celebrates the intellectual death toll of postmodernism and replaces modernism with postmodernism, Marxism with pluralism, class with race, gender and social difference, homogeneity with diversity, metannarative with local narrative. The strength of this work lies largely in its critique of structuralism and, by inference, heavy-metal Marxism. In geography this has taken the particular form of championing the local against the global, place against space, the indigenous against the universal. In its purest form a 'pastiche postmodernism' (Soja, 1988), this approach in geography might embrace a 'limited relativism' that denies any epistemological privilege (Dear, 1985; 1988); it informs a specific vision of locality studies (Cooke, 1989); and it contributes to the semiotic deconstruction of the gentrified urban landscapes of postmodernity (Mills, 1988; Zukin, 1990).

SPATIAL DIFFERENCE

The geographical turn is bound up with the search for ways to express the themes of difference and diversity, fragmentation and dissociation. Long conceived as dead, fixed and immobile, space is both available as foundational metaphor and at the same time being rediscovered as produced, mutable, an intrinsically complex expression of social relations. Not only is the fragility and transitoriness of contemporary social relations expressed 'in' space; the production of space is increasingly the means by which social difference is constructed and reconstructed.

There is a substantial social and philosophical literature on 'difference' (Luhmann, 1984). Some such as Bourdieu (1984) root social difference in a cultural aesthetic of taste; traditional Marxist analysis highlights the generative propensity of the social division of labour (Sohn-Rethel, 1978); feminist constructions of difference range from the biological based (Gilligan, 1982) to socially constituted relations of difference (Barrett, 1987; Di Stefano, 1990). Since the purpose here is to explore the engagement of difference with space, it is not possible to attempt an extended depiction or arbitration of these perspectives. This would in any case be a momentous project. The important point is that the concept of difference is theoretically and politically laden, as such a highly contested concept, and therefore susceptible to ideological appropriation and representation. The political and theoretical opportunities associated with the engagement of geography and difference are significant but they are also tempered by a series of theoretical and political choices. I want to highlight here two specific spatialisations of 'difference' that risk reinforcing in different ways some of the pitfalls traditionally identified in modernism. In doing so, I am sensitive to Bondi's (1990: 160) observation that in some treatments of postmodernism, 'the real import of cultural and intellectual developments is being evacuated in a rush to ensure containment within existing categories'. Rather, I want to explore these questions of spatial difference as a means to get beyond existing categories – specifically to introduce a conceptualisation of the production of geographical scale.

Difference as Eclecticism

It is by now a well-rehearsed warning that by toppling the authority of a structured modernism, the postmodern raises the spectre of a new electicism. The suspension of ethical value on the one side, betokened by insider trading and the Boesky affair and, on the other side, the escalation and destruction of economic value on Wall Street in the 1980s boom are integrally related. The effects of this transience of value were a hallmark of the 1980s. 'Nobody knows what's good' laments a character in Sam Shepard's 'Angel City' as he surveys the institutionalised greed of 1980s Hollywood. 'One minute it's good. Then it's garbage.' 'Difference' is commodified for its own sake as an inherent goal and a style. According even to Lyotard, who celebrates the fragmentary impulses of postmodernism:[3]

> Eclecticism is the degree zero of contemporary general culture: one listens to reggae, watches a western, eats McDonald's food for lunch and local cuisine for dinner, wears Paris perfume in Tokyo and 'retro' clothes in Hong Kong; knowledge is a matter for TV games. It is easy to find a public for eclectic works. By becoming kitsch, art panders to

the confusion which reigns in the 'taste' of the patrons. Artists, gallery owners, critics and public wallow together in the 'anything goes', and the epoch is one of slackening. But this realism of the 'anything goes' is in fact that of money . . . . (Lyotard, 1984a: 76)

The dangers of eclecticism are potentially heightened by an uncritical appropriation of spatial concepts as metaphor. Metaphor functions by asserting the homology or at least resemblance between something *to be known* and something assumed as *already known*. The purchase of spatial metaphor lies precisely in the appropriation and representation of space as unproblematic. In fact, it is a very distinct conception of absolute space to which such metaphors appeal: space is a two-dimensional (or at best three-dimensional) field or surface in which 'subject positions' are definitively located. They have socially defined co-ordinates, a set 'location' from which different subjects conceive and construct or 'map' the world. It is a materially undifferentiated, homogenous space in which all locations are intrinsically equal; the only criteria of differentiation are mathematical via the abstractly imposed system of co-ordinates. Space is also, in this conception, entirely separate from the objects, events and relations that occur 'in' space.

Precisely this conception of geographical space has since the early 1970s been the target of critical analyses seeking to import social theory into geographical theory (Harvey, 1973; 1982; Lefebvre, 1976; forthcoming; Massey, 1984; Smith, 1990; Soja, 1989). The *rapprochement* between geography and social theory – more specifically, perhaps, social theories of science – has encouraged a more sophisticated focus on space as a relative rather than an absolute concept. According to this relative conception, space is not separate from the material realm of objects, events and relations; rather it is precisely the arrangement of this material realm that constitutes space. Space is not so much abstractly given as socially produced within and as a part of social relations.

From this perspective, absolute space is only one of many conceptualisations of geographic space. While it may have provided an appropriate metric for the European conquest and mapping of the globe in the so-called Age of Discovery, for example, it is much less appropriate for understanding the geography of a twentieth-century capitalism that now develops unevenly via relative rather than absolute geographic expansion. In so far as the absolute conception of space is treated as naïvely given, it risks what some geographers, critiquing much of the discipline's work, have called the 'fetishism of space' (Anderson, 1973). Real social relationships between people are transfered to space and seen as spatial relationships. Social conditions are deemed the product of the place rather than social relations, as when 'inner-city problems' is used as a euphemism for poverty. The danger of eclecticism lies precisely in the naïvely undifferentiated character of absolute space, compared to relative space in which space is represented from the start as socially differentiated.

Consider, for example Giddens's attempt to recentre space. In explaining the 'regionalisation' of space into locales, Giddens explicitly rejects the absolute conception of space: regionalisation

> always carries the connotation of the structuration of social conduct across time–space. Thus there is a strong degree of regional differentiation, in terms of class relationships and a variety of other social criteria, between the North and South in Britain. (Giddens, 1984: 122)

Rather than follow this straightforward insight toward a theory of the way in which specific regionalisations take place and specific locales are constructed, Giddens deserts the relativity of space in favour of an abstract binary distinction between 'front regions' and 'back regions'. In effect, he asserts the social structuration of space but with the ontological taxonomy of front and back regions; he fails to grasp the multidimensional, socially woven fabric of space. 'Frontness' and 'backness' are beached abstractions, disconnected from the real social processes that make regions. All front regions, for example, are thus rendered co-equal, there being no reference to social processes that might distinguish them internally.

Giddens announces the 'spatial' project, but geographical space is not brought back to life in any meaningful way. A Giddensian geography is a mosaic of locales, at best front and back regions, each with their own intricacies to be sure but bound together in a simple binarism. Giddens in the end offers no systematic discussion of the social processes that connect this abstract division into regions and the actual social, economic and political geographies of the north and south of Britain. Time–space is insufficiently integrated into structurationism. In fact, produced space is not simply a mosaic but within capitalist society it is intensely hierarchial, according to divisions of race and class, gender and ethnicity, differential access to work and services, and so on.

The difference between a mosaic and hierarchial space is that in a mosaic difference has been reduced and reified to a single *spatial* dimension that abstracts from the more dynamic and multifaceted political differentiation of space. Freed from this political determination of space, a geographically given mosaic of spaces receives its content from the outside, and can thus be endowed with an eclectic infinity of social definitions according to a virtually endless list of criteria. Suffused with meaning as it is, Baudrillard's America is a flattened mosaic, albeit reflective, expressive and liminal. Equally, with its explicit refusal to consider the social constitution of regions, early twentieth-century regional geography depicted the global landscape as a mosaic (Smith, 1989).

Difference as Totality

Michele Barrett makes a very useful distinction between three uses of the concept of difference in feminist research: difference as experiential diversity, difference as positional meaning, and sexual difference. A focus on sexual difference, she argues, is insensitive to social differences among women and within gender divisions more generally. By contrast, a focus on experiential diversity involves a much more subjective emphasis on the specificity of each woman's experience. As positional meaning, difference is most centrally identified with postmodernism. It involves a deconstruction of the 'unified subject', fashioned after the white, bourgeois male, and the reconstitution of 'sites of difference'. Each of these concepts of difference she critiques in different ways: sexual difference involves a basic essentialism; experiential diversity leads to a political 'pluralism', which 'has in fact emerged as the lowest common denominator of feminism' (Barrett, 1987: 32); and the politics of positional difference 'tend towards the textual and local' and fail 'to theorize resistance and political challenge' (Barrett, 1987: 35).

As Barrett emphasises, there is both overlap and contradiction between these different treatments of difference. For the present I want to pick up on this discussion and point to a certain slippage in postmodernist writing between positional difference and difference as diversity. As Bondi (1990: 163) has expressed it, 'positional difference proliferates into a fragmentation of the subject and a differentiation between subjects so total that its effects are indistinguishable from the coherent, unified, stable conception of the subject it opposes'. Graham too (1988: 63) remarks on the anti-essentialist essentialism to which this leads. Such is the case where 'difference' has itself become a totality, where difference is lost in a regresses to 'diversity'.

This argument comes in various forms. Among academics the most radical advocacy of difference as totality may come from the literary critic Stanley Fish (1980; 1988) for whom difference is so universal that it precludes theory. His primary theoretical contention is that there can be no theory. The ' "Against Theory" argument is so effective rhetorically', according to Malkan (1987: 132) because it 'deconstructs itself by using theoretical thinking to discredit the discourse of which it is a part'. Among politicians the implications of the argument are perhaps starker. 'There is no such thing as society'. Margaret Thatcher once proclaimed, 'only individuals'.

Despite the supposed death of the subject, the critique of structuralism and the turn to linguistics and psychology as appropriate texts of social construction have recentred a concern with what we might call the social individual, the making of the social self. Giddens's structuration theory and Bourdieu's habitus represent attempts to be able to deal again with social individuals and the question of agency without separating them from the establishment of social structures and the structuring of social interactions. A parallel shift has affected geographical research. In her influential work *Spatial Divisions of Labour* (1984), Doreen Massey emphasises the need to 'bridge the gap between individual behaviour and aggregate pattern'. The challenge, she notes, 'is to hold onto both the general movement and the particularity of circumstance' since 'neither theorising nor elaboration of general frameworks can in themselves answer questions about what is happening at any particular time or in any particular place'. 'The fundamental message is clear', she elaborates elsewhere, 'that the radical critique of the 1970s – for very understandable reasons both intellectual and political – went far too far overboard in its rejection of the importance of the spatial organization of things, of distance and perhaps above all, of geographical differentiation. ... The unique is back on the agenda' (Massey, 1984: 4, 8; 1985: 9, 19).

Massey's admonition may already have been taken too far, again for very understandable intellectual but especially political reasons, in a broad-based effort to privilege agency as against structure and the locality over regional and global scales of analysis, and to implant a realist ideology. Following its 1979 defeat by Thatcher, the British Labour Party combined a discernible if temporary internal shift of momentum to the left with a geographical shift toward local rather than national politics. The leftward shift of the Labour Party was met by a cadre of disillusioned Marxists moving rightward from the extra-parliamentary left. They sought 'more realistic' ways of remaining politically active. The ESRC localities project[4] in many ways stood at the confluence of this specific political shift with the intellectual challenge to Marxism and, in fact, theory in general. It has come to represent the meeting-point between the metaphorical 'local' of postmodernism, especially in its Foucauldian guise, and the geographical local constructed through everyday social processes. Thus the localities project has ben defended on the grounds that 'everything happens in localities', or that, at least, the locality as the site of everyday life is an inherently privileged scale of analysis. At its most extreme, this vision carried us from a vital research focus on localities to a narrower philosophical localism, at times politically justified by the notion, again fashionable in Thatcherite Britain, that one could *only* act locally. National and global change are effectively resigned to abstraction, or worse, to the prerogative of the right.

Racism, class exploitation, sexism and other forms of oppression – none of these fundamentally 'happens' simply in localities. Specific instances of racism, to take just one example, obviously do occur in 'localities', if by that is meant concrete places. From Bensonhurst in Brooklyn to Bradford in Britain specific instances of racism occur as interpersonal interactions between specific individuals, but racism is as much globally as locally constructed; few would contest the integral relationship between racism, sexism and class-based exploitation. It makes little sense, for instance, to see official Israeli racism against the Palestinians as simply happening in a locality; events in the West Bank can only be understood in relation to US military, economic and ideological support of the Israeli state, the relationship between Israel and other surrounding Arab and non-Arab states, the connections between Israel and South Africa and so forth. We could of course 'construct' the Knesset, the White House or the United Nations as themselves 'localities', but this clearly begs the entire question of localities. 'Think globally, act locally' is in this sense a conservative and unambitious slogan. The right acts globally, why not the left?

Having expressed these misgivings and to try and allay already prevalent confusions about localities (Sayer, 1989), I want to reassert none the less the clear need and the appropriateness of empirical research in and on localities. Nor should there be any doubt of the appositeness of comprehending the rich variety of social, political, economic and cultural meanings bound up with geographical differentiation. The point of contention is not the straw question whether localities ought or ought not to be researched; whether geographical difference is or is not an appropriate research focus. Rather, the question is: how do we conceptually construct localities and geographical difference *as* foci of research, and how are they related to other scales of geographical difference? The danger is not so much that the social discourse will become universally anti-theory or anti-global. There are certainly hints of this move, but a much more likely consequence would seem to be a kind of collective schizophrenia in which global and local scales of analysis, theoretical and empirical approaches, cultural and non-cultural discourses increasingly lose connection, one from the other, along politically established fault lines.

As Malkan (1987: 129) says of Fish, he 'makes a fascinating case study of how ideas originally thought to have a liberating or at worst a value-neutral effect on social change can be made to accommodate a new set of conservative political goals'. Whatever the originating intentions of locality studies, the result is at times a more ambiguous celebration of simple geographical diversity as much as a comprehension of the active production of difference and differences. Locality studies have not to any significant degree embraced the commodification of geographical difference which, as archaic regional ideologies, attend the nostalgic reaction to a trenchant (if never complete) global homogenisation of culture. Such nostalgia for a lost regional identity celebrates a rump experiential 'diversity' as part of, not despite, 'the triumph of a new kind of conformism' (Karnoouh, 1986: 26). Patrick Wright (1985: 16) makes a parallel point when, remarking on the heritage industry, he warns that 'the bourgeois enlistment of particularity' is 'an egoistic ideological principle'.

And yet the connections between locality studies and an ontology of geographical diversity are increasingly apparent. In the history of geography the most extreme advocacy of a received spatial diversity may come from the conservative antimodernism of Richard Hartshorne whose highly influential 1939 book, *The Nature of Geography*, proposed a neo-Kantian conception of geographic research which, while pilloried in the 1960s, enjoys some renewed support today. For Hartshorne geographical differentiation is 'naïvely given' (1961: 237), and this became a fundamental pillar of his methodology. Several authors have sought to reinstate Hartshorne's neo-Kantian distinction between nomothetic and idiographic methods – an emphasis on generality and on the unique respectively (Sayer, 1989; Sack, 1989) – while others have seen in Hartshorne an explicit inspiration for contemporary treatments of place and locality (Entrikin, 1989; Agnew, 1989). Agnew's (1989: 126–30) advocacy of 'areal variation' and the use of Hartshorne to buttress a realist conception of localities makes the most explicit connection. Dear (1988: 271), however, may boast the most cosmic ambition for spatial difference as totality: 'we should make clear [to social theorists] that geography is also everything, because all human life is place-specific'.

In the present mood, the disavowal of 'totalizing discourses' is itself rather total. In so far as difference is rendered total, any kind of radical analysis is effectively foreclosed. Radicalism involves not merely, as its Greek etymon suggests, a comprehension of the roots of a question; radicalism is a process not a result. One gets to the roots but in so doing one better understands the surficial flourishes of the issues. Radicalism is about making links, however enduring or contingent, and that is what is denied or at least circumscribed in the assertion of difference as total.

The useful political insights of postmodernism depend on an ability and willingness to hold on to a concept of difference as actively and integrally established within the array of social relations and processes. Active social relations of difference, not passive diversity or variation, point the way to an emancipatory politics connecting specific experiences of oppression and exploitation with visions of alternative futures *and* a sense of how to get there. The political correlate of diversity is a paralysing pluralism of the 'anything goes' in which there are no criteria for negotiating between competing claims. How then are we to construct theoretical analyses that avoid both an eclectic and a totalistic treatment of difference and at the same time construct a non-pluralistic and spatialised politics based on the potentially liberatory notions of, by Barrett's definition, positional difference?

The work of Henri Lefebvre provides some hints. Lefebvre has conceived the city as 'a space of differences'. The crucial distinction, for Lefebvre, is between a social space constituted by the activity of everyday life and an abstract space laid down by the actions of the state and the economic institutions of capital. The reproduction of the social relations of capitalism is accomplished as a constant struggle between these different modes of reproducing space (Lefebvre, 1979: 293; forthcoming). If Lefebvre was for a long time virtually alone among a generation of older Marxists in taking geographical space seriously and integrating a spatial perspective at the core of his critique of capitalism, it is important, I think, to take further this notion of 'a space of differences' (see also Deutsche, 1988). In particular I want to investigate the structuring of space according to different scales. I want to propose that a political theory of geographical scale lies at the heart of a geographically literate social theory, and further, that such a theory helps to situate one of the central dilemmas emerging from postmodernism: namely, how to negotiate between difference and different subject positions. This is an exploratory idea and I can do little more here than sketch some basic research questions.

THE POLITICS OF SCALE

Much of the confusion in contemporary constructions of geographical space arises from an extensive silence on the question of scale. The theory of geographical scale – more correctly the theory of the production of geographical scale – is grossly underdeveloped. In effect there is no social theory of geographical scale, not to mention an historical materialist one. And yet it plays a crucial part in our whole geographical construction of material life. Was the brutal repression of Tianamen Square a local event, a regional or national event, or was it an international event? We might reasonably assume that it was all four, which immediately reinforces the conclusion that social life operates in and constructs some sort of nested hierarchial space rather than a mosaic. How do we critically conceive of these various nested scales, how do we arbitrate and translate between them? Further, how do we conceptualise such a translation in a way that centres social practices and politics designed to destroy the oppressive and exploitative intent of hierarchial space? The idealism of official 'locality studies' lies in the assumption that this translation is effected simply by asserting the privilege of 'the local', rather than effecting its relatedness to other spatial scales.

I have already claimed that Giddens represented space as a mosaic, although of course with the concept of regionalisation he begins to glimpse scale as an active process. But it is a highly abstract and very limited characterisation of the making of scale, focused on individual regionalisations of time–space. For Giddens a private house is a locale, itself divided into other locales. The house is 'regionalized into floors, halls and rooms. But the various rooms of the house are zoned differently in time as well as space. The rooms downstairs are characteristically used most in daylight hours [he says] while bedrooms are where individuals "retire to" at night.' Locales provide 'settings of interaction' but are not scale specific: 'locales may range from a room in a house, a street corner, the shop floor of a factory, towns and cities, to the territorially demarcated areas occupied by nation-states' (Giddens, 1984: 118–19). Scale here is trivialised to a remarkable degree; there is no suggestion in Giddens that systematically different social processes are involved in the arbitration and construction of different scales of social activity.

Different societies not only produce space, as Lefebvre has taught us, but they also produce scale. The production of scale may be the most elemental differentiation of geographical space and it is every bit a social process. There is nothing ontologically given about the traditional division between home and locality, urban and regional, national and global scales. The differentiation of geographical scales establishes and is established through the geographical structure of social interactions. With a concept of scale as produced, it is possible to avoid on the one hand the relativism that treats spatial differentiation as a mosaic, and on the other to avoid a reified and uncritical division of scales that repeats a fetishism of space. It should become possible, in other words, to interpolate the 'translation rules' that allow us to understand not only the construction of scale itself but the way in which meaning translates between scales. As a global event Tiananmen Square has a very different meaning than it has as a local event; the two are clearly coincident, though not identical, but how do we determine this difference and homology of meaning? Without resolving some of these questions, a more systematic understanding of geographical difference, and hence of difference more generally, will remain closed.

Scale is central in a more conceptual way. It is presumably desirable to have some consistent connection between a hierarchy of geographical scales as produced and reproduced in the landscapes of capitalism and the conceptual abstractions through which we understand socio-spatial events and processes. The concept of scale then takes on a second meaning. It is not only material scale worked and reworked as landscape, but it is also the scale of resolution or abstraction which we employ for understanding social relationships, whatever their geographical imprinting. Many debates and disagreements, including the localities debate, have been needlessly muddled by a confusion concerning these two related but separate meanings of scale. A theory of the production of scale would differentiate but integrate these two meanings, being careful not to equate the local strictly with the concrete, the global with the general (Horvath and Gibson, 1983; Cox and Mair, 1989).

Taken further, this point speaks to the central question of positional difference. Consistent with the metaphorical appropriation of space, the contest and negotiation between different subject positions implies a simultaneous judgement of identity as well as difference, a social judgement about the identity of the subject and its positionality *vis-à-vis* 'others'. In other words, such a contest and negotiation already implies socially established boundaries of difference and sameness (Agnew, 1989), albeit boundaries that are continually forged and reforged in social practice. This in turn implies a theory of the production of scale. To give an obvious example, the question of who is included and who includes themselves as 'black' can be recast as a question of the socially constructed scale at which a black social and political identity is established. Thus amidst the 1981 uprisings in Britain, a whole generation of young Asians who had not hitherto seen themselves as black explicitly adopted this identity, thereby extending the scale of this particular 'subject position'. This was not an uncontested process, of course. Some Africans, Caribbeans and black British resisted this redefinition as a defence of identity; whites resisted even more fiercely to prevent the construction of a larger, more powerful 'other'. Thus the scale of struggle and the struggle over scale are two sides of the same coin.

Patterns of capital investment may well be the most powerful deter-minants of geographical scale, and as capital and capital–labour relations are restructured, so too is scale (Smith and Dennis, 1987; Smith, 1989; Mair, *et al.*, 1989). Corporation such as IBM and AT&T have expansion and contraction strategies that are differentiated by spatial scale; AT&T's investment priorities in northern New Jersey, which it has colonised as a home base, may not be entirely homologous with their national or global strategies. In a 'restructuring capitalism', according to one business writer, 'successful companies must be intensely local and intensely global at the same time – an apparent contradiction wherein lies the formula for success' (Hennessy, 1989). From the perspective of capital, the centrality of geographical scale is that it represents a materialised if always malleable solution to the basic contradiction between co-operation and competition. Within national boundaries, for example, there is explicit co-operation among capitals over labour laws, infrastructure provision, social welfare policies, tax and trade policies and the like. The same capitals compete intensely for internal markets but co-operate in funding a national military capability designed to secure capital abroad and fend off the military, political and economic predations of competing national and even individual capitals. The globalisation of capital does not eliminate the national scale of social organisation, but it does transform and diminish it. Likewise, at the urban scale, the same capitals that co-operate through the local state, chambers of commerce and local growth coalitions, in establishing local conditions for the reproduction of labour power, also compete for wage labour and for local markets. The production of scale is a central means by which capital is both contained and freed, provided with a territory and at the same time a global base. Scott's (1986; 1988) analysis of the construction of new ensembles of production amidst the present restructuring captures this contradiction as it is worked out geographically. Disorganised capitalism is at the same time a reorganising capitalism.

A systematic connection between divisions of labour and capital and divisions into geographical scale has been suggested. The global scale can be conceived as the scale of financial capital and the world market, and is internally differentiated primarily according to comparative conditions, costs and organisational capacities and propensities of labour power. The national scale is constructed via political and military co-operation and competition, but divided into regions according to economic questions also relating to labour. The scale of the locality, by contrast, can be seen as the scale of social reproduction and embodies the geographical territory over which daily activities normally range; ground rent provides the primary means of differentiation (Smith, 1990: 135–47).[5] The scale of the home is established by units of social reproduction and is internally differentiated primarily according to relations of gender construction and reproduction. We might also add, although it is only now beginning to be considered within the geographical discourse, the scale of the body, explored by feminists such as Rich (1986).

Although this schema gives some emphasis to the 'scales of capital', it is important to remember that rarely is geographical scale simply imposed from above. The making of geographical scale also results from and contributes to social struggles based on (and problematising) class, gender, race and other social differences. In so far as scale boundaries, for example those of locality and nationality, quite literally *contain* local and national struggles respectively, scale is constructed as both a technology and ideology of capitalism. Harvey (1973) has argued that while the rich express their freedom in their ability to overcome space, the poor are imprisoned by it. It is scale that delimits the prison walls of social geography. In a similar vein he notes that socialist, working-class and other oppositional groups are 'generally better at organizing in and dominating *place* than they are at commanding *space*' (Harvey, 1989: 236). They are, in other words, relatively empowered in place but disempowered over space. In this sense, scale provides the technology through which space contains struggle unless and until the existing bounds of scale are challenged and broken, to be re-established and rechallenged at a higher level.

CONCLUSION

Heraclitus apparently once complained: 'Everything flows. Give me a place to stand.' Negotiating a place to stand would seem to be an ancient as much as a postmodern dilemma. As I hope I have established here, the predicament is not easily soluble by appeal to spatial metaphors of subject positionality and the like. There is in any case an irony to such a resort. Postmodernism has cast itself as an epochal advance over the narratives of modernism among which an often undifferentiated Marxism was often the major target. It was the heaviest and most metallic of heavy-metal modernisms, by numerous accounts. The language of privileged subject positions, however, reflects a central insight by Marx himself. For Marx, exploitation by capital endowed the working class with a privileged comprehension of capitalism; the privilege lay in an intimate familiarity with exploitation denied to those with a different 'subject positionality'.

The importance of postmodernism lies not so much in escaping Marx and modernism, then, but in expanding this insight to cover other oppressed peoples. The danger of postmodernism lies in the denial of group identity, *à la* Thatcher, the celebration of eclecticism and of diversity as total difference, such that the only permissible privileging resides with the individual. Closely related is the danger of 'gender tourism', or indeed other package tours to the subaltern, in which, as Suzanne Moore (1988) puts it, white male academics cavort in postmodernism as a way of 'getting a bit of the other'. Everybody wants to get their fifteen minutes of 'the other'.

One of the most spirited conceits of modernism, drunk with the influence of history and spurred on by the facility with which twentieth-century capitalism sought the 'annihilation of space by time' (Marx, 1973: 539), is the claim that we are beyond geography. The visceral geographies of a restructuring capitalism, from the devastation of sub-Saharan Africa, deindustrialisation, urban abandonment and homelessness, to the glitzy international simulacra of Disney World, surely disabuse us of that conceit. Yet the philosophical turn, specifically the construction of a spatialised ontology such as Soja (1989) proposes, would leave the contemporary reassertion of geographical space too vulnerable to the whim of philosophical fashion. The history of the production of space and of geographical scale has yet to be written, but if Sohn-Rethel's (1978) hints about the material bases to conceptual abstraction are at all valid, it is to such a history that we should first look for an understanding of the critical uses of geography.

The recentring of space and geographical discourse should not be construed as a further dimension along which postmodernism departs from modernism. The inherited devaluation of geographical space may have material roots, but it also represents the significant underdevelopment of a spatial discourse. Especially in America, but to a lesser extent elsewhere, it may not be too strong to talk of a missing geography between 1919 and the 1960s. Not that geography played no function at all for war is fundamentally beneficent to a discipline that has lent itself in a variety of national and international contexts to postwar reconstruction. Rather, the disavowal of geography itself reflects, as Soja says, the biases of modernism. But hardly the biases of modernity. From colonial expansion to the building of the suburbs, from the destruction of 'local peoples' in the inner city and the Amazon, capitalism always was a geographical project.

The goal of a spatialised politics of the sort Jameson seeks, where 'spatial issues' provide a 'fundamental organizing concern', is, I would argue, to overcome social domination exercised through the exploitative and oppressive construction of scale, and to reconstruct scale and the rules by which social activity constructs scale. The renegotiation of political, as much as economic, competition and co-operation is simultaneously a reconstruction of geographical scale. I doubt that I have managed to do any more than to announce a project here and to ask several questions. How is scale constructed in everyday life, and how are different scales connected? What different roles do questions of class, gender and race play in the construction of different scales and how are these issues connected to questions of the economic, political and social determination of scale? One thing I am sure of is that the answer lies less in philosophy than in an active spatial politics, however that might look. The hope here is that by grounding the spatial metaphors of postmodernism in a theory of the production of a scale, we may produce at least the political language by which *we* – conscious of our identity and our differences, and with a sober sense of the power we oppose – can indeed map the political terrain and decide on 'a place to stand'.

Acknowledgements

Several people have given me comments and criticisms in the various stages of writing this paper and I want to acknowledge all their help: Liz Bondi, Rosalyn Deutsche, Joe Doherty, Andy Herod, Cindi Katz, Diane Neumaier and Ali Rogers. Sheila Moore especially encouraged me to think of the politics of scale in this way.

NOTES

1. For an ironic embrace of the prolific apocalypse wrought by postmodernism, see Derrida (1984).
2. For a critique of construction theory and its psychological roots in Lacan, see Ian (1990).
3. For a pre-postmodern assault on eclecticism, see Therborn (1971).
4. The localities project, sponsored by the British Economic and Social Research Council (ESRC) has been the subject of considerable debate, largely in the pages of *Antipode: A Radical Journal of Geography*. See Savage *et al.* (1987); Smith (1987); Cooke (1987, 1989); Gregson (1987); Beauregard (1988); Lovering (1989); Cox and Mair (1989); Duncan and

Savage (1989). For an incisive treatment of the rise of postmodernism in the context of Thatcher's Britain, see Sivanandan (1989).

5.   In the first statement of these ideas on scale, I used 'the urban' rather than the local. Clearly this excludes the production of rural space at the local scale. Further, despite the problems associated with the 'official' localities studies project, I am convinced that there is a fruitful use of the concept of localities (Cox and Mair, 1989). Also, I am clearly using 'localities' in a different way from Probyn (1989), who correctly notes the inspecificity of 'the local' but whose grounding of this notion itself remains too abstract.

4 Discourse Discourse: Social Psychology and Postmodernity

Ian Parker

In the late 1960s and early 1970s social psychology was in crisis. It still is. However, political debates outside the discipline are more muted now, and this has meant that the rhetoric of dispute and debate over social-psychological theories and methods has softened. Things appear to have settled a bit, and in the place of arguments over the ways in which the discipline has or has not participated in the oppression of ordinary people, we have gentler debates over the conceptual value of attending to the accounts ordinary people give (for example, Antaki, 1988). A consequence is that social psychology today (in Britain and North America) is developing an interest in discourse and in discourse analysis. This topic and its method has emerged in and around Potter and Wetherell's (1987) *Discourse and Social Psychology*.

I want to exaggerate the impact of discourse analysis on social psychology in this chapter, and situate the work on discourse in the context of the 'turn to language' in the discipline which was provoked by combatants in the crisis period roughly two decades ago. It is then a short step to the debates over postmodernism, and I shall set out two possible directions in which the turn to *discourse* can take social psychology. I shall then go on to explain why the reflexive postmodern tendencies in recent discourse work should be supported, even exacerbated, and arrive at a cautionary endnote about the role of politics. So, what was the crisis about?

THE CRISIS AND THE TURN

The dominant theme in the 'new' social psychology critiques of the then dominant laboratory-experimental paradigm was a complaint over the positivist methods and assumptions which underpinned research on social behaviour (Harré and Secord, 1972). A 'new paradigm' informed by a realist philosophy of science was proposed, and the focus of research was to be the accounts people gave of their actions. One line of reasoning here was that accounts and actions had the same origin and that the collection of accounts would be tapping the collective knowledge which constituted the social world (the 'expressive' sphere). In this way the trap of introspection would be skirted, for the object of study was to be shared social knowledge rather than private individual mental processes. A parallel tack was followed by social psychologists who drew upon hermeneutics and they argued that accounts had the function of making sense as a *process* (rather than having, in finished form, 'made' sense). A researcher did not have privileged access to what was 'really' going on; it was assumed that researchers also made their own sense by virtue of their participation in the processes they studied (Gauld and Shotter, 1977). These debates were perceived as being rather esoteric at the time, but it did soon become clear to most social psychologists that a key problem with traditional social psychology was that it studied a silent world. Social psychology needed to turn to accounts, to speech, to language.

These moves reflected wider-ranging academic contests in other disciplines and although the participants in the social psychology paradigm debates rarely refer to structuralism and post-structuralism, the 'crisis' literature was as informed by those conceptual developments as it was by the political upheavals in the academic institutions (Parker, 1989a). Social psychology tends to trail miserably behind intellectual trends outside, and it was inevitable, perhaps, that it should only belatedly shift its attention to the organisation of language, to discourse. It should be noted that the 'new social psychology', deconstructive attacks on texts and the analysis of discourse have been selectively and cautiously adopted, and co-opted, by social psychology.

New Social Psychology

New social psychologists (Harré and Secord, 1972; Gauld and Shotter, 1977) have remained on the fringe of the discipline, and their uses of structuralist and hermeneutic work had the effect of marginalising them. Although mainstream social psychologists recognised the value of the criticisms made of the bulk of the trivial and dehumanising laboratory work, there was never a 'paradigm shift'. Social psychologists could not see in new social psychology alternative systematic methods (with the highly valued possibilities of prediction, control and replication), they could not take on board complex theoretical debates from philosophy, sociology and literature (and would not try to understand them), and they suspected that some underlying political agenda (or, at least, effects) paralleled the critiques. This stream of debate, however, did provide space for other developments.

Deconstruction

Deconstruction emerged from structuralism as part of the post-structuralist package of critical work on texts (for example, Derrida, 1976), and a concern with taking apart texts of different kinds has appeared in social psychology in recent years. Some variants of this work explicitly draw upon Derrida, and deconstruction is used to tease apart dominant concepts in the discipline (for example, Parker, 1988), and other attempts to make deconstruction more accessible and politically useful to radicals in social psychology have included a number of critical perspectives on psychology's texts under the rubric of 'deconstruction' (Shotter and Gergen, 1989; Parker and Shotter, 1990). It is harder to conceal deconstruction in the normal garb of social psychology, and the signs are that the mainstream practitioners will not wear it.

However, the deconstructionist tendencies are not only useful in introducing the work of Derrida to psychologists and exploring the implications of that work for conceptions of 'the self' (for example, Sampson, 1989). Deconstruction is a component in the wave of post-structuralist writing which has mutated in recent years into what we now call postmodernism (Dews, 1987). It also is tactically useful as a way of disrupting theories, opening up *conflicts*. In the case of social psychology, we may want to open up conflicts and not want to see them resolved within the discipline. I shall return to this point later on.

Discourse Analysis

Discourse analysis, on the other hand, has been successful in a short amount of time in marking out a fairly respectable place in the discipline. Some of the new literature does make overt use of Foucault's (1972, 1980d) descriptions of discourse and power and locates social psychology in the midst of discourses of surveillance and subjectivity (Parker, 1989b). One influential strand employs psychoanalytic theory alongside Foucault (Henriques *et al.*, 1984). It is possible to employ post-structuralist ideas to develop descriptions of discourse in social psychology (Parker, 1990). The discourse analysis taken up by an increasing number of mainstream social psychologists, however, is more careful about these Foucauldian filiations; Potter and Wetherell's (1987) work appeals to microsociology, analytic philosophy and (more cautiously) semiological traditions. Now, while it is true that these traditions are, in some senses, as subversive as post-structuralism (and cannier traditional social psychologists recognise this), and that Potter and Wetherell's research has developed alongside politically informed discussions of ideology (Billig *et al.*, 1988), discourse analysis has broken out of the margins of social psychology.

Discourse analysis, in its description of the recurrently used words, phrases and linguistic devices which categorise and reproduce the social world, provides techniques which build on content analysis up to higher levels of meaning, and these techniques *appear* to be systematic. It often plays the scientistic language-game of social psychology (in, for example, the elaboration of systematic 'steps' to analyse discourse), but it also breaks some important rules. It breaks the rules in three ways.

Reflexivity
Discourse analysis is deliberately reflexive about its own truth claims, and draws attention to the discursive construction of its own theoretical position and its 'data'. This invitation to reflexivity is not restricted to statements that any 'social text' can become an object of research and that the text of *Discourse and Social Psychology* 'should not be immune from this kind of examination' (Potter and Wetherell, 1987: 3). The inclusion in their book of earlier drafts is designed to provide Potter and Wetherell with the opportunity to discuss their own activity as writers. This is not to say that they *always* succeed in including a reflection on their own position as researchers (Bowers, 1988), but they do struggle against the scientistic closure which afflicts much social psychology. Elsewhere, Potter (1988a) makes the point that discourse analysis should celebrate the ambiguity and undecidability of social scientific knowledge.

Relativism
Discourse analysis corrodes the truth claims of other supposedly scientific 'discoveries'. Many of the most useful examples in *Discourse and Social Psychology* concern the rhetorical devices that scientists use to support their own findings and to discredit the theories of their opponents. This line of attack applies to psychologists and the readings that they make of one anothers work (Potter, 1987), and to the 'natural' scientists whose rhetoric is problematised by combining the sociology of scientific knowledge with discourse analysis (Potter, 1988b). The relativism that results from this enterprise, of course, can sanction an increased attention to what the knowledge *does*.

Crisis
The relativist and reflexive dynamic of discourse analysis impels social psychology a step further into the crisis. Sometimes deliberately, and sometimes despite itself, discourse analysis breaks the rules by raising broader issues to do with the enterprise of social psychology. Whilst the use of approaches to texts from other disciplines could serve to demarcate social psychology more rigidly from other social sciences, because discourse analysis demands a shift of *topic* to 'social texts of all kinds ... [including] ... conversations, newspaper stories, novels and soap operas' (Potter and Wetherell, 1987: 1), it could also dissolve the boundaries.

At the moment (and the tension between opposition and recuperation will undergo another series of twists before the role of discourse analysis can be fully assessed) the approach does subvert social psychological knowledge. Although the empirical studies of discourse may appear banal and simplistic to those in other social sciences, these developments have been useful to radicals in psychology as a whole. But how does this connect with postmodernism?

DISCOURSE AND THE POSTMODERN: TWO MOVES

Lyotard (1984a) claims that the overarching 'metanarratives' of modern enlightenment culture have given way to the little stories which constitute postmodernity. The big theories of social progress and the scientific work which grounded these theories in truth are replaced by a multiplicity of language-games. In the place of modern political projects which traced the emergence of oppression, we are offered a version of pluralism in which the world consists of a multiplicity of little narratives and language games. In place of truth, we have perpetual reflection on the impossibility of truth. Just as accounts of the social have lost their way in the postmodern, so have senses of individual identity. The personal meanings of each citizen of the modern state have given way to fragmented, contested and situation-dependent experiences which cannot be interpreted to reveal signs of the truth of the human condition. Humanism as a secularised modern translation of religious belief now dissolves into the hedonism (or resignation) provoked by the postmodern condition; the concern is with intensity of sensation instead of interpretation.

What is significant about Lyotard's claims for my purposes is the reflection on the way in which narratives work. Discourse is now seen as responsible for having constituted a particular reality and subjectivity in modern times, and we are invited to believe that the shattered remains of discourse hold together the moves in language in the postmodern. The most useful way to think about these transformations is actually to locate them in the context of theories of language, in the shift from structuralism to post-structuralism (Dews, 1987). In social psychology, discourse analysis is a (very) cautious reworking of post-structuralist approaches. Meanwhile, post-structuralism has spawned a whole worldview. The postmodern is a condition which operates as if post-structuralism was true, and, to a lesser degree, postmodernism in social psychology is the state of things that results when we come to believe that there really is no object of study but discourse, no way of studying it but discourse analysis, and no way of grounding a critical view of discourse but in reflexivity (that is, no way of grounding a critical view).

Discourse analysis is of a piece with this attention to language, and the relativism and reflexivity which discourse analysis prompts constitutes another area of the social sciences as postmodern. There are, of course, contradictions and dilemmas in this area, and the move, for example, from depth to surface in Potter and Wetherell's (1987) study of rhetorical devices is now supplemented by other claims (Billig *et al.*, 1988) that a researcher should also pick up *implicit* themes. But, in so far as discourse analysis turns around to language as 'reality' and prompts reflection on the textual nature of social life, it is postmodern. The turn to discourse is such that all there is in the world is seen as a discursive matter. In this sense, the postmodern is an experience of signification in which everything is invested (equally) with meaning (Lash, 1988), and our understanding of discourse has changed so that it is very different from previous meanings of the term when it could, for example, be contrasted with such things as 'figuration'. There are many oppositions that can be struck between the modern and the postmodern (for example, Hassan, 1985), and I am, of course, selecting aspects which apply to social psychology.

'Post'

However, to say that discourse analysis is postmodern is not to say that this particular expression of the claims of post-structuralists (over-determined in this particular case by microsociology, analytic philosophy and semiology) is part of postmodernity. We need to distinguish two manifestations of post-structuralism as it has mutated from a type of analysis into a way of seeing.

Postmodernism

The term 'postmodernism' describes the conditions of uncertainty, frivolity, relativism and reflexivity in different artistic and scientific fields. These conditions are neither experienced as static (it is a state of flux) nor progressive (in some cases these conditions are viewed as degenerate), and each area has its own point of collapse into the postmodern as well as a particular rhythm of adoption and resistance. It is difficult to generalise from one area to the other, though a symptom, paradoxically, of postmodernism is that one is continually impelled to try and do exactly that. In the case of social psychology, the discipline insulated itself fairly successfully from other academic areas such as sociology, economics, philosophy or psychoanalysis up until the late 1960s, and did not entertain doubts about its serious mission to discover the truth about behaviour and apply it. Postmodern tendencies in social psychology were late-coming and unwelcome.

Postmodernity

The term 'postmodernity', on the other hand, applies to the condition of culture which encloses and informs the abandonment of the grand narratives of humanised science, progress and individual meaning in various areas. It is sometimes useful to describe architecture, music or psychology as postmodern, and to use that term to conceptually fix a contemporary point in the process of acceleration of reflexivity which the enlightenment, modernity, set in motion (Berman, 1982). However, the notion of postmodernity is a little more double-edged. There is, strictly speaking, no such thing as postmodernity. There are, rather, pockets of contemporary culture in which it is possible to identify postmodern themes, and for which the postmodern condition may be 'true'. We have to take care to distinguish the collapse of the modern project in sectors of academic life and avant-garde culture from the delusional projections of that postmodern condition out on to the whole of society. Lyotard (1982a) and critical writers, such as Jameson (1984), who engage with him on his ground are wrong to apply postmodern categories to the *whole* of culture.

The distinction between postmodernism and postmodernity, and the correlative refusal to admit that *everything* is up for grabs, opens up a choice between two directions that a discipline like social psychology could move in. Should social psychology guard against the intrusion of the postmodern, prevent the prescriptions of postmodern writers from becoming, through the operation of a gigantic self-fulfilling prophecy, true, and try to understand the phenomenon of postmodernism? Or should social psychology welcome postmodernism with open arms, dissolve itself into language, and lose its anchor in reality? This choice for social psychology has been raised in other disciplines (Bauman, 1988a), but I want to give an answer which is informed by the particularities of my discipline at this time.

Social Psychology as Modern

From the beginning of the century in America social psychology has been an experimental science concerned with the study of individuals behaving in the presence of others. It has been a thoroughly modern discipline. Social psychologists have been obsessed with trying to discover universal truths about social interaction, and have maintained a disarmingly naïve faith in their steady accumulation of facts. It is possible to interpret the *effects* of the 'new paradigm' critiques as forcing a shift of perspective within this progressivist picture, and as succeeding in merely adding in a focus on the personal meanings of the subjects. When subjects became viewed as accountees capable of giving a (partial, flawed, imperfect) description of their social worlds, this modern science was not sabotaged but improved.

We could generate a social-psychological programme of study of the postmodern, and perhaps this would both improve the discipline and add to our understanding. Within the array of traditional techniques are a number which could be brought to bear on this topic: (a) experimental and interview studies of attribution which focus on commitment to personal relationships, and the degree to which desired moral characteristics are ascribed to an other (modern interpretation) or rated second to attractiveness (postmodern sensation); (b) questionnaire studies which could tap attitudes to the modern and discover who is, and to what degree they have 'lost the nostalgia for the lost narrative' (Lyotard, 1984a: 41), and whether there is a postmodern personality (correlated perhaps with Type B profile, external locus of control, paratelicism and so on); or (c) observational and multidimensional-scaling studies of the cognitive maps of subjects in the Bonaventure Hotel, say, which would (rather worryingly) lock into Jameson's (1984) proposals for a way out of the cultural logic of late capitalism.

New social psychology adds to this some less risible possibilities: (a) ethnographic interviewing which focuses on the experience of the impact of information technology (connected with oral history projects to contextualise these changes), and the ways in which knowledge is used could be connected with contemporary work on leisure practices; (b) there could be studies of the rhetoric and representations (employing hermeneutic methods) of scientific ideas and the ways in which these are turned into a 'common sense', and employed as true stories, urban legends or simple pragmatic language games; and (c) participant research descriptions (using 'ethogenic' approaches) of the small social worlds and subcultures which are postmodern could be linked to work in the sociology of scientific knowledge and an attention to the academic interests served by postmodern notions (cf. Bauman, 1988b).

The task in these examples would be a modern study of the postmodern phenomenon, and would usefully include an examination of the ways in which the postmodern has found its way into sectors of popular culture. Analysis of postmodern discourse could also be added here, but discourse analysis is also – perhaps more – fitted for the postmodern direction social psychology could move in.

Social Psychology as Postmodern

If the heralds of postmodernity are right, then modern studies of post-modernism are fated to fail, and to fold sooner or later into their objects of study. Apart from the (Gergen) quote in the publisher's blurb for *Discourse and Social Psychology* (Potter and Wetherell, 1987) which claims that the book is a step toward postmodern psychology (a claim Potter and Wetherell do not make themselves), the term 'postmodernism' is slowly dribbling into psychology.

From new social psychology, Shotter (1987a) cautiously uses the term to radicalise descriptions of accountability and selfhood. More enthusiastic advocates in psychology refer to the 'postmodernists' as combining constructivism and deconstruction, and moving the discipline forward to give a more liberal (and I use the word advisedly) understanding of gender differences (Hare-Mustin and Maracek, 1988; cf. Owens, 1985, for a more thoroughly postmodern account of gender; and Burman, 1990, for an appraisal of the problems this raises for feminists in psychology). In sociology this astonishingly fast recuperation of postmodern writing is paralleled by claims that social scientists could benefit from the attention of 'postmodernists' to the value base of data, a point at which, we are advised, for example, that 'postmodernists differ little from Weber' (Murphy, 1988: 606).

So far, the term 'postmodernism' is actually used to buttress existing (albeit marginal) approaches, and it may be the case that postmodernism in social psychology will develop through the work of figures whose work was postmodern *avant la lettre*. Lyotard (1984a) suggests some contenders for admission to the pragmatic and pluralist research world which has supposedly displaced the modern.

Language Games

Lyotard's (1984a) use of Wittgenstein and in particular the notion of language games is relevant here. What is important to notice, however – and social psychologists would probably not normally notice it because Lyotard is following a move that the discipline plays with the strength of a repetition compulsion – is that the location of *conflict* is shifted. Conflict is no longer at the level of class or the state, but is to be found at an inter-personal level. The gloss on this is quite interesting. We are told that 'Consensus has become an outmoded and suspect value' (Lyotard, 1984a: 66). The way of coping with the breakdown of consensus is to recognise the 'heteromorphous nature' of language games. However, we are invited into a world in which consensus has broken at a small-scale level, precisely because (though Lyotard does not spell this out) consensus at a larger level is the necessary condition, the backdrop, for the little games to take place.

The use of (Austinian) ordinary language philosophy, and the meaning which is tacked on to the term 'performative', is also designed to have the same effect. It 'realizes the optimal performance' (Lyotard, 1984a: 88) for an account of economic conditions which are now depicted as flowing happily and naturally from the activities of individuals. Discourses, now 'little narratives' rather than metanarratives, which mesh together culture are reproduced in a series of moves which redefine truth when and as is necessary. With this flows an account of legitimation which rests on the performance of the system, the system of moves ('paralogy' which includes, as a function of its operation, but cannot be reduced to, innovation). This, for Lyotard, is also now a description of science.

This, in a sense, is where discourse analysis came in, for many of the examples so far of devices in discourse which have truth effects in the social psychological discourse literature are from the language games of scientists. The sociology of scientific knowledge is an important resource for the development of Potter and Wetherell's (1987) work, and the attention to dialogue and presentation by scientists of their 'findings' effectively subverts their claims to a context-free truth (Potter 1987, 1988b). More generally, the research on particular discourses ('interpretive repertoires') carried out within social psychology cannot but reinforce the view that the essential 'reality' of the discourse lies at an interpersonal level. Discourse analysis participates in this series of games whether it likes it or not, and implies a discourse-user who is either ignorant of the moves or, more often, is restricting their concerns to the pragmatic aspects of encounters.

POSTMODERNISM, PSYCHOLOGY AND POLITICS

At this point I should like to stop and consider whether we should opt for the first direction I signalled above in which we use social psychology as a modern discipline to understand postmodernism, or whether we should support the tendency of social psychology to break with its past and become postmodern. This is a good point to stop and ask that question because a consideration of the putatively consensual nature of social life raises explicit problems, and it is political understanding of the issue that is required. This would be politics in an unashamedly modern sense, and of a kind that is aware of the importance of *conflict*, at least three senses of conflict. First of all it would appreciate the role of conflict between the liberatory aspirations of modern thought on the one hand and the conservative nature of modern *institutions* on the other. Secondly, it would also need to be a politics which opened up the conflict between reflexivity which merely dissolves our experiences in a plurality of different perspectives and *reflection* which grounds our activities in a wider context. Thirdly, it would attend to the conflict between individual experience and social structures. It is the third of these conflicts that I want to examine briefly, for social psychology is founded on the premise that the gulf between the individual and the social can be bridged. Social psychology is supposed to be that bridge, but it is not. The contradiction between the individual and the social is particularly important because the discourse discourse (a discourse which has as its object 'discourse') solves, or *appears* to resolve, it in an unhelpful way.

The Individual and the Social

Modern social psychology is caught between a discipline which constitutes the individual – which is psychology – and the discipline which studies society – that is, sociology. I am not concerned here with the role of psychology and sociology as disciplines, though my focus on social psychology does beg some important questions about the potential for progressive developments in those areas.

Psychology
Psychology is a discipline concerned with regulation and the production of subjectivity (Henriques *et al.*, 1984; Rose, 1985), and it could be argued that it is so deeply implicated in oppressive practices that nothing should be retrieved from it. It is possible, however, to find within the domain of psychology (very broadly conceived), though largely outside the institu-

tion, psychoanalytic accounts which engage with questions of culture, including, recently, issues raised by postmodernism (Frosh, 1989; Rustin, 1989). Psychoanalysis could be one basis for an exploration of individual experience which is not disconnected from social processes.

Sociology

Sociology, on the other side, has both operated as an essentially managerial discipline and nurtured oppositional theories, the most important of which is, of course, Marxism. However, it would be necessary to extricate Marxism from sociology to make it useful and to ground it in politics. When it lies inside the institution of sociology as a theoretical account of the operations of society, it becomes disarmed in the face of postmodernism when it is charged with being typically modern. Jameson (1984), for one, falls victim to the story that Marxism is just as the celebrants of postmodernity paint it, and he has then to play on their ground. We would be able to employ Marxism as an account of the social which is sensitive to individual experience if we took seriously the view that Marxism 'has never functioned as a metanarrative' (Montag, 1988), and should not do so.

Social psychology developed at the beginning of the century in America. It deliberately reduced social behaviour to the activities of an individual in the presence of others. Its laboratory-experimental studies of the individual were modelled on the popular 'scientific management' in the fast-growing modern factories. The individual worker's actions were observed, measured and disciplined. Social psychology, then, flowed out of a type of social organisation which it is now fashionable to call 'Fordism', and, with psychology, contributed to the 'deskilling' of the new labour force (Shotter, 1987b). Modern social psychology is caught, and its function is not to solve the problem but to keep it going. A fundamental premise of the new social psychology, a 'new paradigm' to rescue the discipline, was that the space between the disciplines of the individual and the disciplines of the social could be filled with a more sophisticated theory.

Connecting: Through Practice

Elsewhere, it has always, in modern culture, been possible to bridge the gulf between the individual and the social. The connection between individual singular experience and general social structures is made through political practice. You cannot start constructing a critique of psychology without raising the question of politics, and the same applies to social psychology. The words 'critical', 'radical' and 'progressive' are code-words. They are often merely items in an 'alternative' discourse in the discipline. They only take on a real meaning when a connection is made between studies of the individual and a political understanding of the social. The debates in academic psychology and social psychology are interesting, but they cannot provide a reference point for understanding what social psychology *does*.

Social psychology does not acknowledge that political practice is the key. One of the reasons for this is that the scientific study of individual behaviour was developed, as was scientific management, on the wave of repression of political strikes in America leading up to the First World War. The preoccupation of American social psychologists was with the defence of the rational individual, the good conservative citizen, and with the dangers of the crowd. American social psychology exported a concern with the dangers of the crowd and a discipline concerned to break up this large-scale social interaction into little bits. The discipline was then exported back to Europe. Social activity, political practice, was pathologised (Parker, 1989a).

When psychologists have been radical, it has not been in terms of their theories but in terms of their own political practice. The use of political reference points outside also leads to an understanding of social psychology as a problem, and the modern project of self-understanding, progress and social reconstruction can then be distinguished from the modern social scientific institutions. It is only then that we shall be able to distinguish between the way we would like things to be and the way they actually are. The descriptions of social life and individual choice offered by post-modernism are very appealing, and we may want 'modernity' (in the sense of it being an alienating experience of serial relentless progression and a chase after the 'new') to end (cf. Anderson, 1984). Buying (literally often buying) into the promise of the end of modernity from the relatively privileged position of academics and social science researchers, however, can lead us to slip into a celebration of a politically regressive abandonment of modern political projects. There is some truth, for example, in the claim that as far as the destruction of progressive humanist aspirations are concerned, 'the goal is no longer truth but performativity, not reason but power. The [British employers organisation] CBI are in this sense spontaneous post-structuralists to a man' (Eagleton, 1985: 63).

Connecting: Through Reflexivity

The reason why the role of discourse analysis is at issue here, and why the fate of discourse analysis is so closely connected with postmodernism in social psychology, is that the chasm between the individual and the social *is* being bridged today. The turn to discourse provokes the use of 'reflexivity' as a solution to the crisis that all critical social psychologists experience when they carry out research. Reflexivity is advertised, in some accounts of the postmodern, as the central defining feature of this new state of things (Lawson, 1984), and some of the enthusiasts of the postmodern in the social sciences see in it a way of overcoming the gulf between the individual and the social; 'postmodernists', we are told, advocate an 'anti-dualist position' (Murphy, 1988: 603). Reflexivity *appears* to provide the answer. We turn around and reflect on ourselves and our language. Reflexivity is used to denote our deliberate awareness of our place in things and our difference from others. To reflect thoroughly enough on your activity as a researcher is to problematise your own position as distanced observer, and then to dissolve any space between the topic and the resources you bring to bear upon it. The crueller critics of this state of things say that this is part of a move from parody to pastiche (Jameson, 1984). If you were to reflect on everything, what could be more radical than that?

There is certainly something odd going on when the connection between the individual and the social is made in terms of 'reflexivity' instead of political practice. My caution is that we have to understand the political functions of that connection instead of heaving a sigh of relief because a connection has been made. Reflexivity is an attempt, well-suited to the postmodern condition, to connect which is *depoliticised*. And it leaves traditional academic disciplines concerned with subjectivity, such as psychology, in their place. The new discourse about the nature of discourse and the analysis of discourse in social psychology encourages practitioners to join the spiral of reflexivity.

But I asserted at the beginning of this chapter that the reflexive tendencies in social psychology should be supported. Clearly this is not because, on balance, I like discourse analysis (though I do). It is, rather, because it is possible to allow the reflexive tendencies in social psychology, and confined to social psychology, to disrupt the discipline, while at the same time radical social psychologists can hold on to a reflective but *grounded* understanding of what is happening. Discourse analysis can be put to progressive uses, but only because we also hold to narratives about progress which are more important than social psychology.

Critical Distance

Jameson (1984) takes the notion of postmodernity too seriously, but is right when he insists that we need to construct some 'critical distance' between ourselves and the culture we inhabit (and which inhabits us). The prerequisite for that critical distance is that we mark a critical distance between ourselves and the social sciences. In the case of psychology and social psychology this is particularly important. When a connection between the individual and the social is made through political practice, that practice distances us from psychology. It should. One problem with the turn to discourse, and the way it dissolves the boundaries between social psychology and other disciplines, is that we lose sight of how bad psychology actually is, and the oppressive ways in which it operates when it is not just theorising but also practising on people.

There are pockets of contemporary culture and the social sciences where postmodernism thrives; this book testifies, among other things, to that. But these manifestations of the postmodern are symptoms of something else. When we employ these ideas in social psychology, we should be using them critically. We should not aim to improve the discipline, but to continue the crisis in social psychology so that there will always be room for manoeuvre. We should not be tempted, then, into believing new social psychologies are the truth, into taking our moves in the discipline's language games as ends in themselves, or into *just* joining a discourse about discourse about discourse about discourse . . .

5 Developmental Psychology and the Postmodern Child

Erica Burman

In this chapter I shall address the current and possible areas of intersection between the discipline of developmental psychology and analyses of contemporary society that seek to understand the phenomena of post-modernism. I suggest that theorists of postmodernism must engage with, as well as comment upon, developmental psychology if they are to offer an effective critique, and that there are areas of developmental psychology which postmodern analyses need to take seriously if they are to fulfil a potential of providing critical instruments for change. I shall be discussing developmental psychology, and in particular Piagetian developmental psychology. My intention is not to confirm or reinstate its role but rather to focus on what are in fact pervasive debates about the status and function of postmodernism.

I want to argue, through this juxtaposing of developmental psychology and accounts of postmodernism, that postmodernism is not everywhere but rather coexists with modern accounts. It is sometimes treated as though it replaces modernism. This is a serious mistake because those who see in postmodernism either an expression of or even a resistance to the 'new times' in which we live overlook two things: first, how traditional power structures and relationships are either left intact (or are still being reproduced) by postmodern culture; and secondly, such theorists are wrong to celebrate postmodernity. For when postmodernism does start to inform, for example, family relations it is not progressive. I shall argue that it is deeply complicit in the very structures it claims to have transcended. At the outset, then, a key distinction we need to make is between the claims of those who analyse the phenomena of post-modernism, and the enthusiasm of those who celebrate it. This distinction becomes of crucial importance when we come to consider how we can harness such analyses for progressive political ends.

DEVELOPMENTAL PSYCHOLOGY AS MODERN

First I need to say a little about developmental psychology. Developmental psychology is perhaps a paradigmatically *modern* discipline, committed to narratives of truth, objectivity, science and reason. Like psychoanalysis, developmental psychology participated in the post-Darwinian theorising which linked individual change and growth with evolutionary outcomes (Riley, 1983). 'Ontogeny recapitulates phylogeny' has been interpreted and applied in quite literal ways in developmental psychology: each child being held to reproduce within his own developmental career the psychology of his historical and evolutionary predecessors. (My use of male pronoun here is deliberate and is used to highlight how the model deployed is often implicitly masculine in orientation.)

As currently practiced in the West, developmental psychology is still dominated by the theorising of Jean Piaget whose project of 'genetic epistemology' aimed to link philosophy and biology through the study of the developing organism, the child. Piaget depicted the developing child as a budding scientist systematically encountering problems in the material world, developing hypotheses and learning by discovery and activity (Piaget, 1957) (hence the close association of Piaget with child-centred approaches in education). In Piaget's account, the goal of development is greater adaptation to changing, and ever more complex, environmental demands. The developmental trajectory of children's thinking, by this account, clearly follows the 'up the hill' model of science and progress: a hierarchical model of cognitive structures emerges whereby a more mature logic arises from and supersedes earlier and less adequate structures. In common with others of his time, Piaget, therefore, developing his ideas in Europe throughout two world wars, was deeply concerned to envisage how morality and reason could prevail over what he saw as biological doom and destruction (Piaget, 1918; 1933).

We can see instantiated within the Piagetian model, then, two strands associated with the modern. First of all, it is committed to the project of human emancipation. This not only imposes an enclosed, self-sufficient, autonomous individual, but also foreshadows its end. This is because the achievements of this self are contained within a finite model. Here we have the classic paradox of a modern, teleological model which forecloses its own end or goal by virtue of its envisioning of it. In Philippe Lacoue Labarthe's words 'the modern is . . . the unfolding within all its forms of a finishing philosophy of the subject' (1986: 5). Like most other modernist accounts it is patriarchal and imperialistic in its pretensions to provide universal explanations, both in its conceptualisation and its practice, privileging masculine and Western forms of reasoning, and stigmatising and dubbing inferior the non-rational. Moreover, in its singleminded march to true maturity it is unaware of the cultural and historical origins and specificities of its own project.

At this point it is worth pausing to reflect on whether developmental psychology has simply happened to acquire this modernist perspective, or whether it is in some deeper sense necessarily committed to it. I have taken Piaget as representative of developmental psychology, but of course there are particular reasons and circumstances, not to mention social forces, that have contributed to both the academic and applied popularity of his work. The very project of understanding the nature of the child has a long and prestigious history in western philosophy, which has been explicitly linked to political theories of origins and functioning of society. This is not the place to enter into the substance of the critiques which highlight Piaget's biologistic (Rotman, 1977), idealist (Venn and Walkerdine, 1978) and gendered assumptions (Henriques *et al.*, 1984), not to mention its reproduction of Cartesian oppositions between reason and emotion (Urwin, 1986). Suffice it to say that, as has been pointed out by many critics, Piaget's work presents a clear articulation of the political philosophy of individualism: society is seen as composed of separate, isolated and autonomous subjects interacting with each other only according to rationally evaluated social exchanges. The whole child-centred approach can be seen as a celebration of *laissez-faire* capitalism (Sullivan, 1977). It also celebrates a traditional masculinity which values detachment and objectivity over connection and relationships (Gilligan, 1982).

Critiques of the basis of developmental psychology which draw on post-structuralist approaches trace how the very emergence of the discipline can be seen as a response to social pressures to classify and segregate individuals and populations at the end of the nineteenth and into the twentieth century. At this time public and political anxiety was focused upon 'moral degeneracy', the poor physical health of recruits to the army, and the need to develop some criteria to exclude 'slower' children from mainstream schooling once compulsory elementary education had been introduced (Walkerdine, 1984). Some of the founding fathers of the domain of psychology were active exponents of eugenic ideas, and the concepts of 'ability' and 'temperament', together with their associated statistical apparatus and innatist assumptions, form part of their legacy to contemporary developmental psychology (Rose, 1985).

If the history of developmental psychology demonstrates its role as (in a paradoxically conspiratorial Foucauldian terminology) an administrative technology of classification and segregation (of which the Piagetian notion of stages forms merely a contemporary version), what implications does this have for our understanding of its possible effects and functions? The question arises, then, of whether developmental psychology can be other than modern in its intent. Linked so firmly to practices of education and welfare, developmental psychology will always function as an arena of intervention and social regulation. In this context, it is interesting to note that, although much has been made in recent accounts of Vygotskii's cultural historical model as providing a socially constructed individual subjectivity, the modern Soviet developmental psychology to which it has given rise is even more closely associated with practices of education, training and parental guidance (Valsiner, 1988).

If we are to move beyond the idealised epistemic subject of Piagetian theory and insert an account of development *within* social practices, then developmental psychology necessarily has to engage with the issues raised by postmodernism.

THE POSTMODERN WORLD

At this point I shall sidestep some of the more contentious debates such as whether there is in fact a rupture or a continuum between the modern and the postmodern; when each period began, if indeed such modern distinctions can be made; and the homologies and compatibilities between debates in aesthetics, French philosophy and cultural analysis. I shall confine myself to the following question: given that these debates do seem to offer fruitful insights into the adequacy and functioning of a social science practice such as developmental psychology, can we use them to make progressive interventions? I appreciate that what I am doing may be heresy to those who see in postmodernism no prospect, indeed perhaps even a rejection of the very *possibility* of political engagement. Such are precisely the tendencies within postmodernism that I find most disturbing. In particular, the diminishing sphere of political activity permitted within postmodernism, the shrinkage from socialist revolution to Foucauldian resistance to Lyotardian reflection, lends itself to, and indeed celebrates, a politics of despair and fatalism that constitutes the most dangerous aspect of postmodern existence (Callinicos, 1985).

It follows, then, that the characterisation of postmodernism on offer varies with the political perspective of the commentator, and of course my account is no exception. My understanding of the 'postmodern condition' is that of a crisis of confidence in the narratives of truth, science and progress which epitomised modernity. Meaning is no longer secured,

subjectivity is fragmented and contradictory – with a corresponding proliferation of sexed positions and sexualities – and purpose is replaced with
play. Using one of Jameson's (1984) distinctions, artistic productions have
moved from the rich allusiveness of satire and parody which located the
modern in its relation to previous traditions, to the irresponsible and
superficial narcissism and self-referentiality of pastiche. Fragmentation,
uncertainty and difference are held to govern our worldview, reflected by
a culture intent on style, pleasure and consumption.

   However, the lexicon of postmodernity (itself as self-referential and
prone to proliferation as the culture it is said to describe) merits some
closer scrutiny, in particular in relation to the categories of the very
subject it claims to have dissolved. And here juxtapositions with the
portraits offered by developmental psychology are instructive.

POSTMODERN SUBJECTS: ALIENS, SCHIZOPHRENICS AND CHILDREN

Let us take first of all the tendency to describe the opposition between the
modern and postmodern in psychopathological terms – modernism as
neurotic, postmodernism as schizophrenic, a distinction elaborated by
Jameson (1984) among others. This is perhaps due to a combination of
lingering 1960s British anti-psychiatry with more recent influences from
some French writers (Deleuze and Guattari, 1977). However appealing as
a set of metaphors to describe the collective sense of delusion and diver-
sion that such writers see as gripping contemporary culture, I think such
terminology should be resisted, since it works to reinstate the legitimacy
of the psychiatric discourse it partakes of, and it romanticises mental
distress in ways that undermine and are offensive to those who are victims
of psychiatric oppression.

   A second metaphor of postmodern subjectivity elaborated in discussions
of films is that of the 'other'. An analysis of Joe Dante's film (1985)
Explorers comments that the creatures from outer space are 'the perfect
postmodernist subjects *à la* Baudrillard – pure "viewing screens", mere
intersections of radio and television waves that are incapable of recognising any difference whatsoever' (Collins, 1987: 13). The aliens are
portrayed as sitting in a spaceship surrounded by huge television screens
which relay successions of earth television programmes. Their experience
of human culture and history is entirely mediated through their viewing of
television, providing a superficial acquaintance with its signs but no
framework for understanding or interpreting them. This is reflected in the
way their speech is composed of fragments of lines from cartoons and

cinema classics: the first words they say to their human child visitors is: 'What's up doc!'. This is only one of a whole genre of films such as *Transformers, Making Mr Right, Alien* and *Moonwalker* which are pre-occupied with confusing the boundary between man and machine, or, in the case of *Blade Runner*, woman and machine. (In this last case the coincidence of femininity and robotics works to emphasise androcentric definitions of humanity and permit the rape of the woman/robot.)

Whatever else such preoccupations express, they present clear examples of the postmodern theme of *bricolage* – the fragmentation and haphazard reconstruction of culture in which the image or signifier has come to replace, or at least has broken free from, the reality it once was held to represent, to arrange itself in new configurations and meanings. The current media preoccupation with soaps, where relationships between organs of mass media have come to stand in for, rather than reflect external events, is a further instance of the celebration of the medium over the message of contemporary popular culture: what is happening in *Neighbours* or *Eastenders* has *become* the news.

However, a third metaphor springs to mind that fits accounts of post-modern subjectivity: that of children who, it should be remembered, have at other historical times and in different cultures been viewed in precisely these terms of alienness and psychopathy. In particular, Jameson's (1984) account of postmodernism, as bringing into being a subjectivity of depthlessness ('the waning of affect'), a preoccupation with appearance rather than reality, with surface rather than depth, has quite striking resonances with Piaget's account of the egocentric character of children's thought. Piaget talked of young children having a kind of distributed subjectivity, whereby the boundaries between self and other were not distinct, and subjectivity was not fixed into a coherent static notion of 'self'. He said: 'Reality is impregnated with the self and thought is conceived as belonging to the category of physical matter . . . there is integral egocentricity through lack of consciousness of self' (Piaget, 1982: 188). Egocentrism was the term Piaget used to describe the tendency of children to latch on to one perspective (he wrote of children's thinking as being 'immobile', 'viscous' or 'sticky'), to be diverted or misled by perceptual features of objects they saw and thereby miss or mistake their more enduring properties. (This provided the rationale for his famous conservation tasks.) Piaget considered the transition from what he called pre-operational to concrete operational (or logical) thought as 'the victory of conception over perception'. Clearly the military as well as the progressive connotations of this description are interesting, but isn't this the reverse of the movement from transcendence to immanence, from quality to decoration, that postmodernism is said to represent?

The parallels are yet closer. Like young children, postmodernity is time-less. Jameson presents an account of the postmodern subject as existing outside history, as trapped within a notion of time conceived as a succession of present moments rather than integrated into a coherent chronology of historical time in relation to which individual experience can be linked to collective endeavour. For Piaget an adequate (and logical) concept of time presupposes the ability to construct several independent series and to relate or co-ordinate them together. He regarded young children's abilities to maintain thematic continuity across picture arrangements as a prerequisite to such developmental achievements and discussed the social basis of the construction of personal narratives: 'It is by learning to tell stories to others that the child learns to tell stories to himself and thus to organise his active memory' (Piaget, 1969: 249).

DEVELOPMENTAL PSYCHOLOGY AND POSTMODERN ACCOUNTS: RECIPROCAL CHALLENGES

My purpose in drawing these connections is not simply to make the point that postmodernism reverses developmental accounts (a sort of *cultural recapitulation of*, or rather *retrogression to*, *ontogeny*), but rather to high-light the close connections between accounts of postmodernity and those of children's development. I am not, of course, suggesting that contemporary culture is regressing to some earlier childhood state but rather that features of postmodernism do involve a celebration of qualities that we can now recognise as a return to an idealised childhood, and a bourgeois childhood at that. Postmodernism, for all its rhetoric of the 'death of the subject' thus presents an implicit return to an idealised and essentialised subject, that of the child.

If this argument holds, then, we can use it to interrogate further the adequacy of the 'free play' of qualities postmodernism is said to permit. Postmodernism's resurrection of the humanist and even romantic category of childhood may import the 'emotional' into the model of human subjectivity so far envisaged, but the predominant emotion it is preoccupied with is sentimentality and nostalgia – both too passive to generate the political engagement sought by those who seek to reintroduce the project of social change and emancipation. In addition, gender, that category so significantly and glaringly omitted from traditional developmental and humanist accounts, now occupies an ambiguous place in postmodernity. While subject positions are sexualised, gender identifications have been unhinged from sex and proliferate in de-politicised (effectively reactionary) forms.

Take Michael Jackson as the prime example of the postmodern subject – a Peter Pan figure, signifier or sexual and racial ambiguity (Mercer, 1988). Some of the consequences of postmodernism for a feminist politics start to come into focus at this point. In the first place, the notion of androgeny works to de-sex rather than transcend traditional sexual oppositions; secondly, it reduces power relations to parallel differences; and thirdly, it falls back into a default male model. These are points I elaborate in the rest of this chapter.

What I have sought to demonstrate so far is the necessity for a reciprocal relationship between developmental psychology and post-modern accounts. To sum up, a critical understanding of postmodernism allows us, first, to see that subjectivity is historically and culturally specific; and, secondly, it affords an account of subjectivity that acknowl-edges and places as central (although with the qualifications I have already noted) the multiplicity of positions we occupy.

On the other hand developmental psychology presents certain chal-lenges to postmodernism. Without being crudely realist about this, celebrants of postmodernism need to account for the 'facts' of develop-ment – we are not abstracted subjects existing in some state of pure and static consumption. There is a certain continuity imposed on our experience by virtue of our existence as biological entities that grow and develop and age. We *live out our biology* within a social world. We are not aliens or robots in spaceships. Accounts of postmodernism need to rise above their celebration of timelessness and attend to how the phenomena they seek to explain differentially affect and engage with people of differing ages. The second challenge to postmodernism is to move from difference to critique: for postmodern critiques to be effective in intervening in developmental psychology they have to adopt a critical position in commenting on psychological practices, otherwise there are dangers of leaving intact the whole regulatory apparatus of norms, ages and stages that stigmatise or harass children and families and subject 'failures' to meet these criteria to victim-blaming explanations based on familial or cultural deficit.

CONVERGING TERRAIN

In the remainder of this chapter I shall take two examples of areas of con-vergence between the terrain of developmental psychology and analyses of postmodernism. The first of these concerns familial ideologies and parenthood, and the second, children and television. In considering these areas I am working on the premise that postmodernism is a condition not only of research style (an approach in the social sciences) but of culture. The celebrated postmodern condition is supposed, according to its celebrants, to be everywhere. Well, let's see how useful that claim is.

Familial Ideology: How New is the 'New Man'?

Developmental psychology ignores at its peril theories of culture and cultural change. The entire practice of developmental psychology, with associated paramedical agencies, is committed to a particular perspective on families through its aim to foster facilitating and beneficial environments for children. Indeed it might not be too far-fetched to regard the history of developmental psychology as the history of familial ideology. As is now well documented in both social scientific accounts (Gittins, 1985; Riley, 1983) and the water political domain,[1] 'the family' is located as the site of cultural as well as biological production and reproduction. Postmodern existence clearly affects and even disrupts traditional conceptions of familial relations prevalent within developmental psychology. Although my perspective is part of a broader feminist critique of regulation and devaluation of women through the apparatus of social welfare (and one which is noticeably absent in other chapters in this volume), of which developmental psychology forms a part, I shall sketch out a few points here.

An indication of the way developmental psychology has come to reflect ideas of the postmodern world is in the breakdown of traditional gender roles. In particular, we can interpret the explosion of research on and about 'fatherhood' in the psychological literature as a response to and expression of wider social changes. Until recently the social gaze fell almost exclusively upon mothers – how they mothered, if they mothered enough: did they play enough, did they talk enough, did they foster autonomy and security in their offspring by being attentive, responsive and almost always there? Fatherhood (unlike motherhood) was portrayed as a social rather than a biological category, and the father's role depicted by such stalwarts of the postwar era as Bowlby and Winnicott as a shadowy presence whose primary role was to provide financial support and some psychic reminder of the dangerous world outside the home (Riley, 1983). In contrast, both popular and technical developmental psychological accounts now emphasise the importance of men being involved with and taking pleasure from being with children. This brings with it new pressures: enjoying parenthood is now obligatory.

Yet, as the film *The Good Mother* indirectly indicates, the positions afforded to men and women within this general liberatory parental free-for-all turn out to be in reality quite restricted. The variety of family organisations envisaged is largely confined to heterosexual cohabiting couples within which men are accorded the role of being 'special playmate' for their child, engaging in rough and tumble physical play (Parke, 1981; Clarke Stewart, 1983), and men are still depicted as requiring surreptitious pressure to help them take on paternal responsibilities. The lead article in September 1988's *Practical Parenting*, for example, is entitled 'How to get your man to be a father' and is full of useful tips on how to entice him into the nursery. And if we look beyond the proliferation of media coverage accorded to new men and fathers in particular, as in the films *Three Men and a Baby* and *Baby Boom*, and step back to find out how pervasive and far-reaching these social changes are, it becomes clear that so-called 'progressive' men do less in the way of housework and nitty-gritty childcare than do their traditional counterparts (McKee, 1982), that all do less than working-class men did hitherto (Lumnis, 1982) and, further, that 'role reversed' families tend to shift back into traditional positions (Russell, 1987). We would do well to reflect on the extent to which contemporary postmodern existence offers any genuine change in sexual positions when posters of men holding babies can turn out to be adverts for building society investment accounts or cars.

Corresponding with the rise of fatherhood, changing demands are now placed on women for them to qualify as 'adequate mothers'. Now rather than continuous maternal care acting as the measure of children's future adjustment, women are exhorted to become better mothers by fulfilling themselves at work; hence a recent childcare book entitled *The Woman who Works, the Parent who Cares* (Sandler and Kelly, 1988). That certain questions are begged here, including the availability of work, the satisfaction of work (especially given women's low status and low-paid position in employment), and class issues about the choice to work, should be clear.

We can extend this analysis of developmental psychology's response to and participation within contemporary cultural changes to interrogate celebrants and commentators of postmodernism. Just as men's entry into childcare can be seen as a challenge to women's traditional power, as undermining the one arena in which women wielded undisputed authority, so we can also question whether postmodern existence fulfils its claims to transcend traditional gender roles, or simply extends the domain available for colonisation by the 'new man'. Despite the key focus in postmodern culture on the category of the feminine, it is unclear whether women are getting a fair share of the postmodern cake (and the postmodern world – if such we live in) both practically and theoretically. Developmental psychology accommodates to changing social organisations by depicting maternal and paternal roles as *complementary*, maintaining traditional power relations between men and women. Equally, postmodernism can be seen to be guilty of a similar confirmation of traditional roles through their infraction. Indeed an increasing number of feminists writing within film theory and contemporary cultural analysis are casting doubt on the extent to which postmodernism benefits women (for example, Moore, 1988). In practical terms, women's entry into the public realm (as producer or consumer) constitutes a wider arena in which the 'new woman' (in full post-feminist glamour) is sexualised and depicted as sexually available – portrayed as assertively in control of her sexuality and therefore culpable in her own harassment. At a more theoretical level, the undermining of the traditional sexual polarity and proliferation of sexual positions afforded through notions of androgeny can thus be seen to empower men at the expense of women. Hence traditional power relations remain the same, albeit dangerously cast in the rhetoric of affirming denied and devalued femininity. Even accounts, such as Jameson's (1984), which seek to illuminate a materialist basis for the phenomena of postmodernism turn out to be surprisingly gender in-different (Creed, 1987).

What I am drawing attention to, then, is the way commentaries and critiques addressed to developmental psychology – in this case concerning familial and in particular gender relations – are also of relevance to the evaluation of accounts of postmodernism as a state of culture – as post-modernity. But at the moment the passage of criticism'is only one way, since those who comment on postmodern culture seek either to dismiss it as illusory, or to see in it a developed resistance to the alienation of modern society. Yet what are we left with by these analyses? I am suggesting that the intrinsically modern practice of developmental psychology, together with its inevitable cultural expression in the pop psychology of family roles, incorporates with ease some of the para-phernalia of postmodern culture into its own narrative, while maintaining its regulatory and normalising function intact.

Television Literacy

My second example is more a topic area within and outside developmental psychology than a cursory review of its entire project. Television literacy is a topic which has exercised cultural analysts since the early 1970s. Until very recently little work was devoted to *children's* relation with television. This issue, however, gained media attention from the 1970s onwards through the debates about violence on television and the effects this has on children, together with more recent anxieties about the future, and future quality, of children's television with the advent of deregulation and satellite TV (British Film Institute, 1989). The significance of this topic for analyses of postmodernism lies in the conceptualisation of subject positions provided within these developmental accounts and their inter-section with the contemporary discourses of image and consumer choice.

Psychological research on children and television falls into two main paradigms. The first, social learning theory (the application of a cognitive version of the principles of behaviourism to humans), emphasises the role models provided by images on television and attempts to evaluate the likelihood that children will imitate them (Bandura *et al.*, 1963). The second, cognitive approach, focuses on skills and strategies involved in attending to and processing televisual information. While attracting much attention by claiming that children are more likely to hit a doll after seeing this on film, the social learning approach has failed to provide reliable results to back this up (see Sayers, 1986). These would in any case be suspect due to the basis of this work in experimental research conducted in laboratory situations – hence also confounding results with issues of conformity. The second, cognitive, approach analyses the skills pre-supposed in being able adequately to understand television programmes – ranging, for example, from knowing that the successive pictures of a figure of slightly different size and orientation may be the same figure moving, to the understanding involved in grasping plot and narrative, and to the metalinguistic skills of being able to stand back and reflect on language that is necessary to be able to recognise the 'persuasive intent' of advertising. What this work highlights is that young children may have different preferences and processing orientations to television (that is, they like different programmes, especially cartoons, perhaps because they attend more to visual than verbal information). But from the age of about nine children are capable of understanding, enjoying and analysing programmes directed at adult audiences.

I don't have the space to go into a full evaluation of these strands of research, which anyway has been done by others (Buckingham, 1987; Phoenix, 1987). I mention them, rather, to put into perspective a new genre of developing research into children and television which emphasises that, far from being a 'plug-in drug' (Winn, 1977), children are *active* in their televisual habits and that television can be educationally and socially beneficial. Such accounts are cast in terms of rescuing a much-maligned medium from unnecessary disrepute, treated as a scape-goat for rather than a cause of contemporary society's problems. Not surprisingly, since it is expressed within a liberal human-rights framework, this research lapses back into arguments that tend to reinstate the old individual–social divisions through its rhetoric of choice. This is seen particularly in relation to discussion of advertising where attempts to counter the conspiritorial 'television as seducer' and the idealised 'child as innocent and gullible' theory lead to such dubious or vacuous arguments as 'we can choose to be persuaded to buy a product' and 'Parents and children tend to do what they want to do' (Messenger Davies, 1989: 200). This account even suggests 'we should be reassured by the fact that one of the first words learned by human children everywhere is "no"' (Messenger Davies, 1989: 201). What should be clear from this is that this framework fails to interrogate the origins of the much acclaimed 'fun, humour and entertainment' which guide children's preferences for both programmes and adverts. It cannot therefore problematise the construction of these aesthetic qualities in its audience and thus lapses into a consensual and social contractual model of society which renders unproblematic, and even celebrates, the position of the consumer.

Yet this is to disregard, or to misrecognise, the reality of our current social lives. We live in an era when advertising has become an art form in its own right. Now the success of an advert is no longer evaluated in terms of crude market research measures of buying patterns. Rather, we are now witnessing a classic postmodern feature in action: the decoupling of medium from the message, with the medium being given free play to create and proliferate meanings (even though guided by marketing strategies). Advertising companies now create their own consumers through constructing typological models based on the confluence of products purchased, treating, targeting and creating patterns of consumption as distinct psychological types. Hence what is being marketed is not a product but the – socially segemented – lifestyle the product has come to evoke.

There can be no doubt that children provide an, increasing and expanding market, both in terms of the products they buy and, more importantly, the products that are bought for them – although current trends suggest that children are accorded more decision-making power in this (Sweeney, in Messenger Davies, 1989). Children's participation in pop culture is the obvious example, with the age margins receding at an ever increasing rate so that five year-old children are going to fancy dress parties as Kylie Minogue, and a substantial sector of the readership of *Smash Hits* is under the age of ten (Barton, 1989).

Yet, what the approaches to children and television I outlined earlier fail to deal with is precisely those features that are highlighted by a postmodern culture. Take toy-led programming. All that the 'television is good for your kids' approach can say about toy manufacturers making children's programmes to promote their products is to point to the controls exercised on this in America, whereby a character cannot be shown in an advertisement adjacent to the programme in which it figures. Or they comment on the variable quality of (and corresponding children's preferences for), for example, the *Care Bears* movie over *My Little Pony* (Messenger Davies, 1989: 197). They cannot begin to address the issues of the construction of desires, nor indeed the specific and urgent questions of not only how children are addressed by television but how different children are addressed in different ways according to their sex, 'race' and class as well as age positions. It may be helpful or reassuring to be told that the meaning a child takes away from viewing is constructed or mitigated by the context of viewing, that children rarely confuse reality and fantasy so that violence on TV becomes simple entertainment or else catharsis (Hodge and Tripp, 1986). But it tells us little about how children are constructed as consumers, nor about how relations between adults and children are so constructed within contemporary society that children are not only markets for consumption, but have themselves become commodities which, through the products they wear and possess, signify to others the class and 'lifestyle' position of their parents as well as themselves.

I am aware that such claims demand elaboration and justification beyond the space I have available. So let me simply point out what I see as the significance of this position. I have suggested that developmental psychological approaches to children and television have, through their failure to challenge it, reinstated a notion of subjectivity as pre-existent and hence both essentially asocial and ungendered. Taking the argument a step further, analyses of postmodern culture can be seen to be guilty of precisely the same lapses in two ways. This happens either through their failure to consider how children function within the postmodern economy of the celebration of consumption, or through deploying the category of 'child' as a metaphor for the qualities of postmodernity. Analyses which seek to provide a materialist account of postmodern culture have to address the production of childhood and its multiple meanings and positions, including that produced by developmental psychology. These moves are prerequisite for envisaging a purpose and resistance beyond the passivity and dehistoricisation of postmodern culture.

CONCLUSION: THE BABY AND THE BATHWATER

I shall finish by drawing together some of the issues I have raised, together with some qualifications and extensions.

First of all, in order to fulfil the project of creating a materialist account of postmodernity capable of envisaging challenge and change, we need, as well as focusing on the construction of children, to accord agency to children as constituted subjects. So, for example, we can interpret children's delight in buying sweets which represent objects considered unacceptable as 'food' such as 'monkey brains', or 'terror eye' gob-stoppers, or 'dustbins' filled with (sugary) bones, tins, boots and fishheads, or even 'hedgehog splats', as manoeuvres which emphasise the children's resistance to adult authority and 'aesthetics' through the disapproval their purchase incurs (Miller, 1987). We can see similar conceptual moves emerging within wider discussions of postmodern culture, with commentators identifying a 'return' to the subject (Dews, 1989).

Secondly, the attention to developmental issues highlights that we must beware of assuming that postmodernity exists hegemonically and carries the same meaning for all consumers. The roving fingers of a child over the TV remote control device, flicking from channel to channel, has been seen as symptomatic of the postmodern preference for little narratives through the new stories that the activity of channel-hopping constructs. But this symbolic account should not mislead us into thinking that children are not capable of privileging one narrative over another. Indeed, the very notion of the postmodern child may be a postmodern fiction. Children may well construct a modern world for themselves, irrespective of the world around them. Returning to the film *Explorers*, it is noteworthy that the aliens (who are, significantly, also children – and grotesquely gendered children at that) can be interpreted as postmodern by the pastiche of their discourse, composed of fragments from other films. However, in contrast, their child visitors are positioned as steadfastly modern in their commitment to the adventure narrative of science fiction – and they are even depicted as unified in this despite the crude classification of character types they portray – of scientist, dreamer and 'thug' (Collins, 1987).

Thirdly, analyses of the phenomena of postmodernism need to deal with issues of power in order adequately to comprehend the position of children, families and the role of developmental psychology. This is necessary so that we can intervene rather than comment from the sidelines. I have argued throughout this chapter that we need to distinguish between those who analyse postmodern culture and those who celebrate or 'practice' it. Making this distinction represents a first step towards gaining a critical understanding of the dynamics and effects of postmodernity without getting so seduced by its dazzling facets and theoretical possibilities that we overestimate its impact on people's lives and, as a consequence, fail to counter the continuing impact that traditionally modern practices and agencies such as those associated with developmental psychology have on our lives. I have tried to indicate how the terrain of developmental psychology and current analyses of postmodernism necessarily intersect in some areas, and I have commented on the possibilities of each informing the other. I have drawn attention to how analyses of postmodernism have fallen into some of the same traps as developmental psychology did, and also where and how their accounts conflict. However, as I have demonstrated through the examples of ideologies of the family and of the child, we need to be aware of how modern regulatory agencies that developmental psychology requires assimilate potentially challenging ideas to their overarching narratives, leaving their oppressive practices intact. Changing this can only begin through taking up again a fully developed analysis of power relations, and recognising the accounts of power as resistance provided by commentators on postmodernism as informative but insufficient for our purposes.

In the early 1980s it was fashionable in developmental psychology to discuss the individual–society relationship in terms of 'the baby and the bathwater'. In postmodern allusive style, therefore, I shall conclude by commenting on how these terms reflect on the relation between developmental psychology and analyses of contemporary postmodern culture. On the one hand, we've seen how such accounts of postmodernism, for all their protestations, tacitly return to a theory of the subject – a backdoor way to the baby through the bathwater. On the other hand, developmental psychology posits a baby that exists independently of its cultural bathwater. While conceptually and politically developmental psychology needs to develop a more adequate account of the cultural construction of subjectivity, its failure to do so reconfirms its position as arbiter and monitor of the modern regulation of childhood. Paradoxically, analyses of postmodernism need to reconstruct the very baby, or subject, they have claimed to dissolve like soap, or even to drown, in order to envisage an agent capable of resisting and changing the modern practice that originally gave rise to it.

NOTE

1.   'There is no such thing as society. There are only individual men and women, and families' (Margaret Thatcher, 1987).

6 Postmodernity and the Globalisation of Technoscience: The Computer, Cognitive Science and War

John Bowers

INTRODUCTION

In spite of the most devout hopes of many cynics, the allure of postmodernism and the problems that are attendant upon this term and its cognates – postmodernity, postmodern, 'postie' – is undiminished. The salon lizards of theory – to adapt Margolis's (1989) dig – are yet to move *en masse* to any newer, more attractive fad. Indeed, since 1984, with the publication in English of Lyotard's *The Postmodern Condition: A Report on Knowledge* (1984a), and the fullest version of Jameson's often reworked 'Postmodernism, or the cultural logic of late capitalism' (1984), there has been a proliferation of theorisations of postmodernity and suggestions for practice.

Of the intoxicating myriad of possibilities connected with postmodernity, my concern in this chapter is to investigate theorisations offered in reference to science and alleged changes in scientific activity – changes usually periodised as occurring during and after the Second World War. Since Lyotard (1984a), debates about science have had an especial importance to postmodernism and often have implications for political postmodernisms. Indeed, this paper can be read as offering an account of science which has rather different conclusions from Lyotard's about the constitution of science, the relation between science and narrative, and the possibilities for oppositional practice. I shall do this by examining so-called cognitive science, discussing the tropes by which it seeks legitimacy, tracing their consequences in the form of links with technology and war, and offering a characterisation of postmodern science in terms which owe something to the work of Bruno Latour (for example, 1987). In some respects, this paper can be read as an attempt to politicise the kinds of understanding which a 'sociology of scientific knowledge' (in the sense of Woolgar, 1988) might give us.

COGNITIVE SCIENCE AND COMPUTERISED KNOWLEDGE

Cognitive science (which we can take provisionally as an amalgam of disciplines including cognitive psychology, artificial intelligence, linguistics, philosophy of mind, computer science, cognitive anthropology, cognitive sociology) is, I believe, especially interesting to study because it largely lacks any internal debate in connection with postmodernism. However, I should like to conjecture that cognitive science so exemplifies a postmodern science in its knowledge producing *practice* that it need not (or, perhaps, cannot) articulate postmodernity at the manifest level of its theory.

Indeed, theoretically, cognitive science is wedded to that most anti-postmodern figure: the rational Cartesian individual subject, as is acknowledged by both critics and advocates of its research programmes (see Henriques *et al.*, 1984; Fodor, 1981). There seems to be no death of the subject here. Rather, the subject is filled to overflowing with mechanisms and representations – mechanisms and representations which are frequently captured in formal calculi. Neither the subject nor the theorist goes with the flow of playful signification. The formalisms seem to put a (transcendental) stop to that, while presenting individual (usually speaking) subjects as the source and origin of intention and all meaning (for such Derridean critiques of cognitivism and contemporary psychology, see some of the contributions to Parker and Shotter, 1990). However, it is in the figure of the computer that cognitive science becomes postmodern. In cognitive science the computer is not merely an aid for, say, data analysis but the dominant source for metaphors of mind (see Johnson-Laird, 1985). Above all else, the commitment to theorise minds as information-processing devices keeps the amalgam together.

The special significance of the computer to the postmodern condition has been noted by many writers. For example, Lyotard (1984a: 4) writes that knowledge can:

> fit into the new channels, and become operational, only if learning is translated into quantities of information. We can predict that anything in the constituted body of knowledge that is not translatable in this way

will be abandoned and that the direction of new research will be dictated by the possibility of its eventual results being translatable into computer language. . . . Along with the hegemony of computers comes a certain logic, and therefore a certain set of prescriptions determining which statements are accepted as 'knowledge' statements.

But Lyotard does not spell out why knowledge which is not translatable into quantities of information will be abandoned rather than, say, finding its own level and extent of dissemination through the media appropriate to it. For Lyotard, the 'hegemony of computers' is a *given*; he does not treat it as the *outcome* of an analysable process (and perhaps only a partially achieved one at that). Nevertheless, it is clear that a discipline like cognitive science, which often *defines* acceptable theories in terms of their computability, will have absorbed Lyotard's translation process *into the very activity of theoretical work itself*. If one way to address postmodernity is in terms of the computerisation of knowledge, then a science which produces computational devices as its theories may be more deeply emblematic of the postmodern condition than one which uses computational devices only as analytic aids or for data storage.

However, we need to examine more closely what is at stake in 'translatable knowledge' and the rhetorical means by which the 'hegemony of computers' has been achieved in cognitive science. This should enrich our provisional coupling of postmodern science to the figure of the computer. It is with this intention that I look at the well-known early writings of Alan Turing whose attempts to solve various metamathematical problems in cracking the Nazi's Enigma code led to the investigation of computers as universal simulation devices, a moment often claimed as foundational for cognitive science (see Bowers, 1990).

TURING AND THE NARRATIVE *A PRIORI* OF COGNITIVE SCIENCE

In *Computing Machinery and Intelligence*, a paper first published in *Mind* in 1950, Turing addresses the question: 'Can machines think?' by narrating what he calls the 'imitation game'. The game involves two participants, A and B, one of whom, A, has to claim (falsely) to be B. A third participant, C, is in a separate room and, after a period of asking questions of A and B, has to guess their identity. In Turing's version, A is a man and B is a woman. It is A's task, then, to simulate being a woman so as to cause C to make the wrong identification. Turing thinks it best that communications between the two rooms take place via a typewriter so that the quality of the voice cannot influence the outcome.

Turing (1950: 54) said: 'We now ask the question "what will happen when a machine takes the place of A in this game?". Will the interrogator, C, decide wrongly as often when the game is played like this as he does when the game is played between a man and a woman?' A machine capable of simulating some characteristic (here gender) to this degree is often said to have passed the 'Turing Test' and Turing expresses faith (57) that computers will be developed which will be able to simulate human intelligence in such scenarios.

The Turing Test has kept cognitive psychologists, artificial intelligence workers and philosophers of mind in steady controversy for 40 years. However, rather than debate questions that the imitation game *raises*, I want to look at what might be called the game's *a priori*: what you have to accept for Turing's question – what will happen when a machine particpates in the game? – to get raised in the first place. This involves looking again at the composition of Turing's narrated scenario itself (see also Bowers, 1990).

Adapting a distinction Deleuze (1988) makes in his interpretation of Michel Foucault's work, we can associate with Turing's *narrative a priori* what can be called two regimes: one of *vision* and one of *articulation*. The game contains particular constraints on visibility. The man/machine and the woman (A and B) are removed from the interrogator (C) who stays in a separate room. It sets up an impermeable boundary between the interrogator and the others. It divides and differentiates the participants. The game also contains particular constraints on what can be articulated. The interrogator articulates a certain sort of speech (questions) to which the man/machine and the woman are constrained to respond (with intelligible answers; Turing does not allow that they might respond with concerted disruption of the game itself). In this way, associated with the game's constraints of visibility and complementing them, there is a regime of articulation which ensures that some forms of communication are privileged over others which are excluded.

Although the imitation game is a kind of narrated thought experiment, its implementation – whether imagined or real – is productive of determinate forms of knowledge: knowledges which are non-materialist (inspection of the stuff of which the participants are made is ruled out), which reduce language to questioning and answering; knowledges which arise without a coeval negotiation or disputation between the knower and the known (cf. Fabian, 1983). All this is built into the very fabric of the imitation game. And, indeed, these are some of the theoretical and practical prejudices of the forms of knowledge we can call cognitive science. If you forget the constructedness of the 'Turing Test' or if you regard it as 'fair' in its selection of the features of the world that matter, you have *already* been initiated into cognitive science.

ABSTRACTION, CONCRETISATION AND UNIVERSAL SIMULATION

The imitation game is constructed through forcing a differentiation between those features that matter to the question of the similarity of thinking beings to machines and those that do not. As long as two things are similar with respect to the *things-that-matter*, we can treat them as being the same with respect to some newly fashioned abstract category of which they are both members. In the case of minds and machines, this might be the category of intelligent artefacts (Simon, 1981). Abstraction is the process whereby the different gets reduced to the same. Once two things are made the same in abstraction they become exchangeable as equivalents, one can substitute the other. With Turing, we have the rhetorical means to enter Baudrillard's (1983) 'third order of simulacra', where simulation, reproduction and substitution come to dominate. Abstraction – etymologically, a dragging away – is the necessary trope for simulation.

Indeed, while considering Turing's metamathematical preliminaries to breaking the Enigma code, Manuel de Landa (undated) argues that Turing's work marks a new phase in the historical development of abstraction. However, as de Landa also notes, we much understand formal, abstract systems as lying within a *circuit* of abstraction and concretisation. Some metamathematical problems are given a solution through the postulation of a highly abstract computational machine which can stand for the functions of real, concrete machines. However, this abstraction is complemented by a concretising manoeuvre in which actual machines come into existence to break the code. Furthermore, Turing accomplished this not by merely reconstructing the Enigma machine and, as it were, running it in reverse to decode encrypted messages; rather, he abstracted a *universal* simulation device which could stand for, not just Enigma, but all other computational machines. And, according to the *Mind* paper, the serial digital computer could be such a universal device with minds becoming mimicable machines.

In Turing, then, we find the abstractive tendency, the desire to reduce the different to the same, to de-differentiate (Lash, 1988), developed to its highest form. But this very abstraction makes possible a multiplicity of (re)concretisations, equivalences and substitutions: computers as surveillance devices, as production-line automatons, as minds. Along with abstract knowledge and theory there come concrete practices. To theorise abstractly is not to remove oneself from the affairs of the daily world. On the contrary, a universal simulation device can enter into indefinitely more circuits of abstraction/concretisation than devices which substitute only one other. Indeed, 40 years on, under the Strategic Defense Initiative (SDI, 'Star Wars'), Turingesque abstractions have made possible new links between computers and war, with cognitive theory engaging in a thorough-going metaphor-exchange with militarism (Bowers, 1990).

ABSTRACTION, POWER, REPRESENTATION AND NETWORKS OF ASSOCIATION

It is important to examine further what is at stake in abstraction and how abstraction intersects with scientific practice. For this I turn to the work of Bruno Latour. Like de Landa, Latour (1987: 241) does not see abstraction as an operation of thought in the minds of scientists. Rather, abstractions arise to resolve problems of power and representation. Let me take these in turn.

First, power: Latour notes that the sheer numbers of scientists in the world is really rather small. So how is it that science is claimed to be so powerful, even the dominant way of conceptualising the world? Is it because scientists themselves are incredibly powerful or have especially large brains? No, scientists can only be said to 'have' power to the extent that they are able to enrol *others* who are willing to serve as allies or supporters, act at a distance as instructed and report back. Power is not something scientists can have and hold *in potentia*; it is only something that can exist *in actu*, as others translate knowledge, instructions, 'tokens' of any kind, shaping them in accordance with their different projects (Latour, 1986). This means that, for Latour, scientists are implicated in the construction and extension of long networks of association which permit action at a distance and the many to act as one:

> If technoscience may be described as being so powerful and yet so small, so concentrated and yet so dilute, it means that it has the characteristics of a network. The word network indicates that the resources are concentrated in a few places – the knots and the nodes – which are connected with one another – the links and the mesh: these connections transform the scattered resources into a net which may seem to extend everywhere.   (Latour, 1987: 180)

The coining of the term 'technoscience' is felicitous because – if we attempt to follow scientists as they construct or traverse networks – we shall find all sorts of entities and allies associated with one another in ways which cannot be reckoned with if pure–applied or science–technology distinctions are taken for granted (or abstract–concrete in de Landa's argument; see also Callon, 1986).

Secondly, representation: The extension or traversal of a network of association is valueless unless *something* can travel along it, accompanying the scientists or coming to them as ordered. In either case, the 'something' must be mobile, durable and capable or inciting action at a distance. It must, in other words, have the form of a trace, an inscription, a representation. However, as soon as the networks become large in scale, the scientist is in danger of becoming engulfed, overcome by cascades of representations. To solve this problem, the representations have to be made manageable. Again, scientists do not possess especially large brains. Rather, they make the multiplicity of inscriptions manageable through the activity of *re*-representation, through the translation of a large set of representations into a smaller more manageable one which nevertheless retains the detail and richness necessary for keeping the network together. Thus, before re-representation – we have an overwhelming multiplicity, afterwards – a manageable many; before – a separation, afterwards – a unification. This is how we should understand abstraction, not as an operation of thought, but as a product of the concrete activity of re-representation, an *n*th order inscription (Latour, 1987: 241).

However, if re-representation is to achieve unification, rather than involve merely throwing some of the multiplicity away, the inscriptions at each stage must be potentially combinable. Insisting on combinable inscriptions also solves another problem: how to connect otherwise separate networks of association. As Latour (1987: 237–41) shows in discussions of Reynolds's work at the turn of the century on fluid mechanics and Edison's contributions to the development of American domestic electricity, the combinability, mobility and durability of inscriptions is massively enhanced through number, computation and abstraction. Abstractions multiply possible associations, while warding off inscription-overload. Without computation and translatability of traces, networks of association – if they are sustainable at all – tend to remain local.

POSTMODERNITY, THE COMPUTER AND THE GLOBALISATION OF TECHNOSCIENCE

If paradoxes of power are resolved through the extension of long networks of association and, further, if long and intersecting networks are sustained through cascades of re-writing inscriptions as other inscriptions, then the computer is an especially important device in the power–knowledge nexus of technoscience. It permits the storage of a mass of inscriptions in spaces of much smaller granularity than, say, libraries or filing cabinets. It permits their retrieval and translation at speeds outstripping the human body, which musters, maybe, a leisurely perambulation by library shelves or a swift stroke of the pen. When networked to other computers as part of a distributed communication system, it promotes the mobility of traces at light-speed surpassing any transportation method.

The important corollary to these points that we can obtain through Latour's work is that, by increasing mobility, durability and combinability of traces, the computer can sustain networks of association on a *global* scale. The extension of a network with global pretensions without the computer is now well-nigh impossible: the strain at the centres where multiplicities of traces have to be disciplined but not discarded would become intolerable. It is in this regard that I should like to formulate postmodern science. *Postmodern (techno) science is marked by the globalisation of networks connecting people, objects, resources, elements of all kinds.* Such networks can only be kept together and aligned if their elements can be incited to produce or relay traces and if these can be speedily rewritten at the centres where they accumulate. Postmodern technoscience secures action and realises effectivities at distances-now-global. And its underlabourer and midwife is the computer, no longer the philosopher (*pace* Locke).

The global scale was not achievable by Reynolds or Edison with the elements available to them. Indeed, the accomplishment of a scale coinciding with the reach of the nation-state is precisely what Edison was acclaimed for, as the title of Hughes's (1979) account of him – '*The electrification of America*' – betrays. However, I want to claim that Edison and Reynolds share with postmodern technoscientists the same practical problem of keeping existing networks together and extending new ones. On this view, rather than a matter of rationality or legitimation alone, the difference between modern and postmodern science concerns the conditions to be satisfied for networks of different scales to come into existence. For any scale of interest, the conditions – though intertwined into an ensemble – may well be quite heterogeneous: from the use of computers to the dissemination of abstractionist tropes. Of course, if the conditions involve reference to entities of all sorts, then the transition to postmodernity is likely to be an uneven one and no glib periodisation will be satisfying or helpful.

In referring to globalisation, I do not merely want to draw attention to a question of geographical scale or to the geopolitical fact that the networks of postmodern technoscience go beyond the reach of nation-states, though these are important matters. The networks of technoscience are also global in the topological sense that a globe provides more varied possibilities for the interconnection of nodes on its surface than does, say, a plane. In the networks of postmodern technoscience any point may connect with any other. Any point has an indefinitely large number of circuits connecting itself with itself. Though the points still constitute centres in that many connections converge, there is no clear beginning or end to the network, nor can the inside/outside distinction be made with confidence. That is, to use the terms of Deleuze and Guattari (1987), the networks of postmodern technoscience have the form of a *rhizome*.

GLOBAL NETWORKS AND THE MILITARISATION OF SCIENCE

It is worth pursuing the consequences of long network construction still further. As Latour notes, it is not a strange coincidence that work able to muster a long network, or seeking to create one, eventually comes across military interests or aligns itself with them:

> For centuries, [the military] have enlisted people and interested them in their action. ... As far as enrolling, disciplining, drilling and keeping in line are concerned, they have proved their mettle and on a much larger scale than scientists have ever tried. ... The similarity between the proof race and the arms race is not a metaphor, it is literally the mutual problem of *winning*. Today no army is able to win without scientists, and only a few scientists and engineers are able to win their arguments without the army. (Latour, 1987: 172)

Importantly, the connection between technoscience and the military is non-accidental because *both* experience the necessity of the mobilisation of resources so that the many can act as the one, *both* need to resolve paradoxes of power through efficiently manipulating and relaying representations, *both* have an interest in the reciprocal relation between abstraction and concretisation. With the globalisation of technoscience, military interest is almost impossible to avoid. This is why *postmodernity is coextensive with the militarisation of science.*

One might suspect that cognitive science – through manifesting highly developed abstractive tendencies and taking the nature and management of representation as one of its central themes – would be of particular interest to the military. Indeed, direct funding links between cognitive science and the military are well documented (see Shallice, 1984). However, in tracing long networks, we can expect that economic relations of paymaster to employee will constitute just one kind of association. Associations *born of abstraction* can be more subtle. Scientific work which conceives of the computer as a universal abstraction and simulation device and regards computability as a criterion of theoretical adequacy will be an almost essential ally in the computerisation and globalisation of war, whether the work is directly paid for or comes gratis. I claim (and develop elsewhere, Bowers, 1990) that one consequence of cognitive science being an emblematic postmodern technoscience is that it has non-accidental associations with the most determined attempt to computerise a global war – SDI. With Star Wars, the conduct of war becomes another programming task, cognitive science being a ready-to-hand source for how the task should be done. These associations are made possible by the abstraction and universal simulation elements of the Turing drama.

POSTMODERNITY AND A POLITICS FOR RESISTING TECHNOSCIENCE

I have argued that postmodernity – as it relates to technoscience – is to be discussed in terms of the globalisation of networks associating elements of all kinds. The rhetorical component of the task of keeping a network together and combining it with others can be enhanced through tropes of abstraction of the sort Turing exemplifies. Turing's abstraction was accomplished through projecting – in the form of a narration – both a regime of vision and a regime of articulation which enabled the production of newly relevant equivalences between minds and computing-machines. With Turing's Test as a rhetorical commonplace for cognitive science, the possibilities for extending long networks are facilitated. Indeed, as Turing promises *universal* abstraction and simulation in the figure of the computer, *global* networks become possible for cognitive science, along with an indefinitely large scope for re-concretisation and intervention. The yield of inscriptions given up and relayed by a global network requires enhanced techniques of re-writing at any centre where there is accumulation. For cognitive science, then, the computer becomes doubly determined as both re-writing device and metaphor. Any science which can extend near-global networks of association will inevitably bump up against the military as they extend theirs. *Postmodernity marks the flowing together of technoscience, the computer and war.*

This account of postmodern technoscience is worth comparing with some other formulations. In particular, contrasts can be made with the Lyotard of *The Postmodern Condition*. For example, throughout that book, Lyotard argues that science and narrative have an antagonistic relation:

[Science] has always existed in addition to, and in competition and conflict with, another kind of knowledge, which I will call narrative . . . (Lyotard, 1984a: 7)

The scientist questions the validity of narrative statements and concludes that they are never subject to argumentation or proof. (Lyotard, 1984a: 27)

However, I have suggested that narration is a crucial component of scientific practice. Recounting a story may be a key element in the rhetoric of network construction and maintenance. Indeed, I have claimed that a narrative can act as the *a priori* for a science, making the science possible. This seems to be the case with Turing whose text contains the typical narrative elements of character, setting, event, even problem and resolution. Similar points can probably be made concerning the narratives of Einstein which are foundational for relativity theory (the 'thought experiments') or those of Freud for psychoanalysis or, for that matter, those routinely disseminated in the induction of students or the construction of scientific papers. Narrative is a means of manipulating a number of chronicities so as to make present and re-ordered at the time of narration elements otherwise absent and, perhaps, chaotic (Genette, 1980; Bal, 1985). As such, one can suspect that narrative is an important resource for the mobilisation of allies.

That scientists may call upon *both* narrative and argumentative, proof-seeking repertoires (cf. Gilbert and Mulkay, 1984) is an instance of what Latour (1987: 7–13) calls the 'Janus face of science', which – when appreciated – will make it quite plausible to resist Lyotard's suggestion that narrative and science are forever in conflict. For Latour, a rich enough conception of scientific practice is only to be had once we look upon the more frequently ignored of the faces – 'science in action' – and pursue scientists in their disputes, their attempts to win over allies, their struggles against all manner of adversities. The other face of Janus – ready-made science' – presents us with established facts, 'black boxes' whose innards are near-inscrutable and miraculously sealed up.

However, in his definition of scientific knowledge, Lyotard seems to see only the black boxes (1984a: 18, 25):

> Learning is the set of statements which, to the exclusion of all other statements, denote or describe objects and may be declared true or false. Science is a subset of learning. It is also composed of denotative statements. ... Scientific knowledge requires that one language game, denotation, be retained and all others excluded.

To regard science as the production an dissemination of denotatives is to pick out from the myriad of concrete activities that occur in the practice of technoscience only its end products, its *a posteriori* ignoring its *a priori*. In Latour's terms, it is to privilege the black boxes of ready-made science over sciencè in action, or in other terms, it is to be hoodwinked by the commodification of science. Lyotard's philosophy seems to allow the invisibility of the means of technoscientific production. Note also, in our case, that concentration on the denotative black boxes of cognitive science would have side-tracked us into debates about its rationalism, Cartesianism, formalism and individualism, and whether a science manifesting these could be properly postmodern.

If the conflict between narration and science is queried, then some of Lyotard's account of the alleged demise of the grand narratives of emancipation and speculation is also undercut, for this seems to depend in part on there being such an antagonistic relation (Lyotard, 1984a: 37–41). An alternative account: *if* the grand narratives have demised, perhaps it is because *grandeur* is not required to pull together the elements in the one place. Other tropes, techniques and artifacts will suffice. For example, mere possession of a computer may obviate the need to connect a scientist's project to that of the whole human race through narrated protestations of an emancipatory interest. The computer will help to keep the network in place. The associations may not need to be rhetorically projected in a grand narrative. Any narrative-work which remains can be handled by a small yarn (to bind the forces together, of course – *sic*!). While Lyotard (1984a: 60) admits that the little narrative still has a place in science, the alternative just given allows a useful possibility which Lyotard cannot: *the grand narratives may be mobilised again if a network looks as if it is breaking up.* Indeed, grand narration seems to be precisely the dominant rhetoric of resistance to budget cuts, loss of tenure and departmental closures. In contrast, Lyotard writes too much as if grand narratives suffered from original sin ('inherent' nihilism, p. 38; 'intrinsic' erosion, p. 39). This cannot constitute an *explanation* for their alleged demise, nor can it recognise the possibility that grand narratives might be re-excited.

Finally in connection with Lyotard, we can be sceptical about the degree of politicised resistance that can be offered by pursuing 'paralogy' – the search for slippages and instabilities between scientific discourses (Lyotard, 1984a: 60–7). Indeed, paralogy may be precisely the way to connect networks rhetorically. Pointing out an irregularity between two discourses and signalling a reorientation of the discursive field doubles your audience at a stroke. Administrators of the SDI budget frequently respond to arguments against the technological feasibility of Star Wars (for example, Parnas, 1985) with calls for 'blue sky' rather than 'proof-of-principle' research, for revolutionary science rather than paradigm tinkering (see Thompson and Thompson, 1985; Bulkeley and Spinardi, 1986). What stops the paralogical scientist from responding to such calls?

As long as science is conceived of principally as the production of denotative statements capable of assessment for truth-value, the referential dimension of discourse will be privileged – no matter how indirectly – in ways which limit debates over the possibilities for political action. A politics for technoscience which takes as a central issue *the nature of the existing associations and the possibility of their undoing or transformation* could not be articulated in Lyotard's scheme. Similarly, the familiar call for local theorisations and knowledges again manifests a partial view of political possibility if localism is confined to reference. A locally referential theory, while eschewing invocations of grand subjects or grand processes, may traverse global networks at light speed. *If* we are to celebrate local knowledges as Foucault, Deleuze and de Certeau have all recommended, shouldn't it be to the extent that they fall through the net of technoscience, cannot be captured in it and beamed around the world? The association networks in which knowledge is produced have to form part of the reckoning if such a strategy is to offer resistance by refusing to connect or by offering up something which – to the networks-in-place – is sublime, unrepresentable.

Put crudely, I suggest that we need a politics for postmodern technoscience which asks what connections are made at least as often as it asks what is and what is not represented. To do so, of course, is to politicise the conditions of production of technoscience, rather than to moralise over the implications of the black boxes, their use, their abuse, or celebrate their dexterous, paralogical juxtaposition. Such a strategy allows us to raise the possibility that currently existing conditions might be resisted or transformed. If we concern ourselves with analysing the conditions under which a technoscience of global scale is produced and what might threaten it, talk of postmodernity need not be a rhetoric of defeat.

But can the global association networks of postmodern technoscience be undone? A global network may seem impossible to undo but, in fact, it is exactly the anxiety that such may happen overnight that keeps scientists mobile, continually having to accomplish anew or reproduce the tenuous networks that they find themselves in. If the network disappeared, so would the equally tenuous lines of power: power *in actu* turning to power *in potentia* and hence lost. After all, a network is just that: net-*work*. A global network may seem like a hydra, and indeed the severing of one link will not cause the whole net to unravel, but it is vastly more difficult for a single centre to keep together a network which contains many elements than one which contains just a few. For one thing, a global network itself would be impossible to represent in full, and hence dominate, from any one centre. And this for all the reasons that can be found in Gödel and Borges: what would constitute 'in full'? Where could the representation reside? Could it ever be known if a full representation had been achieved? Could it be accomplished, checked and used before the represented had significantly changed? In one of Borges's stories (noted by Lyotard, 1984a: 55), an emperor wishes to have made a completely accurate map of his empire. The project causes the empire's destruction as the entire population become enforced cartographers (Borges, 1972).

However, if we can obtain optimism from the impossibility of the perfect and, hence, perfectly dominating representation, is this not destructive in turn for the oppositional cartography proposed by Jameson (1984, 1988e) in his advocacy of cognitive maps of the postmodern world? Well, I would like to suggest that it depends on the *reader* that the map projects or, alternatively put, it depends whether you map from on high or on foot.

Mapping from on high with a god's eye panoptical view, a universal scale and key has always been a project associated with preparation for combating internal disorder (think of the Ordnance Survey: why Ordnance?) or gloating over accomplishments (Borges's emperor, the view from the top of the World Trade Center as described by de Certeau, 1988) or external domination and conquest (think of the cartographic advances at the time of the Portugese conquest of the spice trade; see Law, 1986). The reader projected by such maps is the king or, at least, the kind of imperious Cartesian ego supposed in cognitive science and underpinning cognitivist work on mapping such as McNamara's (1986). For these maps, oriented to dominance as they are, the ever-present fear of the incomplete representation can frequently be assuaged only by normalising the real so that it takes the form of the representation.

In contrast to the view from on high, maps for those on foot emphasise the path rather than the territory, speedy transversal displacement not sedentary domination. The map from (embodied) eye-level invites others to tread the same path but with greater confidence than those who went the first time. It is maps of this sort that we need in tracing the global networks of postmodern technoscience. These maps may help us to undo a network without necessarily substituting a similarly constituted network in its place. I take it that the last thing an oppositional politics wants to get embroiled in is another proof race, as occurs all too easily when we take the black boxes for granted and start debating about the possibilities for their 'social use'.

To map the lines of technoscience which are now the lines of power in postmodern societies, we need to follow scientists as they traverse their long networks. We need to track the associations they make and renew, and at every juncture we need to find out what escapes the network and why, what contrary voices are silenced and how. Perhaps it is to these voices and not to the scientists that we should report back (*pace* some responses to the fashionable call for reflexivity; for example, Mulkay, 1985). In this sense, mapping the global seems to be essential and, hence, stepping outside of representation is not compulsory for an oppositional postmodern politics. Indeed, rather than seek the sublime, some position outside, before or after representation, it is viable to multiply representation still further. After all, one of the great anxieties scientists have to counter stems from the possibility that they might be suffocated by inscriptions. As Latour expresses it, the represented have to be let in but not for too long. But if the represented not merely burst in but force an unmanageable multiplicity of traces, the global networks may yet give.[1]

NOTE

1.   A few loose ends. I want to leave it open whether an oppositional politics should establish what might be called counter-hegemonic networks of association. Similarly, I want to leave open the question as to whether oppositional *sciences* are possible. For example, a reader of Habermas might find this chapter characterising only sciences with a technical interest and an instrumental rationality. Perhaps networks – if they be such – born from an emancipatory science would have rather different properties. I do not know. The politics outlined here stops at approximately the same place as Foucault did when he suggested that we should work to create the circumstance where the experts no longer know how to function.

However, to develop a more complete politics, further work should address these issues directly and also interrogate the relation between accounts of postmodern technoscience and the development and nature of capitalism.There are some promising possibilities here. I have alluded to the relation between the commodity form and black–box–knowledge, and Braudel (1975) formulates capitalism in terms of extending long networks. Additionally, in developing his account of postmodernity, Harvey (1989) notes Marx's observation that capitalism is implicated in the annihilation of space through time. For Harvey, the economic imperative to cut down turnover time under conditions of competition has become urgent since the early 1970s and has yielded a variety of cultural and political effects. The imperative to speed up the processing of inscriptions in order to compete in the proof race is no accidental parallel for – as Lyotard (1984a) himself notes – knowledge has become a vital element in the production process.

7 Modernity, Postmodernism and International Relations[1]

Nick Rengger and Mark Hoffman

INTRODUCTION

There is a certain irony in discussing postmodernism and the social sciences in relation to the study of international relations. This results from the subject matter of international relations and the manner in which it is approached. As Philip Windsor has noted, international relations 'literally considers the fate of the world'. As such, 'it is bound to be comprehensive by virtue of its preoccupation, but it can not be unitary because of its preoccupation' (Windsor, 1987: 187). It has a unifying concern, but no unifying methodology or philosophy. The result is a subject area which it is difficult at times to hold together. In consequence, international relations is by nature a fragmented 'discipline'. This fragmentation is unavoidable. However, it is not necessarily a weakness and may even be seen as desirable.

There are several things which follow from the above comments. First, it is difficult to conceive of the study of international relations as either a social science or a discipline in the usual meaning of either term. Secondly, it means that to study international relations is to engage naturally in a 'discourse'. This discourse is concerned with the relationship between power/knowledge and social relations and the tensions between the search for survival and the articulation of values: order versus justice; state interests versus humanity. It is a discourse concerned with the limits of particularism and the limits of universalism (Walker, 1984a; Linklater, 1990a, 1990b). Thirdly, because of its intellectual concerns and its status as a 'non-discipline', international relations is naturally open to critical theory and postmodernist approaches. Indeed, it has been argued that the study of international relations is itself an exercise in critical theory (Windsor, 1987). However, its natural inclination towards critical theory has been submerged beneath the successive waves of positivism. This view is reinforced if we examine the development of international relations as a 'social science'.

INTERNATIONAL RELATIONS AND THE SOCIAL SCIENCES

For the most part, the intellectual history of the various disciplines within the social sciences is one of an organic evolution and development out of fifteenth- and sixteenth-century philosophies. This development was based on a growing differentiation between 'scientific' and 'philosophic' modes of inquiry and led to the establishment of, for example, economics, sociology, anthropology and psychology as separate disciplines. Despite this process of differentiation, there was a unifying feature to these various disciplines in the form of positivist epistemology. Each accepted that there were universal laws which governed social behaviour and that these were objectively discernable through empirical investigation.[2] More importantly, such 'scientific' investigations would provide the basis on which to resolve long-standing philosophical disputes. The positivist approach to knowledge provides the backdrop to the evolution of the social sciences.

However, the intellectual history of international relations is markedly different.[3] The study of international relations developed out of diplomatic and international history. These traditions of thought emphasise the particular, the contingent, the indeterminant and the idiosyncratic. Their concern is not with the metanarrative of universal laws, but with the narratives of particular decisions or events. *Intellectually*, therefore, international relations was rooted in an interpretative rather than a positivist tradition.

Institutionally, however, the academic study of International Relations did not develop organically out of this interpretative tradition, but as a reaction to events in the real world. It was the carnage of the First World War which provided the impetus for the systematic study of international relations. Paradoxically, the establishment of International Relations as an academic area of study, as a 'discipline', resulted in a shift away from its interpretative roots and an embracing of the positivist tradition. The inroads of the positivist tradition can be identified at five junctures.

The first positivist juncture is found in the focus of the newly established academic 'discipline'. The initial concern of the discipline was with the *causes* of war.[4] This entailed a fundamental shift away from the focus on the diplomatic history of individual wars to a concern with the phenomenon of war in general. It laid the basis for the later development of general theories of international relations and implicitly incorporated positivist assumptions about the nature of causation and the bases of knowledge. It also precipitated a focus on international law and international organisations as the means to promote, develop and maintain peace.[5] Technical, instrumental and rationalist in nature, this 'peace through law' approach dominated the study of international relations in the 1920s and 1930s.[6]

The second positivist juncture is found in the development of the subject in the 1940s and 1950s. Given the failure of interwar Utopianism – practically with the collapse of the League of Nations and intellectually as critiqued by E. H. Carr (1939) – the study of international relations became dominated by political realism.[7] The most important development in this context was the publication of Hans Morgenthau's *Politics Among Nations* (1973). The significance of this book, for our purposes, is twofold: first, it constitutes one of the earliest, and certainly most widely referenced, efforts at a comprehensive, general theory of international relations; secondly, it emphasises an objective set of laws governing international behaviour as the basis of that theory. The epistemological premises of Morgenthau's arguments are summed up in his Introduction: 'there exists an *objective* and *universally valid truth* about matters political ... [which] is accessible to human reason'.[8] This epistemological turn was reinforced by the shift towards positivist approaches to international law by figures such as Hans Kelsen.

The third positivist juncture occurs in the late 1950s and early 1960s with the effort to promote the 'scientific' study of international relations. Explicitly drawing on the methodology and epistemology of the physical and natural sciences, the behaviouralists argued that the general theories of international relations on offer were not 'scientific' but 'intuitive', intermingling 'facts' and 'values'. These critiques provoked sharp confrontations in the discipline. Scholars lined up to be counted and went into battle on behalf of the traditionalist and scientific camps.[9] As a consequence of a debate which generated more heat than light, the behaviouralist approach came to dominate the discipline in the United States leaving a small but influential traditionalist rump in the UK.[10] However, while the behaviouralists were highly critical of the reflective approach, the imprecise concepts and the use of *ad hoc* examples favoured by the 'traditionalists', it did not fundamentally disagree with the Realist view of international relations. Rather than overthrowing Realism, it reinforced its classically derived conclusions with quantitative 'scientific' research.

The fourth positivist juncture occurs with the publication of Kuhn's *The Structure of Scientific Revolutions* (1962) and his arguments regarding the nature of paradigms and paradigm change. Published just at the point when the study of international relations was being made more 'scientific', Kuhn's work had a dual impact. On the one hand, along with other work in the philosophy of science and the sociology of knowledge, it undermined the very idea of 'science' on which the behaviouralist argument was based. The implication of Kuhn's argument was that there is no possibility of knowledge which stands apart from or independent from the values, beliefs and preferences of the observer. What Kuhn showed was that these were not the products of individual research values, but of paradigms – disciplinary matrices which depended on a prior set of untestable assumptions and which structured the field and its research. Knowledge was subjective and 'paradigm dependent' rather than 'objective'. The implications of this view of knowledge were important. It undermined the positivist enterprise in international relations and undermined Realism's faith in the objective law of power. These intellectual debates coincided with a recognition that the contemporary international system was undergoing dramatic changes. The combination of changes in theory and practice was to challenge the orthodoxies at the centre of the discipline. There was now a changing set of assumptions about the nature of the discipline, the units of analysis, their relationship, the issues at stake and the structures within which they existed. The result was a series of crisscrossing developments which coalesced into Pluralism and Structuralism as two alternative paradigms to Realism. Each of these 'paradigms' focused on different actors, different concepts, different questions and embraced different values.

However, the confusion surrounding the concept of a 'paradigm' and the use, misuse and abuse of the term within the social sciences also reinforced the nascent scientism in the study of international relations. This resulted primarily from emphasising the necessity for 'normal science' and the need for a 'paradigm shift' in the discipline, rather than emphasising 'revolutionary science' as the desirable norm. The effect was an intellectual schizophrenia in which positivist epistemology was held in abeyance during periods of paradigm change but would reassert itself with the return to 'normal science'.

The fifth positivist juncture takes place in the 1980s with the publication of Kenneth Waltz's *Theory of International Politics* (1979) and the focus on neorealism. Waltz's book became the focal point for the most recent and significant of the debates in the study of international relations. In the effort to develop what he thought was a truly systemic, as opposed to reductionist, theory, Waltz reasserted and reinforced the positivist premises of the second and third junctures. As Ashley (1984) has argued, 'neorealism is by, of and for positivists'. Neorealism in general and Waltz's arguments in particular came under sustained attack from a number of different directions.[11] Most importantly, it triggered a self-conscious wave of theorising which turned to critical theory, postmodernism and the interpretative social sciences in an effort to undermine the dominance of positivist and neo-positivist social science in the study of international relations.[12]

IMPLICATIONS OF THE POSITIVIST HERITAGE

It is worth noting some of the implications of this characterisation of the development of International Relations as a social science. First, the intellectual history of International Relations is one of movement *from* the humanities *into* the social sciences and embodies a tension between its interpretative and positivist traditions. In consequence, international relations as a subject area has its intellectual roots in, but developed *academically* outside, the context of a rich tradition of philosophical debates. The effect of this on the study of international relations has been to leave it hesitant about its own intellectual justifications and defensive in its relations with other areas of study, producing a constant introspection which is in many ways unique in the social sciences.[13]

Secondly, it has produced a fragmentation of international theory into a multiplicity of paradigms, perspectives, theories, partial theories and concepts. This diversity is a double-edged sword: on the one hand, it constitutes a tremendous strength and apparent vitality in the study of international relations; on the other hand, it is confusing and destabilising – particularly for students as there is no longer an agreed central core to the discipline regarding the nature of the subject matter, the questions to be addressed or the methods of analysis.

Thirdly, despite this apparent theoretical diversity, the study of international relations is dominated by a set of modernist (largely positivist) assumptions that its various theories and concepts represent true understandings of the world. These, in turn, provide the basis and justifications for attempts at manipulating and controlling the international environment. But they ignores the degree to which the theories themselves do not simply provide the means for describing, discussing and directing phenomena, but help to constitute such phenomena.

Fourthly, all the mainstream theories of international relations rely on a set of modernist dichotomies and often emphasise only one element. For example, in the case of the agent–structure distinction, international relations theory chooses to focus by and large on the latter half of the dichotomy, ignoring the necessary duality of their interrelationship.[14] This means that anti-systemic or 'emancipatory' developments that take place in domestic civil society or at the individual level are seen as having little or no meaning at the international level.

Fifthly, the development of the discipline has resulted in the adoption of an often unstated, narrow understanding of politics and what constitutes the political. These limited understandings and definitions constitute a form of closure which leaves no room for an open-ended, open-textured understanding of politics or what constitutes political space.

Finally, because of its underlying modernist assumptions and the degree to which it draws both on political and social theory, it has become increasingly difficult for international theory to remain isolated from wider debates. Indeed, the roots of international theory compel it to locate itself within the current debates at the heart of social and political theory regarding theories of knowledge, questions of rationality, foundationalism, modernity and postmodernism.

TWO MODES OF CRITICAL INTERNATIONAL THEORY

The increasing discontent of many international theorists with the parameters of the mainstream debate has led, over the last few years, to a wide range of different approaches being applied to the study of international relations and world politics. The most prominent of these have been the development of 'critical international theory' and 'postmodernist' approaches. However, as more and more make recourse to these appellations, we need to develop a degree of caution in their use and a clearer understanding of what they entail and embrace.[15] Within this growing body of literature two broad approaches can be identified. Drawing on a variety of sources from the Frankfurt School to post-structuralism, they can be sufficiently differentiated on the basis of their views regarding modernity and post-modernism and provide the basis for a sophisticated and illuminating debate about the status, character and implications of postmodernism for the study of international relations.

These two approaches can be characterised as *critical interpretative theory*, on the one hand, and *radical interpretativism*, on the other.[16] These characterisations are meant to stress, first, the similarities in the two sets of approaches even while we are concerned primarily with their differences, and secondly, to underline that they have more similarities with each other than with most (though not necessarily all) mainstream international theory. It is also worth noting that many writers display elements of both in their work.

Critical interpretative theory made the key break with the positivistic, rationalistic tradition of the mainstream. Its roots are in the critical theory of the Frankfurt School which has received its most elaborate formulation in the contemporary work of Habermas. In international relations, its arguments are found in the works of authors like Robert Cox (1980), Andrew Linklater (1986, 1990, 1990a) and, to a certain extent, Mervyn Frost (1985). Underlying this approach are three fundamental premises.

First, a belief that the epistemological assumptions of mainstream, traditional theorising are incorrect. Paralleling the arguments of the Frankfurt School, Cox argues that mainstream international theorising has concerned itself with 'problem-solving' theory *within* the confines of the existing world order; it does not ask the important questions about *how* that world order itself came about and what possibilities for transformation exist within it. As with all critical theory, it rejects the positivism and the *technical* rationality of the mainstream. Secondly, it argues that technocratic and bureaucratised forms of knowledge promote certain kinds of normative interests regarding order within the international system which are hidden and therefore unexamined. When examined they are seen to be contradictory, incoherent, constraining of human potentialities or all three. Following from this, critical interpretative theory entails a 'normative Utopian element', offering a 'radicalised', 'historicised' notion of Enlightenment rationality as an alternative guide to action (Cox, 1980; M. Hoffman, 1987). Indeed, one of the hallmarks of critical interpretative theory is a very pronounced normative emphasis which, it is held, is inextricably entwined with the task of explanation and which is also precisely the point most obviously ignored or down-played by the mainstream. Thus central to critical interpretative theory is the emphasis on a knowledge–interests nexus which, it argues, needs to be radicalised in the pursuit of emancipatory rather than technical interests.

Critical interpretative theory thus implies a 'minimal foundationalism' in that it accepts that a cautious, contingent universalism is possible and necessary in both ethical and explicatory fields. This does not, however, imply any facile degree of certainty in its conclusions. Indeed, most critical interpretative theory implies a strong element of epistemological humility (the opposite of the epistemological arrogance which characterises the mainstream tradition's explanatory matrix). Thus, if critical interpretative theory is 'foundationalist', it is so not only to a different degree from the mainstream tradition but in a wholly different way as well (M. Hoffman, 1987; Rengger and Hoffman, 1992).

Radical interpretativism shares the antagonism of critical interpretative theory towards traditional, positivist theorising but moves beyond critical interpretative theory in adopting a post-structural methodology and developing dramatically different ethical and epistemological assumptions. In this regard the mapping-out of the general terrain of radical interpretativism has been done by post-structuralists such as Foucault and Derrida, much as Habermas provides a map for critical interpretative theory. Within international relations its arguments are most fully represented in the works of James der Derian (1987a, 1987b; and der

Derian and Shapiro, 1989) and Richard Ashley.[17] Others, such as Rob Walker (1987a, 1987b)[18] and Jean Elshtain (1987)[19] also draw on this approach. For these authors, the radical interpretative turn in international theory allows us to 'undertake a theoretic investigation of the textual interplay behind power politics' (der Derian and Shapiro, 1989: 6).

In this approach the interpretativism is radical because it is all there is: even the minimal foundationalism of critical interpretative theory is abandoned. It is not so much that the ethical and/or normative assumptions of the mainstream are hidden, and anyway wrong, though this may be so, but that the mainstream cannot understand the way it closes off and privileges its view of the world and therefore can offer us no real understanding of itself, world politics or, indeed, anything. The adoption of this post-structural method (or anti-method) leads to a rather different problematique with a focus on the power–knowledge nexus.

It is important to emphasise, of course, that both critical and radical interpretative theories stress the positive role of interpretation, both are epistemologically humble and both are sceptical of the characteristic modes of utterance of mainstream international theory. What ultimately separates them is the answer they each give to the question: what do we mean when we talk about (in this case) international relations or world politics? To put it simply – and very crudely – for the critical interpretative theorist the mainstream tradition is misconceived because it does not ask the really important questions about world politics and, because of its epistemological premises, can never answer them; for the radical interpretativist, the whole notion of there being 'really important questions' about world politics in any meaningful sense is to betray adherence to the standards of epistemological judgement that must needs be abandoned if we are to examine properly the intertext of (post)modern world politics. Of course, radical interpretativists are no more mere followers of a map than are their critical confrerés. What differentiates them, however, is that the deconstructionists are governed by a power–knowledge rubric rather than the knowledge–interests one which is more prevalent in critical interpretative theory. The difference in emphasis leads to a further important differentiation: the focus of radical interpretativism is on the *reinterpretation* of international theory, while the critical interpretativism emphasises its *restructuring*.[20]

MODERNITY, POSTMODERNISM AND INTERNATIONAL RELATIONS

Within International Relations, the impact of these two approaches has been variable in two ways: in terms of approaches adopted; and in terms of subject areas discussed. In terms of approaches, broadly we can see a movement from one to the other. In the early 1980s it was Habermasian-influenced critical interpretative theory which made the first inroads (Cox, 1980; Ashley, 1981, 1984). From the mid-1980s most authors developing post-positivist international theory had moved to Foucauldian and Derridan-influenced radical interpretativism.[21] The subjects covered by both approaches has been somewhat limited in range. In terms of the substantive research making use of either approach, most deal with issues relating to strategic and defence issues, war, violence, terrorism and conceptions of peace.[22] There is a more limited number of works dealing with issues of political economy,[23] but very little dealing with areas such as foreign-policy analysis[24] or international organisations.[25] Not surprisingly, much of the published literature is concerned with critiques of mainstream international theory, establishing critical international theory as a legitimate part of the theoretical discourse and assessing the relative merits of each approach.

The debate between the two versions of critical international theory can be seen as part of the wider debate within social and political theory as to whether or not modernity (by which is meant the shared intellectual inheritance of the Enlightenment) can be salvaged or whether it should be dropped and alternative conceptions adopted (though usually with similar results). A parallel question, of course, follows from this, at least for our present concerns. If critical interpretative theory seeks to save, reformulate and restructure the 'Enlightenment Project', is this, in any sense, a postmodern reading of world politics? Or is the essential characteristic of postmodernity for international relations pre-cisely the recognition that such a salvage operation is impossible and that, consequently, the types of understanding, the world order and the political assumptions that go with it must be abandoned?

The realisation that traditional forms of social science enquiry are not adequate to explain contemporary international relations still leaves us, however, with the problem of which, if any, of the varieties of critical theory might best serve as an alternative, or perhaps, corrective. This chapter seeks to suggest that, for all its ability to illuminate neglected and hitherto unsuspected areas in the discourse of contemporary world politics, radical interpretative approaches, at least in their present modes, fall short and that an alternative exists in the form of a linkage between approaches which conjoin some version of a knowledge–interests nexus with the power–knowledge nexus (Rengger and Hoffman, 1992; forthcoming).

There are many points of agreement between the different approaches within critical theory beyond the obvious opposition to the positivistic rationalism of the mainstream tradition. However, while agreeing with der Derian on the importance of addressing the 'space between the intertexts constructed between knowledge and power' and on how ideas travelled from the margins to positions of 'natural' dominance (der Derian, 1987a; Derian and Shapiro, 1989) it still leaves open the question of whether, on its own, deconstructionism can offer us an alternative reading of world politics that can explain or contribute to an understanding of that phenomenon rather than simply point up 'spacings, fissures, lacunae and breaks (Steiner, 1989) within the discourse. This question, in turn, raises the rather more general deconstructionist problematic as to what there might be outside the intertext and whether it is in any important sense 'meaningful' – to use the term in its strongest possible sense. It is on the answer to this question that the radical interpretativists and critical interpretativists begin to part company.'

A good way of starting to map the divergence is Steiner's remark that the 'spacings, fissures and breaks' in deconstructionist arguments are postulated on, as well as emblems of, 'absence' (Steiner, 1989: 122). It is precisely this aspect of deconstructionism that has come to be the fulcrum about which radical interpretativist international theory pivots. The problem is that such readings of world politics must assume that 'world politics' is in fact as much a 'non-signifier' as terms like 'author', 'subject', 'context' and 'intention'. In Derrida, as in Barthes, we are told that a text is not a sequence of words, that it communicates no single, decipherable meaning (nor even, as Steiner remarks, a constellation of meanings) and that it cannot, therefore, be 'interpreted' more or less 'accurately' since there is nothing against which to judge its alleged 'accuracy'. Thus, whereas much may be gained in terms of breaking old caricatures, stereotypes or models, attaining new normative or even aesthetic perspectives by a piece on the diacritic relations of the sports–war intertext or the spy 'reality' and spy 'fiction' intertext (Shapiro, 1987; Der Derian and Shapiro, 1989; der Derian, 1987b), we do not gain a greater understanding of 'world politics' (nor even 'international relations') for there is literally nothing, on strict deconstructionist premises, to be 'understood'. Ashley makes this point forcefully when he remarks that 'poststructuralism cannot claim to offer an alternative position or perspective, because there is no ground upon which it might be established' (Ashley, 1987b: 278) – all it can do is invert dominant hierarchies.

Connolly suggests that this view is too narrow, imposing too severe a self-restriction. Instead, Connolly argues that deconstruction must be combined with constructivism. Each must be seen as a moment, 'as indispensable elements bound in a relation of dependence and conflict in its own practice' (Connolly, 1987). Connolly's arguments embody a conception of radical interpretative theory which is different to that sketched by Ashley. This debate reveals a 'lacuna' or 'fissure' at the heart of post-structuralist international theory. What is exposed is a 'difference' over the idea of 'absence'. Thus, while all radical interpretativist international theorists display what Lyotard famously called an 'incredulity towards metanarratives', the character of that incredulity varies from theorist to theorist.

This difference is not a fundamental one, but points to an uncertainty in the radical interpretativist project. Connolly is again interesting here because he most specifically takes up the general question that is often asked of all critical theory (of any sort), but most especially of radical interpretativist arguments: how to construct a political agenda from a disbelief in the 'truth' of any agenda. Connolly's answer to this question is worth quoting at length:

> The postmodernist contends, in a way that overtly presents itself as a contestable supposition, that we live in a time when a variety of factors press thought into a rather confined and closed field of discourse. . . . The political task, at a time of closure and danger, is to try and open up that which is enclosed, to try to think thoughts that try to stretch and extend the normal patterns of insistence. (Connolly, 1987: 338)

The modernist fear, suggests Connolly, is that if a transcendental standard is not somehow proved (or at least presupposed to have been proved) then all hell will break loose. The inevitable modernist question to the postmodernist then becomes: do you not yourself presuppose truth in repudiating it?. The answer, Connolly suggests, is not given by the postmodernists within the same problematic as that of the modernist:

> While modernists univocally apply a code of coherence and consistency to discourse based on the implicit faith that only this one code can save us, the postmodernist thinks within the code of paradox because only attentiveness to paradox can loosen the hold monotonic standards of identity hold over life in the late modern age. (Connolly, 1977: 338)

While Connolly's arguments provide the potential for a synthesis of critical and radical interpretativism, his notion of the radical interpretativist project still depends upon a crucial ambivalence towards the notion of 'absence'. For, as Connolly describes it, there is no need for us to dissent from his picture of the condition of contemporary global politics, or his description of the need to open up that which is enclosed while at the same time asserting the possibility, indeed the necessity, of a notion of the transcendental standard. Yet if we do follow Connolly's vision, the radical interpretativist position (redolent of paradox and irony) becomes fatally incomplete, for only if we assume the postulate of absence does the deconstructionist strategy, in its full and unimpeded form, become appropriate. The central questions therefore become the extent to which the postulate of absence can be sustained and what we might conceive of as an alternative.

As a preliminary to answering these questions, we might ask what, if anything, can be said about the discourse of world politics which could identify a 'presence' and not an 'absence' at its focus and which, in some sense, it is the business of international theory to explore and investigate. One possibility is to start with the premises that most societies or communities will have certain sets of customs, principles and understandings for dealing with other communities, even if, as in the case of post-sixteenth-century Japan, such sets of customs in fact virtually forbade contact with others (see Lehman, 1982). It further assumes that these sets of customs, principles and understandings are, at least in principle, recoverable, investigable and understandable. It might, of course, be the case that there are some counter-examples to this which do nor necessarily invalidate the premises.

A second premises of the argument is that these 'rules' (in their Wittgensteinean sense) will perforce be intimately entwined with the internal arrangements of a particular society or community and are not somehow categorically distinct. Thus any attempt at understanding these 'rules' must be predicated on a sufficiently sensitive understanding of the communities' social and political understandings more generally (See Onuf, 1990).

These two premises lead to our first main argument that any conception of 'world politics' must involve some delineation of the relevant 'world' and that implies that there could be a sense of incorrect usage. If, for example, following an example discussed by Connolly (1987), we were examining European conceptions of the rules governing the limitations of sovereign authority in the sixteenth-century, we would have to be aware that there was a serious dispute in both Protestant and Catholic world-views over the ascription of rights claims and, therefore, over who was to count within the *ius gentium*. It would do very little good to offer a deconstructionist reading of the Las Cases–Sepulvada debates if it were intended as a contribution to our understanding of how sixteenth-century Europe was evolving in terms of the ideas governing what would later be called international society unless it was also premissed on an assumption that there was a real change in progress. Therefore the texts (and intertexts) of sixteenth-century Europe must be read as a sequence in chronological time or an sense of their meaning is lost. For all the illuminating leaps of subject matter and the deconstructionist brilliance of his studies of madness and civilisation, the birth of the prison, or the history of sexuality, this was a point that Foucault understood very well (as Connolly suggests) but that some other deconstructionists would appear to dispute (see Hoy, 1986).

This suggests that the 'presence' that exists for students of 'world politics' is one that both entails the decoding of the relevant sense of the words 'world' and 'politics' and relates them to their referent as it manifests itself in the world. Thus, we are not bound, as are some (realist) mainstream writers, to suggest that there is a 'fixed' international system governed by the 'structure' of the system (Waltz, 1979) because, of course, the notion of 'system', as contemporary (mainstream) international relations understands it, is a very recent conceptualisation and would make no sense applied to, for example, seventeenth- or eighteenth-century Europe. Moreover, if we disagree with the (neo-)realists we are not forced to adopt some variant of (neo-)liberalism or interdependence theory as an alternative, nor even world systems analysis; for each implies, at least as much as realist writing (and sometimes more), that there is a fixed 'core' to understanding world politics which has to do with system structure, system change, the forces of production: all three or any number of other possibilities.

While both critical and radical interpretative theories deny that there is any such 'core', critical interpretativism stresses that 'world politics', like any other kind of politics, can only be understood from the inside out, never from the outside in. This is because it sees the 'presence' as a constantly evolving, changing matrix. However, this matrix must be seen as an identifiable 'presence' and that as a result it must be located and understood in a context which conditions the full free-play of deconstructionist readings, at least if such are meant to imply a Barthean, Derridan or even Rortyesque 'absence' at the heart. In this respect, critical interpretativism and Foucauldian radical interpretativism are as one.

The above argument implies that understanding world politics involves a normative as well as an explanatory commitment. Although the former will usually precede the latter, the relationship is inevitably a symbiotic one and never more so than when the 'presence' one is explaining and evaluating is that which motivates the system closest to ourselves: the contemporary international system itself.

CONCLUSION

This leaves the question of whether such an approach which seeks to interrelate the critical interpretative knowledge–interests nexus with the radical interpretative knowledge–power nexus constitutes a 'postmodern approach' to international relations, and the implications of this approach for social enquiry more generally. In an effort to address this question, and by way of conclusion, we offer both a summary and a suggestion.

The summary is as follows. In our view, the contemporary study of international relations and world politics requires a threefold project of deconstruction, conversation and reconstruction which incorporates both modes of critical theory (see Grant, 1989). The first stage, deconstruction, provides a means of unmasking the hidden and the absences in our existing accounts and explanations of social relations. The (critical and interpretative) rereading and reinterpretation of foundational texts offers an initial means of opening up an apparently closed debate on our under-standing of key concepts. Rereadings of classic texts or understandings of the meaning of key concepts – states, security, power, anarchy – allow us to examine the intertextualities of presences and absences and provide a basis for destabilising the dominant discourse which is premissed on accepted, unitary understandings. In denying the possibility of an *ultimately objective* discourse in favour of intersubjectivity, the modernist, positivist vindications of political power begin to be questioned. It leads to a recognition that we are dealing with complex, contingent 'rule-governed behaviour' which can only be understood in the context of the discourse, conventions of argument, habits, customs and political actions which produced it.

This process of defamiliarisation becomes an essential step in rethinking ourselves and our political circumstances. But this step is not enough in itself. As Elshtain notes, 'problematizing the state is not an end in itself but an incitement to discourse and perhaps to action as those references by which state power has legitimized itself are destabilised' (Elshtain, 1989: 11). Therefore, no single discourse can give us a transparent picture of reality; rather, a multiplicity of voices is necessary to expand the horizons of conversation and make our thinking more supple, more sophisticated. This necessarily leads to the second stage: conversation.

The second stage of 'conversation' is the antithesis of much of main-stream international relations theory and practice, which ignores multiple understandings of social reality. In opposition to a single, dominant discourse, it offers a conversation which is open-ended and has no fixed agenda. The conversation must be opened up to include new issues and new participants, particularly those 'voices' that previously have been marginalised.[26] Such a conversation is likely to foster social relations which are conducive to redefinitions of politics and political space, which enhance understanding, awareness of difference and an empathy with other cultures and societies.

It is important to recognise that such an approach may lead to a surfeit of 'voices' in the conversation and that this is not without difficulties. It raises questions about who is to participate, whether every 'voice' is to have an equal standing and whether any 'conversation' will do. The implication of these concerns is that this multiplicity of conversation cannot be endlessly self-regressive. The point of the conversation cannot be simply to critique dominant discourses, as this would constitute a delimitation and closure of possibilities, an 'objectified' conversation. Moreover, to do so would lead to a critical theory devoid of its intellectually radicalising elements. 'Conversation', therefore, is a method of understanding; it cannot itself be the goal of such understanding. This means that the starting point for the conversation must inherently be a concern with the kind of normative, emancipatory interests which lie at the core of critical interpretative theory. It also necessarily impels us towards the third stage: reformulation and reconstruction.

The third stage of reconstructing and reformulating draws on the various critiques of the existing structure of international relations. The most important component of this is the reformulation of 'being' as 'becoming' (see Windsor, 1985; Grant 1989; Rorty, 1989), as contingency rooted in a view of human consciousness itself having history, an evolution and a series of contexts for understanding and interpretation. It would also entail a reformulation of the view of the formation and nature of the modern state, the inter-state system and international relations. This would lead to addressing the traditional questions and concerns of international relations in a different way, as well as incorporating questions, issues and problems which should lie at the centre of international relations but which have been marginalised by the way in which the subject has been traditionally constructed. While deconstructionism provides a radical starting point, the central focus of the third stage is the reformulation and redefinition of the political in international relations. This is, and must be, a critical interpretative project, however much it might welcome, admire and even use deconstructionist techniques and methodology.

This, then, is a summary of our position. We said, however, that we also had a suggestion. Elaborating it takes us back to the several instances in the text where we sidestepped the question of to what extent our approach can be said to be a postmodern one. While not being overly concerned about labels (and, indeed, recognising the danger of labels), it is important to stress that in many ways we believe that the approach outlined above can be characterised as a postmodern one, at least on a certain reading of what constitutes postmodernism for the human sciences. This reading would hold that a rejection of the structure of modernity as we now perceive it *does not* involve the necessary rejection of all elements held to make up that structure. In this respect, though not necessarily in other aspects of our work, we would agree with Richard Rorty that rejecting 'modernity' does not mean rejecting the Enlightenment, or at least not all of the Enlightenment (see Rorty, 1989). Here, of course, we stand opposed to a very prominent strain of post-structuralist writing running from Adorno and Horkheimer, through Foucault, to Derrida and beyond. We would argue (as indeed Foucault himself can be interpreted as doing on at least one occasion) that in any situation of radical change, of intellectual and political fragmentation, of uncertainty, danger and potential closure there will always be movements of life or of thought, or both, that refuse to accept the modes of experience and knowledge that are instantiated in the ruling structures of the time. They will therefore be in whole or partial rebellion against the 'modernity' of that time, just as some are against 'our' modernity. To believe, as some radical interpretativists seem to do, that the hallmark of 'postmodernism' is the unalloyed subscription to the post-structural intertext (it could not, after all be a 'text') is to assume that all those who wish to break radically with the forms and structures of much of the contemporary world must either be post-structuralists or else they are really 'modernists' of one sort or another.

This is not necessarily the case and, paradoxically, is a view that results from demarcating and policing the boundaries of modernity and postmodernism too strictly. While it may well be that all post-structuralists must be postmodernists, not all postmodernists need be post-structuralists. The nature of our critical project can therefore accommodate a number of different and often contradictory impulses within it. It will involve rethinking the ways in which traditional problems of international relations are perceived and conceptualised, perhaps dropping some and adopting others. It will involve, for instance, the recognition that we cannot properly analyse foreign policy without examining the general context of the constitutive rules in which foreign-policy formulation and implementation take place. This will require a more reflective awareness of the changing nuances that characterise such rules. Similarly, it will involve the recognition that we cannot properly analyse the problems of international security without understanding and moving beyond the existing constitutive framework to one that places less emphasis on security and more emphasis on politics (Weaver, 1989). It will involve a deepening awareness of the problems of ethnocentrism and cultural diversity, and how and when to relate and hold together different traditions, if indeed this is possible at all.

This process of reintegration and restructuring will not be easy and will involve losses as well as gains. It will involve the loss of paradigmatic certainty and the loss of the belief that International Relations either can or has unlocked the 'arcane secrets of world politics'.[27] However, what will be gained will be a recognition of the contextuality of our social circumstances and therefore of their 'plasticity' (Unger, 1987a, b, c). Such a realisation makes the task of properly understanding the sets of constitutive rules that humans have evolved for the management of their social life even more vital than has been commonly supposed. The knowledge that nothing is fixed or inviolate, that everything can be changed (for better or worse), involves us in the pressing task of assessing what might *be* better or worse, whether we like it or not.

We do not suppose that many radical interpretativists would find much to dissent from here (though some would), but it does mean that many of those in the mainstream who hope for a dialogue with aspects of critical theory that leave the cornerstones of modernity untouched delude themselves. The opportunity for dialogue is open; it certainly does not preclude the many contributions of 'mainstream' scholars to the understanding of contemporary world politics. But dialogue is a two-way process and part of the mutual recognition must be an acknowledgement that the fragmentation of the world, intellectually as well as politically, means that eclecticism in method is sometimes the only way to achieve understanding. Therefore, for international relations at least, postmodernism means starting a dialogue premised on the recognition of the fragmentation before us and abandoning the belief that a fixed 'scientific', 'rigorous' method will help us to understand the world or that there is a set of key, privileged problems which constitute 'International Relations'. If these two premises are born in mind, then critical theory and the mainstream will begin to resemble one another, in form at least, if not always in content, and that will be the first indication, perhaps, that the postmodern era is truly upon us.

NOTES

1. In this paper this term is used as synonymous with 'international politics', 'world politics' and 'global politics'. However, it is worth noting that the term 'international relations' is a contentious one. Coined by Bentham in the nineteenth century to denote activity among nations, it has come to be understood in both very narrow and very broad terms. The narrow definition views international relations as concerned only with formal political relations between states. Broader definitions extend the units of analysis beyond the state to include non-state actors and the issues beyond the military–political to the economic. The broadest definitions understand the term to cover the internationalised or global dimensions of social, economic, political and cultural phenomenon. It is the latter definition which informs this paper. When used with lower case initials, the term refers to this phenomenon of international relations; when used with upper case, it refers to the study of that phenomenon.

2. 'Positivism' is of course a disputed term. Here it is taken to mean the 'received model' of the natural sciences and, in the context of the social sciences, entails five elements: (a) that there is a reality that exists in accord with certain fixed structural or causal relations which is independent of human subjectivity; (b) that this independent reality can be described in a value-neutral scientific language; (c) that such a language provides the basis for technically useful knowledge that enhances human capacities to make predictions and exert control; (d) that truth claims made in this language can be tested by their correspondence to a field of external experience; and (e) that the phenomena of human subjectivity do not create any barriers to social conduct being treated as an object' in the natural world. For a detailed discussion of these issues see Giddens (ed.) (1974) and Hesse (1980).

3. For a more detailed discussion of this, see Little (1980). For general discussion of the development of the academic discipline of International Relations see Banks (1985); Holsti (1985); Alker and Biersteker (1984); and M. Hoffman (1987).

4. The standard text which addresses the causes of war is Waltz (1959). For an insightful discussion of the problem of 'causation' in the causes of war literature see Suganami (1990).

5. Scholte (forthcoming) has noted that there were previous attempts in the late nineteenth century to identify international relations as an aspect of the developing discipline of sociology, thus firmly placing it within the history of the social sciences. These attempts to define the study of the international system as the sociology of world politics were unsuccessful in overturning the intellectual grip of international law. It is only within the last decade that there have been concerted efforts to try and reformulate the study of international relations in an historical sociological framework. This approach is exemplified, for example, in the works of Scokpol, Tilly, Barrington Moore, Halliday, Mann, Gellner and Hall.

6. For a discussion of the legalistic approach to international relations see Suganami (1977 and 1989).

7. Part of the reason for this dominance was the rapidity with which the study of international relations established itself to coincide with 'reality', it also

coincided with the perceived security needs of the US in pursuit of its Cold War policies of containment. These quickly came to dictate the research agenda of the discipline, leading Stanley Hoffmann (1977) to characterise International Relations as an 'American social science'. This in turn reinforced realist international theory's emphasis on the military–political dimensions of international politics and the concern with deterrence, nuclear weapons and the viability of military power in a nuclearised bipolar world.

8. Morgenthau (1973: xi), emphasis added. It is important to note that there are other readings of Morgenthau's book which would push towards a different characterisation of his work. Nevertheless, this points to a tension within Morgenthau (mirrored in the study of international relations as a whole) between the positivist and the interpretativist approaches.

9. The flavour of these exchanges is best exemplified by the exchange between Hedley Bull (on behalf of the traditionalists) and Morgan Kaplan and Bruce Russett (on behalf of the behaviouralists) reprinted in Knorr and Rosenau (1969).

10. It is worth noting that the classical approach associated with the tradition of international theorising in mainstream UK scholarship has a strong undercurrent of an interpretative epistemology. Indeed, some see this, in conjunction with critical theory and postmodern approach, as providing the basis for a 'post-classical' approach to international theory. See Rengger (1988).

11. The best single compendium of these critiques is Keohane (1986). It also contains an interesting reply to these critiques by Waltz himself.

12. It is important to emphasise that interpretative approaches to the study of international relations endure at each of the positivist junctures identified. At the first juncture they are embodied in the continued emphasis on voluntaristic assumptions and the idea that war could be eliminated by altering the motivations of decision makers through the enhancement of international law and international institutions. At the second juncture it is embodied in the emphasis on the need to understand history and Morgenthau's implicit recognition of the importance of the psychological dimensions of power. At the third juncture, by the survival in the UK of the 'English school' or 'classical approach to the study of international relations. At the fourth juncture by the inroads that the sociology of knowledge made in highlighting the subjective nature of knowledge and the development of alternative 'paradigms'. At the fifth juncture interpretative approaches come into their own with the rise of 'non-problem solving' theories of international relations which draw on critical theory and postmodernism.

13. It might also be added that international relations is largely a reactive area of study, often lagging behind important intellectual debates in other areas by 10–20 years.

14. For a discussion of the implications of this dichotomy for international relations theory, see Wendt (1987).

15. The danger is that the usage of the phrase 'critical theory' – and parallel terminology such as 'post-modernism' 'deconstruction' and so on – might become the buzz words of the 1990s and end up being used, misused, abused and discredited in much the same way that the notion of a 'paradigm' was in the 1970s. A recent example of this is evident in James

Rosenau's effort to coin the phrase 'post-international relations'. See Rosenau (1990).

16. This is instead of post-structuralism, an epithet that is favoured by some and disavowed by others as a characterisation of their approach, and post-modernism, which is too ell-embracing to accurately describe the approach.

17. Richard Ashley is the most prominent of those working within a radical interpretative/postmodernism perspective in international relations. His most important articles are: Ashley (1981, 1983, 1987a, 1988a, 1988b). A reading of these in chronological order provides an interesting insight into the movement in Ashley's perspective from that of critical interpretativism influenced by Habermas, to a form of radical interpretativism influenced by Foucault, to a radical interpretativism influenced by Derrida.

18. However, it is difficult to place Walker squarely within the radical inter-pretive tradition as is evident in some of his other writings, for example, his (1988) book. Indeed, Walker may be most representative of the convergence between critical and radical interpretativism which we discuss in the latter sections of this essay.

19. Elshtain's work, as well as that of others, highlights the interesting radical interpretive intersections between feminist political theory, postmodernism and international theory. See Elshtain (1988) which includes a useful bibliography; and Sylvester (forthcoming).

20. To some extent this is a rather different way of expressing some of the points developed in the exchange between Yosef Lapid, K. J. Holsti, Thomas Biersteker and Jim George in *International Studies Quarterly*, 33 (1989) 3. However, there are important differences of emphasis between their respective positions and in relation to the argument made here. For example, Lapid in the *ISQ* discussions, and elsewhere, has argued that these approaches are the basis for developing a 'third way' in international theory, but one which may be allied with some form of 'paradigmatic science'. The emphasis of the exchange in *Millenium*, 17 (1988) 1, was that not only was the critical 'conversation' meant to open 'international theory' to many other influences for too long shut out of its view, but it was meant to do so in a way that does not of itself suggest anything about the *direction* of the debate. Equally important, it sought to emphasise the importance of eclecticism in method.

21. This shift is best exemplified by the shifts in Ashley's theoretical position. See note 18 above. The shift is also evident in the approaches taken in the first edited collection of postmodern international relations essays in der Derian and Shapiro (1987). However, the critical interpretative approach still has a major advocate in the work of A. Linklater (1990a, 1990b).

22. An example of the degree to which these issues dominate the critical international theory agenda is evident in the der Derian and Shapiro volume. Nine of the fourteen chapters in the book deal directly with these issues. One explanation developed for this seeming fixation may be that critical theory developed in reaction to neorealism and in the context of the revitalised militarism of the Reagan years and the second Cold War.

23. Arguably, from a critical interpretative perspective, much of the historical sociological research on international political economy associated with Immanual Wallerstein and world-systems analysis would be empirically

relevant, though lacking a consciously self-reflective emancipatory component. See M. Hoffman (1987) and Linklater (1990a). For an example of a
radical interpretative approach to political economy, see Grunberg (1991).

24. Works which indirectly draw on critical international theory in this area are
Hollis and Smith (1989) and (1990). More self-consciously, and in
particular drawing on Giddens's structuration theory, is Rosenau (1990).

25. Some of the literature dealing with regime theory directly or indirectly
draws on critical international theory approaches, but most of it fits squarely
within a neorealist framework. A recent effort at drawing directly on
Foucault in discussing international regimes is Keely (1990).

26. The most important of these is to be found in feminist theory. As Elshtain
(1987: 1) argues, there is a need for 'critical explorations ... promoting a
fruitful engagement between and among those who see themselves
primarily as feminist scholars or international relations scholars or those
who position themselves knowingly inside both universes'.

27. This is characterisation of the role of theory in the study of international
relations found in Ferguson and Mansbach (1987).

8 Postmodernism and Economics
Sheila Dow

INTRODUCTION

Postmodernism has not been well-articulated as such in the field of economics. Nevertheless, there has been a series of developments in economics which may be better understood with reference to postmodernism as it has been articulated in other contexts. Indeed, since there is a disparateness about these developments, the possibility of identifying a positive unifying theme is an attractive one. At present, the unifying theme is a rejection of modernist and, as we shall see, late-modernist economics. But reinterpreting this rejection in the form of the embracing of postmodernism may help us understand better what it is envisaged will be put in the place of modernism, or late-modernism.

Already a problem arises in contemplating postmodernism as a unifying concept. Postmodernism involves a move away from unifying theories to a more particularised epistemology. It is therefore inherent in postmodernism that those attracted to it will have particularised notions of postmodernism itself; this is even more of a stumbling block to discourse when postmodernism is applied across disciplines. But this feature of postmodernism calls into question the validity of its general application. However, in order for discussion to proceed, we shall treat the general application of a concept which denies general theories as a paradox, emphasis on paradoxes being another noted feature of postmodernism (see Schulte-Sasse, 1987: 6).

In the next section, we specify modernism and late modernism in terms of economics. This specification is well-founded in recent economics literature. We then explore the problems with modernist, and particularly late-modernist, economics which have brought economics in the view of some to a state of crisis which involves a turning-away from modernism. The more difficult task of specifying postmodernism for economics is attempted in the following two sections, first, by discussing developments in economic methodology, and secondly, by outlining the nature of the non-modernist schools of thought in economics. Postmodernism is discussed in terms of pluralism, although the issue is confused by the fact that pluralism means different things at different levels. It is concluded that the notions of pluralism (at the theoretical level) and schools of thought are contradictory. However, it is argued that all economic analysis conforms in at least a loose way to a school of thought which guides choice of technique, perception of reality and so on. If postmodernism is defined as involving pure pluralism at the theoretical level, it is therefore in danger ultimately of being empty. If it is to be at all useful, the notion of postmodernism (as opposed to non-modernism or anti-modernism) must allow for some structured theorising according to some methodological principles.

MODERNISM AND LATE-MODERNISM IN ECONOMICS

It is the clarity of the definition of modernism which makes it relatively clear to identify, and also accounts for much of its success as an approach to economics. Its main features can be listed as follows: (see Klamer (1987a) for a slightly different expression of these features):

1. desire for progress in thought, so that each successive generation uses all that is useful from the past (no specific reference therefore need be made to history);
2. search for universal theories, independent of history and context;
3. although belief in unity of science, tendency to professionalisation and separation of disciplines;
4. achievement of 2 and 3 by formalism in terms of classical logic, particularly favouring axiomatic, reductionist, dualistic reasoning and mathematical expression;
5. self-referential approach to methodology and theory, achieved by formalism applied to fictional, as opposed to realist, concepts;
6. split between normative and positive analysis.

The development of modernism in economics can be traced to the nineteenth-century determination to model economics on classical mechanics (see Mirowski, 1984; Drakopoulos, forthcoming). This was achieved by the increasing use of mathematics and the concomitant reliance on 'economic man' (the selfish, pleasure-maximising individualist) as the basic building blocks of determinate economic behaviour. It was reinforced by the move away from regarding economics as a moral science and the advent of logical positivism.

The first major challenge to these antecedents of modernism came with the Great Depression; mass unemployment was precluded by the self-referential theoretical system of the time. John Maynard Keynes's challenge to the orthodoxy involved demonstrating that injecting even minor elements of realism would dismantle their full-employment results. In fact, Keynes's challenge was a fundamental methodological one. Explicitly rejecting the epistemological foundations of what was to become modernism, Keynes put forward a different mode of thought; this emerged from his early work on probability but was reinforced by his subsequent experience as a practical economist and policy advisor (see Carabelli, 1988; Fitzgibbons, 1988).

A distinctive feature of Keynes's work was his theory of effective demand which, in simple terms, states that the level of output and employment in an economy is determined by the aggregation of individual demands, in so far as they are made effective by firms' production plans. This marked the birth of what we now know as macroeconomics: the study of economic aggregates as something distinct from the sum of their parts (whose study is called microeconomics). As a direct challenge to the reductionist reasoning of the orthodoxy of the time, Keynes demonstrated the complex interrelationships between different levels of aggregation. His most powerful conclusions were that microeconomic solutions did not apply at the macro level: for example, a fall in the money wage on the part of isolated workers might ensure their employment, but a wholesale fall in money wages would not, because it would depress aggregate demand.

Modernism in economics arose from the successful translation of Keynes's theory into orthodox terms (a classic case of paradigm defence in the face of Keynes's extraordinary science). Keynes's theory became a mechanistic adding-up of sectoral demand. If the total fell short of full employment the government would make up the difference with its own spending; if demand were so high as to spill over into inflation the government could withdraw demand directly by raising taxation or indirectly by raising interest rates. Hydraulic Keynesianism, to use Coddington's (1976) term, lent itself to the formal expression advocated by modernists, and to the construction of large econometric models to assist governments in their policy-making. It was conventional to perceive a sharp divide between positive model-building and testing, on the one hand, and normative policy recommendations, on the other. The major methodological issue in the late 1950s and 1960s was sparked off by Friedman's (1953) argument against realism of assumptions (see Caldwell, 1984; 1989).

The resolution of the ensuing debate on the realism of assumptions, particularly as it related to macroeconomics, was to lead to what we can now recognise as late-modernism (see Klamer, 1987b). Macroeconomists were chastised in the literature for being insufficiently reductionist, and thereby for perpetuating a logical split between macroeconomics and microeconomics. General equilibrium theorists, Hicks, Arrow and Debreu (all Nobel prize-winners) and Hahn all paved the way for macroeconomics to be built up from the axioms of rational individual behaviour applied to the fictional concept of economic man (thus destroying the last vestiges of Keynes's challenge). Developments in macroeconomics over the last twenty years can be best understood in terms of this pushing to the limits of modernist principles. In the case of some, notably Hahn (1983), the self-referential principle is taken to the extreme of arguing that no connection may be made between theory and reality. For others, particularly rational-expectations theorists, theory is still self-referential although defined as being coincident with reality. One manifestation of the resulting circular reasoning is the argument that there is no involuntary unemployment. If all individuals are rational, pleasure-maximisers, then, if they are unemployed, it must be the result of a voluntary choice.

As in the Great Depression, so in the 1980s there has emerged a crisis in economics. The professionalisation and specialisation of the discipline has been entrenched in textbooks and teaching methods, the importance of which has been pointed out by Kuhn (1962). The result has been a conflict between an interest in policy issues and the technical requirements of the discipline, as is evident from a recent study of American graduate students (see Colander and Klamer, 1987). In particular, there is concern among many economists that mainstream economics does not adequately address issues of apparently involuntary unemployment, uneven income distribution on local and global scales, and the potential for financial crisis. It does not address these issues adequately because they have no place in general equilibrium models which assume that all individuals already take fullest advantage of all opportunities available, and where the benchmark is stable equilibrium.

It must be said that recent developments in mainstream theory have attempted to address these points, to avert disciplinary crisis. Indeed, these developments could be classified as representing a move towards post-modernism. Reductionism employed 'economic man' as the basic unit, whose hedonistic behaviour had universal validity, allowing generalised theorising. But attempts to introduce elements of realism (such as diversity of information on which rational decision-making is based), have broken down the generality of the early models. The most notable result has been a denial of macroeconomic analysis; that is, the argument that no aggregative results are feasible. But the methods employed to analyse disaggregated units remain modernist in every other sense. Indeed, while there is pressure in some quarters of mainstream economics to break down boundaries between economics and other disciplines (not least to modify the limiting concept of 'economic man'), the more notable trend has been for mainstream economics to extend its coverage (on grounds of universal validity) to areas traditionally occupied by other social sciences (see Nicolaides, 1988).

It is the contention of critics of the mainstream that economic theory built on modernist principles is incapable of modification to produce satisfactory economic analysis. In the next two sections we discuss the content of this line of argument; first, in economic methodology, and secondly, in the different schools of thought which counterpose themselves to the mainstream.

THE METHODOLOGICAL CRITIQUE OF MODERNISM IN ECONOMICS

Methodology in economics was until recently dominated by adherence to Lakatos's theory of research programmes. This stance was most clearly and most recently put forward by Blaug's (1980) methodology textbook. From the standpoint of logical positivism, Blaug chastised economists for falling short of the requirements for theory to be tested empirically in order to be meaningful. But the renewed interest in methodology to which Blaug was catering had arisen because of what was seen as an emerging crisis in economics. It was not long before a new literature appeared in methodology which suggested alternatives to the traditional, prescriptive approach. This new literature, led by Boland (1982), Caldwell (1982) and McCloskey (1983, 1986) held in common a rejection of the modernist goal of a universal, unique prescriptive methodology, particularly in the form of logical positivism, and the advocacy instead of some form of pluralism.

The critiques of modernism in economics took the form of pointing out its inherent logical inconsistencies (see, in particular, Boland, 1982, and Caldwell, 1982) and pointing out, like Blaug, that practice did not conform to modernist principles anyway (see, in particular, McCloskey, 1983); these two aspects are interrelated in that economists in practice must seek methods outside logical positivism to handle its inconsistencies. The underlying problem is that modernist, mainstream economic theory is constructed mathematically around a series of fictions (notably rational economic man), but logical positivism requires testing with respect to real entities or events. Further, formalism requires that all aspects of the economy which cannot be expressed formally are automatically excluded, and the tendency for formalism to restrict analysis to equilibrium states excludes formal consideration of states out of equilibrium other than those on a path returning to equilibrium. Most applied economics requires some means of overcoming these logically necessary limitations, which inevitably leads to logical inconsistencies.

The advocacy of pluralism in recent economic methodology may be classified as an emergence of postmodernism, since for some (for example, Klamer, 1987a, b), pluralism is a notable feature of postmodernism. (Lash and Urry (1987: 14) refer to 'transgression of boundaries' as a feature of postmodernism, a notion which includes pluralism.) Pluralism can be defined at a variety of levels. Caldwell (1989) advocates it at the metamethodological level; that is, that methodologists should be pluralistic with respect to the methodologies of practising economists. Rather than imposing a set of rules by which these methodologies should be judged, methodologists should assess each critically on its own terms. Boland (1982) argues as a methodologist that economists should be pluralist in the sense of considering a range of methods, recognising that some may be more suited to particular problems than others; the rôle of methodologists is to guide economists' choice of methods. McCloskey (1986) denies a rôle for methodologists altogether, and therefore argues at the level of theory. Economists themselves, he argues, should be pluralist in being open to the full range of methods, choice and appraisal being governed by reasoned discourse amongst economists themselves. It is the first and last forms of pluralism which Klamer seems to identify as postmodern: methodologists avoiding prescriptive methodology and theorists open to a range of theories and methods. The middle level of pluralism is more difficult to classify as postmodern. Boland constructs a methodological argument that economists be pluralist; this would seem to be a general application of methodological principle, which is antithetical to postmodernism.

It is noteworthy that none of this literature constitutes a critique of mainstream economics *per se*, simply of the methodological standards it purports to adopt. Further, it is notable that, in general, mainstream economics seems to have continued regardless in its late-modernist mode. The methodological critique of modernism has made most headway among alternative schools of thought, and it is to this angle that we now turn.

NON-MODERNIST SCHOOLS OF THOUGHT IN ECONOMICS

The methodological critique of modernism was in fact well advanced within the theoretical literature of non-mainstream schools of thought well before it emerged in the economic methodology literature. Since, by definition, all non-modernist schools of thought employ a fundamentally different methodology from the mainstream, their critique of the mainstream involved a methodological critique of modernism. In particular, the modernist notion of the inevitable progression of thought, and the uniqueness and universality of the best methodology (modernism), had to be undermined.

The power of modernism in our educational system is so strong that elements of it appear in all schools of thought (particularly in Marxian economics). But its explicit rejection is common in some degree to those that I shall discuss briefly below: neo-Austrian economics, post-Keynesian economics and Marxian economics. These schools do not cover all non-modernist thought in economics, but are sufficiently representative to provide an indication of the alternatives available in economics. (They are discussed in detail in Dow, 1985.)

Neo-Austrian Economics

The individual's motivation to action is the starting point for this school, as a real entity rather than a fiction. But the complexity of human motivation and behaviour and the subjective nature of perception preclude the formal analysis of individuals, far less aggregates. The resulting methodological individualism puts in the place of modernism a case-study approach to knowledge, focusing on motivation and behaviour, and the role of institutions, in particular contexts. General statements are limited to the advocacy of withdrawal of the state from the economy, other than in helping to promote competition between individuals and individual firms, so that full play may be given to human action to bring about socially optimal outcomes. These general statements have their basis in intro-spection and case-study analysis, since it is illegitimate for methodological individualists to generalise formally by means of macroeconomic models. (It must be said, too, that these general statements received much support from the Thatcher government which, many argue, was more influenced by Hayek than by Friedman.) Recent work in neo-Austrian economics draws on postmodern terminology; Lavoie (1990), for example, advocates a hermeneutic relationship between economists and their object of study (entrepreneurs).

Post-Keynesian Economics

This school of thought carries forward the innovations of Keynes, in conjunction with those of his contemporary, Kalecki. It occupies a methodological middle ground, whereby formalism is rejected as a universal method but is used in conjunction with other methods. Like neo-Austrians, post-Keynesians focus on historical process and the rôle of institutions; but the macroeconomy is regarded as a legitimate object of enquiry, not least because it impinges on individual behaviour just as much as the reverse. Formalism is limited in its scope particularly by the uncertainty with which knowledge and expectations are held by economic agents; but the resulting theory is not subjectivist. Post-Keynesians see an active rôle for the state in offsetting the inability of capitalist economies to maintain a high and stable level of employment, or what is seen as an equitable distribution of income.

Marxian Economics

This school occupies the other end of the non-modernist spectrum. Individual behaviour is derived from the macro, or class, level. Also there is more scope for formalism, so much so that some Marxian analysis verges on modernism. But the emphasis on historical process, the rejection of the notion of rational, economic man, and the pragmatic adaptation of Marxian theory to such diverse contexts as rural China and urban North America demonstrate the non-modernist character of elements of Marxian economics. As with neo-Austrian and post-Keynesian economics too, there is an openness to a range of disciplines to be drawn on together with economics.

These alternative schools of thought recently seem to have attracted increasing interest, concomitant with the growing unease with mainstream economics. Their major stumbling block, however, has been the wide-spread adherence to modernist principles (even if not carried through to practice). While presenting a critique of modernism in economics, dissent-ing economists have not been altogether successful in specifying their alternative and justifying it methodologically. It has been the negative rejection of the mainstream which has been the most powerful, rather than the positive embracing of an alternative.

If the methodological stance of the various alternatives to the main-stream can be defined in terms of a positive (that is, non-negative) position such as postmodernism, then the satisfactory specification of the alter-natives may be more easily achieved. This project was attempted in Dow (1985) where the distinction was drawn between Cartesian/Euclidean thought (synonymous with modernism) and Babylonian thought; the latter term was adopted, on the basis of some obscure precedents, as a label for a non-modernist mode of thought, and one which did not bring with it any potentially confusing intellectual baggage.

The possibility of classifying non-modernist thought as postmodern is therefore an appealing one; it would have the distinct advantage of being specific to the current era and of allowing economists to draw on intellectual developments across a range of disciplines. It would be up to particular schools of thought in economics to map out their territory within postmodernism.

POSTMODERNISM AND SCHOOLS OF THOUGHT

While modernism is readily defined and recognisable, the concept of postmodernism in general seems less clear-cut, other than involving a rejection of modernism, that is, non-modernism. Even then, Jencks (1986: 7) refers to postmodernism as 'the continuation of Modernism and its transcendence'. This implies that postmodern economics would use some of the advances made in modernist economics, albeit embedding them in a historical and cultural context, with an openness to other disciplines which might contribute to understanding. But since mathematical sophistication has been the hallmark of modernist, and particularly late-modernist economics, does postmodernism entail the use of mathematics? If so, then neo-Austrian economics could not be regarded as postmodern. Yet neo-Austrian economics, with its emphasis on small-scale case studies, seems to conform to what is understood by postmodernism in other disciplines (economic geography, for example). While all fields of economics have no doubt sharpened the edges of their analysis along with modernist developments, it is not clear that 'continuation of modernism' is a notable feature of non-modernist economics which one might be tempted to term postmodern. The most likely candidate would be mainstream economics which has moved away from macroeconomics, stressing diversity of information at the micro level, and the possibility of multiple equilibria. But the other features associated with postmodernism are notably absent (openness, appeal to other disciplines, grounding in history and so on).

The classification of economics in terms of postmodernism is hindered by the fact that there is no overtly postmodern literature in economics, that is, discussion of postmodernism in terms of specific theories or approaches. Indeed, while one would tend to look to non-mainstream economics for evidence of postmodernism, a leading critic of modernism (and implicit advocate of postmodernism) is McCloskey who works in the neoclassical or mainstream tradition. We must, therefore, fall back on discussions and developments in other disciplines for guidance.

Understanding postmodernism in terms of other disciplines is helpful, but must be treated with due caution. The arts provide the most concrete examples of modernism and postmodernism and is the field most often used to convey their meaning (see, for example, Jencks, 1986). Within architecture there has been a clear change among some practitioners from a self-referential, technique-oriented profession, whose goal was functionalism narrowly defined, to a more open profession concerned with the physical, social and cultural context of buildings, with goals which include decoration and making connections simultaneously with different historical periods.

But it is easier to envisage postmodern architecture using techniques developed under modernism than the same for economics; that is, for postmodernism to be seen as developing out of modernism. This is not to deny that some techniques may be used, but that their use must be limited by the fact that modernist economic techniques actively preclude the attention to historical time, uncertainty and evolving institutions and so on which are the hallmark of non-modernist economics.

Following our account in the third section of developments in economic methodology, which focus on pluralism, we could start with a very broad definition of postmodernism as: 'openness to a range of methods, disciplines and influences, accepting that no theory can be regarded as true in any absolute sense'. This definition is equivalent to non-modernism as anti-modernism; that is, together modernism and postmodernism by this definition form the kind of dual (mutually exclusive categories, with fixed meaning and universal application) beloved of modernists. On the one hand, therefore, it reinforces the notion of rejection of modernism as a negative intellectual force: anti-modernism. On the other hand, in the form of a concept like postmodernism, it allows for a more positive expression of non-modernism as the embracing of the principle of openness.

However, while openness is advocated by many economists, it can only take economic discourse so far. On what grounds is one theory to be preferred to another in any particular instance? What criteria are to be employed in selecting from among the available methods and disciplines and influences? Without any such criteria, however particularised to a given context, theorising risks being incoherent. The problem is more clearly recognisable in the context of architecture, where haphazardly drawing on different influences can generate very unappealing buildings. It is because of this danger of incoherence that we should exclude as unhelpful the notion of pluralism at the methodological (rather than metamethodological) level; that is, a methodological argument for openness without provision of further methodological principles. To be useful, therefore, the 'non-modernism' definition of postmodernism needs to be modified to allow for mechanisms to generate coherent theorising.

The notion of coherence seems fairly clear in the context of architecture (although, even so, aesthetic judgements are notoriously controversial). But in the broader context it raises the vexed questions of standards and criteria of appraisal. What constitutes coherence within a pluralist approach to economics? Are some non-modernist approaches better than others, conforming more to what we might think of as 'good' postmodernism? Pluralist methodologists are not in fact 'pure' pluralists in the sense of denying any criteria of appraisal. McCloskey (1989) envisages agreement on approaches to particular problems by means of 'effective persuasion'. Caldwell (1989) has moved to a position of envisaging some sort of consensus on an acceptable range of methods. Neither envisages this agreement to be modernist in the sense of setting permanent, universally applicable standards. But neither provides a satisfactory account of how agreement might be reached. Rhetoric, for example, includes devices like humour which, although often persuasive, cannot provide satisfactory grounds for choosing methods of analysis. McCloskey makes matters even more difficult by arguing that the whole notion of schools of thought impedes constructive discourse by arbitrarily limiting use of concepts. Such a view does seem to conform to expressions of postmodernism in other disciplines (see, for example, Lash and Urry, 1987: 14). McCloskey would therefore appear to support a narrower definition of postmodernism for economics than that suggested above, that is, one which precludes discussion of methodological principles.

I wish to argue here, on the contrary, that the notion of schools of thought provides the necessary channel between the Scylla of nihilism and the Charybdis of vagueness when reliance is placed on pluralism. A school of thought can be understood in terms of a Kuhnian paradigm, adopted by an academic community with shared views of the world as a whole, and as to the preferred techniques to analyse it. Rorty (1980) argues that paradigms can successfully prescribe their own choice of methods and appraisal criteria, in conjunction with a hermeneutic approach to other paradigms. Thus, we can classify postmodernist schools of thought as sharing a pluralist approach to technique, in the sense of being open to a range of techniques whose selection would be governed by the context of the problem addressed. But within this postmodernist grouping are different paradigms characterised by different world-views and criteria for choosing techniques and appraising the results. The brief descriptions of non-modernist schools of thought in economics outlined in the fourth section should give an idea of some differences in world-view with respect to the workings of capitalist economies, the rôle of the state and so on; that is, differences of vision.

Two of these schools of thought, post-Keynesian and Marxian, put forward what might be regarded as general theories; they certainly put forward theories applied to the macroeconomy, that is, an aggregation of micro units. So, if the definition of postmodernism were to be qualified to preclude general theorising, these schools of thought would be excluded. Only neo-Austrianism would qualify because of methodological individualism. But even then, the neo-Austrian vision is a general one, about the functioning of capitalist economies. And neo-Austrian theory generates policy prescriptions at the macroeconomic level (about the size of the public sector, the rate of growth of the money supply and so on). So it too is in danger of being excluded from postmodernism. Indeed, it could be argued that postmodernism which precludes general theorising must be empty, since all theorising, however particularised, draws on general theories of some sort, even if they are not articulated.

In any case, the Kuhn–Rorty approach allows for general theories to be held, but not held to be absolutely true, so that openness can be maintained when theorising in particular contexts. Thus, for example, a post-Keynesian might argue against the wisdom of controlling inflation by means of monetarist policies in one context but not in another. Postmodern schools of thought can therefore be characterised also as having a pluralist, or hermeneutic, approach to each other. If no paradigm holds claims to the truth, then mutual tolerance is to the advantage of all. The modernist paradigm (or paradigms, depending on how boundaries are defined) not only espouses a unitary choice of technique but is also methodologically unitary, regarding alternative paradigms as being by definition unsatisfactory and not part of the progression of knowledge.

But just as postmodernism denies any claims to absolute truth, so, to be useful, it should also deny claims to absolute pluralism at the methodological level as well as at the theoretical level. No economic theorist or methodologist approaches any theory independently of culture, training, history or psychology. As noted above, even advocates of pluralism ultimately accept that some criteria must be employed; the postmodern view is simply that these criteria should not be regarded as independent, universal rules. The criteria themselves are up for discussion as much as the theories being appraised. What has been missing from some of the pluralist literature is the recognition of this fact, and the recognition that the regress cannot be infinite: ultimately disagreements may have to stop at an underlying disagreement on vision.

But for practical purposes, much of economics must be conducted as normal science, as Kuhn (1970) himself advocated, Popper (1970) notwithstanding. There is good reason for paradigms: much progress can be made if economists working together hold a shared vision and a shared view as to the range of feasible methods. McCloskey's vision of everything being open for discussion all the time, like Popper's, is scarcely feasible in reality.

Individual economists generally recoil from classification according to paradigms; this seems particularly to be the case in Britain. But this need not detract from my argument. First, it is useful to classify bodies of thought (if not bodies) by paradigm, as a reference point for the work of individual economists. But secondly, if we accept the Kuhnian, and postmodern, argument that science cannot be independent of the context of discovery, then the work of any one economist is inevitably grounded in some paradigm. Discourse across paradigms can only be constructive if this is recognised and the contents of each paradigm discussed. Otherwise non-modernist theory can fall into incoherence.

CONCLUSION

Discussion of postmodernism in relation to economics risks circularity. Either we define postmodernism and decide which type of economics fits the definition, or we define postmodern economics and arrive at a definition of postmodernism. The discussion here has, along non-dualist (postmodern?) lines, avoided this bifurcation and attempted to draw both on a general understanding of postmodernism, on the one hand, and a general perception of economics which some regard as postmodern, on the other.

The very notion of considering disciplinary developments in terms of broad intellectual developments is an intriguing one. Certainly, there seems to be some generality in the perception of modernism as it affects a range of disciplines. But if the economics literature is anything to go by, what is most apparent as possible postmodernism is a rejection of modernism. If it is this rejection which is general across disciplines, it does not necessarily follow that what is put in its place, which we may call postmodernism, is also general across disciplines.

With that caveat we have proceeded to suggest a definition of postmodernism which is most helpful for economics: pluralist metamethodology, in the sense of allowing for a range of possible methodologies, and pluralist theory, in the sense of allowing for a range of possible techniques and methods of theorising. For these two together to generate theory, the different methodologies studied within pluralist metamethodology must necessarily involve their own internal criteria of method selection and theory appraisal. In other words, while theorists may be pluralist in the sense of being open to a range of possibilities, they can still be grouped into schools of thought which employ different means of selecting among the possibilities.

The openness and tolerance associated with postmodernism would certainly be constructive if more generally held in economics. But that alone could not survive in the face of the power of modernist thought. If postmodernism is to hold its own, it must explicitly allow for, and indeed encourage, structured theorising and discussion of methodological principles.

9 Postmodernism or Modernism?: Social Theory Revisited

Scott Lash

Postmodernism, in social theory and in social practices, is understood usually as a categorical rejection of modernism. Postmodernism in this interpretation thus signals the death of *humanism*. Foucault (1977b) in this sense speaks, not just of the dismembered totality of the *oeuvre*, but of the 'death of the author'. Structuralism had already meant the rejection of theories which featured the independence of the social actor or of 'agency'. In France this took a largely philosophical turn, and heralded a break with the autonomous agency of existentialism and phenomenology of Sartre, Merleau-Ponty and Hippolyte. In its Anglo-Saxon, sociological reception, it meant the rejection of Max Weber's action theory in favour of structural determination. For Freudians it suggested the dismissal of a similar domination of psychoanalysis by ego theory, and its replacement with the orthodox Freudian primacy of the id, whether or not the latter appeared in the colours of Lacan's symbolic. In film theory it pointed to rejecting *auteur* notions in favour of a focus on structures of Barthesian or Lacanian signifiers. *Post*-structuralism and post-modernism radicalised this refusal of the human agent. Now no longer did even the text constitute the author, but both author and text were deconstructed into Derridan *écriture*. Humanism entails the existence of not just author and autonomous actor but also of 'meaning'. And it was just this humanist warmth of meaningfulness that Baudrillard dissolved into the cold winter of his mediascapes.

Postmodernism ostensibly counters modernism in its disavowal of *history*. This has several dimensions. One is the rejection of teleological and totalising accounts of history; a refusal of a general, overarching march of history, complete with origins and teleological endpoint. Structuralism had already disputed the orthodox Marxian version, as the rhythms of structures – proposed by Althusserians – called into question the importance of actual historical time, and posed a challenge to Whig notions of history. Lyotard's condemnation of the 'metanarratives' pushed this critique further, rejecting any sort of even recast Marxian vision.

Foucault (1972) and Deleuze (1972) questioned the validity of any possible notion of linear time, challenging, in a Heideggerian vein, a notion even of empirical (as opposed to totalising) history in which events follow, one after the other, as causes and effects. Their conception instead was one in which events float fully haphazardly in a veritable sea of contingency. The other side of their opposition to such linear notions was, of course, Nietzsche's *ewige Wiederkehr*.

Postmodernism is further understood as putting modernism into perspective. In coming after modernism, postmodernism has thus been identified as a rather latter day avant-garde. Post-structuralism and postmodernism have in this sense not uncommonly been referred to as 'avant-garde theory'. If the modernist abstraction of Pollock and Barnet Neuman was old-hat, then Warhol and Pop Art, as well as the figural revival of the 1980s, were logically the new avant-garde.

Architecture followed suit as Charles Jencks pronounced the demise of the modernist tower block to make space for the new postmodernist avant-garde of Graves, Venturi and Helmut Jahn. The postmodern architectural avant-garde themselves even began to draw directly on the theoretical avant-garde as architect Peter Eisenman cited Barthes and Foucault and Jencks opened a 1988 London architectural conference by playing a video tape of the talking head of Jacques Derrida, the latter obviously too busy to take the first-class transatlantic flight over. Such postmodern theorists fit perfectly Pierre Bourdieu's (1988) sociological model of a heterodox avant-garde counterposed to institutionalised and academic orthodoxy. Like previous aesthetic avant-gardes, Derrida, Foucault, Deleuze and the like stood largely in a world apart from France's academic institutions, with one foot inside France's prestigious and money-making publishing houses. Like previous aesthetic avant-gardes, they were darlings of the salons of *tout Paris*.

Finally, postmodernism lays down the putative gauntlet to modernist notions of *referentiality*. Thus the Early Modern displacement of religious symbolism in painting by quattrocento perspective's window on the world was itself eclipsed. And other-referentiality replaced by postmodern's famous self-referentiality. The 'realism', both narrative and pictorial, of mainstream cinema in a very much later modernity was displaced by the well-known 'chains of signifiers' of Metz and the Lacanians (Heath, 1981). Foucault spoke of the concomitant death of the 'philosophy of representation' alongside the sciences of man. And Derrida and Baudrillard imploded the object of aesthetic reference into, in the former's case, *écriture* and, in the latter's, into networks of medial simulacra.

Humanism, historicism, avant-gardes, referentiality; on these four central counts postmodernism is understood to break with the entire *problématique* of modernism. What I want to do in this chapter is to dispute all of this. In what follows I should like to argue that much of what is usually regarded as postmodern culture is in fact really part and parcel of modernism. That is, I should like to maintain that what is characteristically understood in terms of a cultural paradigm (postmodernism) becoming pervasive in the past one or two decades is in fact much more characteristic of the set of modernist movements of the turn of the last century.

Thus, perhaps a majority of today's analysts (a) define postmodernism in terms of anti-humanism; (b) say it is anti-historical; (c) see it in terms of an (often inaccessible) avant-garde; and (d) claim that it is self-referential. It is my contention that it is *modernism* – not a recent, but a late nineteenth-century phenomenon – that is anti-humanist, anti-historical, is initiated by avant-gardes and is self-referential. *Post*modernism, on the other hand, (a) is an attempt to restore humanism; (b) is an attempt at reconstituting a historical dimension; (c) rejects avant-gardes in favour of 'convention'; and (d) is not self-referential but *other*-referential.

This said, the first section of this chapter will argue that most of what are taken as postmodernism's main characteristics (usually seen as arising from the late 1960s and becoming widespread in the 1980s) were in fact part and parcel of the turn-of-the-twentieth-century modernism revolution in culture. And that the postmodernist position, when examined carefully, is in fact a disavowal of this and a return in an important sense to *pre*-modernist tenets. In this context the issues of humanism, historicity, avant-gardes and referentiality will be addressed serially.

The second and third parts of this chapter briefly follow up the implications of this. The second part argues that postmodernism, in its canonical form as exemplified by Baudrillard, Lyotard and Derrida in theory and by the postmodern architects and painters, fails in its attempt to recapture the pre-modern. I contend here that the consequences of postmodern cultural practices are instead (a) a phoney humanism; (b) a de-semanticised historicity; (c) not convention, but an avant-garde leading from the rear'; and (d) a vain quest for a, so to speak, 'disappearing' referent.

The third and final part argues that in its inability to re-establish any sort of pre-modernist roots, postmodernism, in its canonical form, winds up being *hyper*modernism, a taking to the extreme of everything modernism itself stands for; a final sweeping-away of even the over limited foundations of modernism. In contrast to this failed critique of canonical postmodernism, an alternative, communitarian and ecological critique of modernity is proposed.

I

Humanism

What is meant by 'humanism' is a fairly straightforward matter. Writers on art and architecture – as diverse as Panofsky, Aldo Rossi, Michael Graves, Peter Eisenman, Lewis Mumford and many others – are in broad agreement on this centuries-old, conventional notion of humanism. Humanism has to do with Alberti, Erasmus and Grotius. It has to do with the ontological primacy of 'man' over the Christian God. It has to do with the Renaissance and the eighteenth-century search for Classical and humanist values in Greek Antiquity (Panofsky, 1960).

It has very little at all to do with what French structuralism of the 1960s labelled as 'humanist'. The structuralism of Althusser, Barthes, Foucault and even Bourdieu defined itself in contradistinction to the agency-centred social theory – of Sartre, Merleau-Ponty, Hippolyte – of the generation of their teachers. They called these older theorists 'humanists', But action-theoretical social thought is not at all necessarily humanist (MacIntyre, 1988). Action-theoretical philosophy and sociology (and this would apply to Jon Elster and the ethno-methodologists) assumes a highly abstract notion of agency which is incompatible with humanism. Humanism looks back to Classical Greece when the view of human agency was not abstract but foundational. Moral agency here was not abstract but rooted in the foundations of a social *Sittlichkeit*. Moral, aesthetic and cognitive actions were not conceived of in abstraction, the one from the others, but as integrally intertwined. Rational agency was not conceived of in the same kind of abstraction from the body. The nature–culture disruption was not so radically stated.

Neither structuralism nor the twentieth-century theories of agency of which the structuralists were so critical are humanist. Both structuralism and these action theories are, instead, quintessentially modernist. Habermas and Benjamin's discussions of modernism juxtapose Ancients and Moderns. And humanism in its classicism, its foundationalism, its rootedness in Socratic Greece is not modern but fundamentally ancient. Modernisation, it has been argued following Habermas (1981b), is a process of cultural differentiation and autonomisation. Humanism, whether in fifth-century Greek, Renaissance or eighteenth-century neo-classical guises, represents a certain level of cultural modernisation (pre-Socratic Greece and mediaeval Europe are less differentiated, hence less modern and more 'ancient' than the Ancients). That is, humanism represents a certain level of differentiation and autonomisation of cultural spheres as, for example, when the sacred is differentiated from the profane and secular culture from religious culture but it also entails the foundationalisms mentioned above.

Modernism, a turn of the last-century phenomenon, represents the culmination of this process of cultural differentiation. At this point the different cultural spheres are fully autonomised. Modernism is thus fully non- or anti-foundational and cultural spheres are fully abstracted from one another. This is exemplified in the full autonomy of modernist art, that is, in the aesthetics of 'art for art's sake' and 'truth to the(aesthetic) materials'. It is exemplified in the birth of sociology and its assumptions of the autonomy of the social. Hence Durkheim's 'social facts' are *sui generis*. Further, epistemologies and ethics are not foundational and categorical in the Kantian sense, but are socially conditioned or socio-logistic. Thus the abstract and autonomous agency of the action theorists is only the other side of the (relatively) autonomous structures of the structuralists. Abstraction and autonomy are the rule in both cases. In this sense modernist social theory only reproduces the assumptions of modernist painting. Here action theory is homologous to the abstract agency assumptions of Expressionism, and structuralism to the facet-plane constructions of cubism.

Following this argument, humanist architecture and humanist urban space are anthropomorphic, anthropocentric and anthropometric. Modernist architecture rejects, while postmodernist architecture embraces, anthropomorphism, anthropocentrism and anthropometrism.

Historicity

It is not postmodernism but modernism which has advocated the radical break with history. Let us be certain in this context to distinguish movement and change from history. The modern, as advocated by Berman and (the acceptable face of) Marxism, constitutes a metaphysics of change and movement but it is a rejection of history. Anti-modernist cultural neo-conservatives like Bell, Lasch, MacIntyre and Allan Bloom advocate the recovery of the historical dimension in the interest, not of movement or change, but of stability. Hence Bell and Lasch lament the disappearance of the historical sense in which identity is stabilised by the sensibility of being 'the son of my father who is the son of his father' and so on.

Modernism, for its part, rejects history in order to embrace movement and change. Modernism in Vienna, Paris, Berlin and a number of other European cities, as the nineteenth century drew to a close, was ushered in by a series of effective 'secession' movements (Schorske, 1981). These movements consisted of a rejection of 'academic' standards by artists and architects. This was at the same time a rejection of state sponsored art, given the fact that national states controlled both the academy which taught art or architecture and the selection of paintings to be exhibited at the annual 'salons'. Official, 'academic' painting and architecture in each of these cases was historicist. Paintings were commonly of historical scenes. Architecture taught by the Paris École des Beaux-Arts and its non-French equivalents repeated styles from previous historical epochs. Thus French Impressionism (and realism), Viennese Art Nouveau (*Jugendstil*) and German Expressionism, all took from the institutional context of the reaction against historical art. In each case the rejection was in favour of a modernist or proto-modernist aesthetic of working through the possibilities of the aesthetic materials.

Postmodernism, on the other hand, proposes a return to historical values. The event which consecrated the arrival of modernism in the US was the Museum of Modern Art's International Style exhibition in 1932. The event, according to the editors of *Oppositions*, which heralded the coming of *postmodernism* also took place at the MOMA some 45 years later (Colquhoun, 1984). This was the Beaux-Arts exhibition of 1977. Significantly, the École des Beaux-Arts was the central institutional context of the historicist architecture that modernists rejected. Corbusier in the 1920s and 1930s saw the Beaux-Arts academic style as the main enemy in much the way that the secession movements several decades earlier were revolts against the academy. And the Beaux-Arts style was above all historicist. Training at the École produced architects such as Cass Gilbert and William Van Alen, authors of 'delirious' New York's awesome neo-Gothic skyscrapers such as the Woolworth and Chrysler buildings. Such training is noticeable in the neo-Romanesque features of Louis Sullivan's Auditorium Theatre in Chicago. Beaux-Arts influence informs Speer's monumental Third Reich neo-Classicism.

But Beaux-Arts architecture was historicist rather than historical. That is, its architects reproduced in the present one of a set of varied styles from different historical epochs. The rise of historicist architecture ran parallel to the rise of historicist social theory, in the work of, for example, Dilthey. The very plurality of historical styles suggested a rejection of universalism and an acceptance of a certain relativism corresponding to the 'forms of life'-type relativism of the social theorists. The return to history that the postmodernist architects advocate, however, rejects historicism and relativism. The search instead is for *universals* in history. And these universals are humanist. Hence the neglect of Gothic and Romanesque forms for neo-Classicism by the postmodern architects.

This universalism of the postmodernists is a bit confusing perhaps in the light of criticisms by Habermas and his followers. Such criticisms have taken the postmodernists to task for being anti-universalist. But there are (at least) two types of universalism. Universals can be sought, by modernists such as Corbusier and Habermas, in the 'ought', in the Utopian moment of a possible future. Such universals constitute the moment of critique in Corbusier's harmonically juxtaposed volumes or Habermas's ideal speech situation (Reichlin, 1988). But universals can also be sought in the past, as in the model of humanism described above. Because modernist universals are abstract, this does not mean that all universals have to be abstract. The (historical) humanism outlined above is universalist in the sense that a certain set of values is held to be valid for all historical periods and in all geographic places. Full spatio-temporal validity is also the assumption of modernist universals.

But postmodernist (humanist) universalism is grounded in the rejection of modernist abstraction. The architects' search for historical universals is matched by that of painters among the German *neue Wilden*, such as Anselm Kiefer. It is purveyed by the social theorists such as MacIntyre and Leo Strauss. Strauss and his follower Allan Bloom are critical of modern natural-rights theory because of the very abstraction of the rights involved. Their advocacy of a return to Platonic political philosophy is an endorsement of the more humanist and *sittlich* (that is, grounded in social practices) notion of rights implicit in Classical thought. Alisdair MacIntyre (1981) is critical of the assumptions of abstraction (and absence of *Gemeinschaft* and *Sittlichkeit*) in Enlightenment thought. In MacIntyre's view, Nietzsche and the modernists do not constitute the reversal of the Enlightenment project. They are emblematic instead of the radicalisation of Enlightenment abstraction. They bring about the total break of ethics and epistemology with any kind of foundations. MacIntyre has also advocated a return to the social groundedness of Classical Greece, to Aristotle's ethics and the *Sittlichkeit* of the polis.

Thus the critique of modernism in architecture and in social theory embraces a return to the historical sense that the modernists have abandoned. This critique is perhaps most appropriately, though surely cryptically, formulated by the populist/vernacular postmodern architect Robert Stern. Stern (1980: 86–7) writes that modernism is based on the dialectic of the "is" and the "ought" ', and postmodernism on 'the resolution of the "is" and the "was" '.

Avant-Gardes

One tends almost naturally to see postmodernism in terms of a set of new avant-gardes, in architecture, painting and so on, setting themselves up in counterposition to an entrenched modernist establishment. Surely postmodernism is in an important sense a somewhat *populist* critique of modernism. But so were Surrealism and Dada in the 1920s and these were quintessentially movements of avant-gardes. Equally, Derrida, Foucault and other post-structural theorists are commonly called postmodernists, and they have been widely understood to be a Parisian, theoretical avant-garde; a conception reinforced by their own aesthetic pretensions and their loyalties especially to Surrealism.

Avant-gardes, however, not only originated with modernism, but their whole ethos is quite integral to its logic. The aforementioned universalist abstraction of the modernist 'ought' is, at the same time, the regulating principle of avant-gardes. Both aesthetic and political avant-gardes presume a universalism which, unlike humanism, is abstracted from the social. Avant-gardes which are abstracted and thus separate from socio-political everyday life, impart forward movement to the latter. Thus for Marxism, class struggle, and later the proletarian political party, is the (avant-garde) 'motor' of history. Much the same characterises aesthetic avant-gardes which, separate from the everyday convention of the state and social *Sittlichkeit*, are to impart movement to the latter. In both cases the principle of modernisation, or autonomisation and differentiation, is the rule.

If modernisation is a process of differentiation, then postmodernism is one of cultural *de*-differentiation (Lash, 1990). And such de-differentiation precludes the possibility of avant-gardes. The postmodernist denigration of avant-gardes stands in counterposition to the modernist autonomy of the creative 'author'. Modernism presupposes an Adornian production aesthetics, in which power lies in the hands of the (avant-garde) producers of cultural goods. Postmodernism is not only homologous to consumer capitalism but lodges power in the consumes of cultural goods. Postmodern aesthetics are thus reception aesthetics and this entails the absence of avant-gardes. Hence the 'populism' of Venturi and Scott-Brown in their assignment of an important role to the public in deciding the shape of the built environment. 'Convention' would seem to be the antonym of avant-garde. Venturi and Scott-Brown castigate the idea of the avant-garde architect as legislating hero and instead note, inconspicuously, 'we like convention'.

Avant-gardes, further, mean change, much in the sense of Marshall Berman's ever-transmuting modernist Utopia. But postmodern architect Robert Stern wonders what indeed is so great about such 'constant change and experimentation'? And the (equally postmodern) maverick Leon Krier (1978: 58) calls for the termination of avant-gardes and 'their barbarous profusion of innovations that culminate in the kitsch which perverts every level of life and culture'.

Modernist avant-gardes, as noted above, have always been constituted in opposition to 'the academy'. Thus Corbusier, though admitted to the École des Beaux-Arts, was trained in the art school of his home town in Switzerland. And van der Rohe underwent a crafts-orientated training. Postmodernism, on the other hand, has literally grown up in the academy; that is, in the architecture departments of the most 'establishment' of American universities. Thus the chief voices of postmodernism have been the *Harvard Architecture Review* and Princeton's *Oppositions*. One can only lament here, along with Russell Jacoby, the academy's destruction of the modernist critique of 'the last intellectuals', though Jacoby points the finger rather more at postmodern theorists such as Jameson.

Modernist avant-gardes presuppose the primacy of *movement*. This is foregrounded in discussions of the modernist city by analysts like T. J. Clark, Carl Schorske, Berman and Bell. Key to the modernist built environment on these accounts is the street and the promise of never-stopping circulation, both of vehicles and pedestrians. By contrast, postmodern space would, it seems, hold out the promise of *stasis*. It is not uncommonly held that Japanese culture was postmodern *avant la lettre*, and this ontology of stasis would seem to be borne out by the organisation of space in Japan. Thus the Japanese street, unlike modernist western streets, is organised not for moving through but for living in (Berque, 1982). Those activities which often take place in squares, airports or malls in the West (such as buying, selling, public sociability) commonly take place in residential streets in Japanese cities.

With modernisation, as western space became more and more a medium not for living but for moving through, streets took on names and houses numbers. To this day in Japan streets have no names and houses no numbers. Japanese residences and places of business do have addresses, typically with three digits and a name. The name refers, however, not to a street, but to a quarter. The first of the three digits refers, in its turn, to a district in this quarter; the second to a square block in the district; the final digit designates the building on this square block. It does so, not in spatial and linear sequence, but in chronological order according to when the house was built. Thus *Business Week* has noted the popularity of fax machines in Japanese offices. Japanese companies must send western (and Japanese) visiting clients photocopies of maps showing the location of their corporate headquarters.

Referentiality

If post-structuralist theory is postmodernist (and most commentatators think so), then the Derridan '*il n'y pas un hors du texte*' would be the postmodernist canon. This would also be canonical self-referentiality. The absence of an *hors du texte* would mean a semiotics consisting solely of signifiers, in which utterances have their effect totally apart from any relationship they may have to signified and referent. In fact, signified and referent are banished as '*hors du texte*', and meaning is generated through the differential values of elements and spaces in networks of signifiers.

But Derridan self-referentiality has, for the most part, its roots in Saussure. And Saussure, for his part, is a canonical modernist. Modernist differentiation and autonomisation reached its peak in the early decades of this century, as cultural spheres and discourses achieved their fullest autonomy. Hence there is at this time Kelsen's pure theory of law. There are the beginnings of a political science which does not, as did early modern political philosophy, elide the political and the social. There is the onset of autonomy of the social in Durkheimian social facts and sociologistic ethics and epistemologies. And there is the autonomy of language, both from referent and signified where it had been lodged in the nineteenth-century historical linguistics (that is, philology) of the Grimms and others in Saussure's course in general linguistics. There is finally the theorisation of all these autonomous and modernised cultural spheres in Max Weber's ethics of responsibility. Weber speaks of each sphere becoming self-legislating (*Eigengesetzlichkeit*). And self-legislation is the other side of self-referentiality.

The doctrine of the non-existence of the '*hors du texte*' is pre-eminently exemplified in modernist architecture. For Mies van der Rohe, for example, the form of a building was to follow not function – which would be an *hors du texte* – but the structure of the building itself. That is, van der Rohe's understanding of, say, glass was not in terms of light maximisation for a building's users but instead involved with aesthetic, formal and structural properties. He thus wrote of glass as a building material permitting not 'the play of light and shadows as in ordinary buildings ... but the play of reflections'. 'It [glass]', he continued, 'also permits a particular massing of the building as viewed from the street' (Meyer, 1988). Thus the role of glass, as building material, was to reveal structure. This surely is the language of self-referentiality. Similarly, Corbusier's rendering of the house as a '*machine à habiter*' focused less on the functions of the machine for its users than on the relationship of the elements of the machine to one another. This looks suspiciously like

Saussurean '*langue*' – Corbusier even calls the elements 'terms'. The five elements of the '*machine à habiter*' in a 1925 Corbusier exhibition were (a) the pilotis; (b) the free plan; (c) the free façade; (d) the horizontal strip window; and (e) the roof garden.

Postmodernism, in contrast, revels in the *other*-referentiality of the *hors du texte*. Thus the signified is ressurrected in the rejection of modernist syntactical architecture for an architecture of semantics. Postmodernism also heralds the return of the (repressed) referent in the representational painting of pop art and the *neue Wilden*, or of Americans like Eric Fischl and Edward Hopper.

In brief, modernism signifies via a principle of semiosis, and postmodernism via mimesis. Semiotic signification is self-referential and takes place through the differences among signifying elements in a *langue*. Mimetic signification is other-referential and takes place through the resemblance of signifier to referent (Eco, 1976). Postmodern signification takes place largely through images, through spectacle. And the more closely signifiers resemble images (compare abstract versus figural painting) the greater the extent to which signification proceeds via mimesis. Thus the Lacanian and Barthesian analysts associated with *Screen* could not be further from the truth in their main claim that cinema signifies like a language. Indeed, it would be difficult to find a cultural practice – with its images, its movement, its sound, the size and high definition of its images – that signifies less like a language than cinema. Cinema and video signify almost not at all semiotically, but almost fully mimetically. And postmodern signification through images could not be further from self-referentiality. It could not give a greater role to the *hors du texte*.

II

When Michel Foucault heralded the 'end of man' in *The Order of Things* (1970b) and celebrated the subject's removal from social-scientific centre-stage by structuralist anthropology, psychoanalysis and semiotics, he was celebrating the triumph not of postmodernity but of modernity. The principle of 'man', or 'humanism', with its corresponding mirror-of-nature (which is also quattrocento) epistemology and ontology, is part and parcel not of Foucault's modern but of his classical episteme. The bulk of *The Order of Things* deals with the classical and modern epistemes. Foucault's critique of Marx takes place significantly in the sections on the classical episteme. Elsewhere in Foucault in *Discipline and Punish* (1973a),

Marxism is criticised for its pre-modern, statist conception of power. Foucault's famous chapter in *The Order of Things* on the replacement of the sciences of man by autonomous sciences of 'structure' comes, of course, under the modern episteme. Lyotard' analyses comprises a similar logic. Here Marxism is a 'metanarrative' to be replaced by autonomous and 'local' language games. Thus in Foucault's terms and those of the argument of this paper, Marxist metanarratives would be pre-modern and the local language games modern. Lyotard's aesthetics of 'paralogy' fully parallel a modernist aesthetics of experimentation. The only problem is that what is classical (humanist) or pre-modern Lyotard mistakenly labels modern, and what is modern he mistakenly labels postmodern (Lyotard, 1979a).

In any event, Lyotard's *Postmodern Condition* (1979a) was a hastily written report for a Canadian social-policy agency and bears none of the depth of insight and analysis of his major works such as *Discours, figure*. Foucault's *Order of Things* is a twentieth-century 'Great Book' in which the radical separation of subject from object at the outset of his very Kantian modernity already foreshadows the death of humanism. As Foucault's (1966: 314–54) modern episteme unfolds, the subject of Kant's categorial epistemology and ethics achieves autonomy from categorical (that is, unconditional) status and becomes socially conditioned in Weber's neo-Kantian *wertrational* and *zweckrational* social action. The other side of this autonomous actor is the social structures of Durkheimian sociology, which achieve their own autonomy from all of the humanist foundationalisms described above.

Thus Foucault, as structuralist, is pre-eminently modernist, as is the self-referentiality and basis in autonomous Saussurean linguistic structures of Derrida's post-structuralist '*écriture*'. These modernists, like the modernist architects, celebrate, implicitly or explicitly, the downfall of humanism. The postmodernists, I have argued, want to resurrect it. Have they succeeded?

The answer to this would seem to be largely in the negative. Let us review our categories. As regards *humanism*, the attempt of postmodern architects to reconstitute the anthropometric and anthropocentric scale and fabric of our cities has turned into the highly individualistic and atomised isolation of the buildings of the 1980s' financial districts. This has been only a radicalisation of modernism's loss of foundations. Modernist architecture came under the spell of industrial society's polarisation of manufacturing capital and labour. Industrial capital went into the initial growth of the tertiary sector in our city centres with its proliferation of high-rise buildings for the white-collar employees of manufacturing firms. Industrial labour was housed in the modernist public-housing blocks first in Germany and then in Britain, the US and elsewhere. In contra-distinction, postmodernist architecture has been subject to the imperatives of a post-industrial economy, of the internationalisation of fictive com-modities, of financial, business and cultural services, and of the property developers (Zukin, 1988).

As regards *historicity*, one must be suspicious of the authenticity of the engagement of postmodern architects such as Moore and Graves with historical universals. Their more populist counterparts, like Jahn, Stirling, Venturi and Philip Johnson, are quite openly 'playful' with historical elements. They operate with historical signifiers only for 'effect' or 'impact' on the public. Their focus, surely, is not on meaning. Rather, theirs is a de-semanticised historicity.

As regards *avant-gardes*, Venturi (in Venturi and Scott-Brown, 1980) has admitted that his buildings are intended for two publics: one élite and the other mass. The élite reception group is similar to the audience for the modernist avant-gardes. The same is true of a number of recent postmodernist films such as *Diva*, *Blade Runner*, *Blue Velvet* and *Robocop*. They too, unlike Godard's or Bergmann's modernist films, are aimed simultaneously at two audiences. The assumption, of course, is that much of the significance of these postmodern cultural objects, like that of modernist avant-gardes, will not be accessible to the mass audience. Finally, the engagement with populist commercialism of the postmod-ernists was not unknown among modernist avant-gardes and is exemplified in, say, the Josef Hoffmann and Kolo Moser's design in the Vienna Secession and the mass-production turn of the later Bauhaus. Thus the claim of the postmodernists to reject avant-gardes is not substantiated in their own cultural practices. Perhaps most apposite is the comment made by British architectural critic Martin Pawley that the postmodernists are an 'avant-garde leading from the rear'.

Finally, what about the attempt to break with modernist *self-referentiality*? The attempt of postmodern architecture to re-connect with historical meanings (or 'signifieds') has, as has often been noted, wound up in the trivialisation of the latter. Similarly the putative reunification of signifier with referent, that is, of representation with reality, in (postmodernist) pop art turns out to be a very problematic referentiality indeed. The referent in, for example, Warhol's silk screens, the Elvises and Marilyns and Maos, turn out to be images, or signifiers themselves. This sort of reference differs considerably from modernist self-referentiality. In the latter, attention is called to the signifying practice; in the former, to entities external to the signifying practice. For example, in Godard's modernist cinema, attention is continually drawn to the fact that what the spectator is seeing is not reality but a cinematic signifying *practice*. In a postmodernist film like Beneix's *Diva*, the spectator is not told that he/she is watching a cinematic convention or a signifying practice but is instead drawn into the murky reality of the film itself. Elements of Diva's *mise-en-scène* turn out to be lifted from Nicholas Ray's *Rebel without a Cause*. This draws attention not to *Diva* as a signifying practice (or set of conventions) but to how much (this) reality itself is like an image. Thus the quest for stabilisation of reference is travestied by the very 'flimsiness' inherent in the nature of the postmodernist signifieds and referents.

We can now finally begin to present an answer to Habermas' *j'accuse* of neo-conservatism versus the postmodernists. As we have seen, important strains of postmodernism are, in parallel with social theorists such as Bell, Lasch, MacIntyre, Strauss and Bloom, cast in the intention of some sort of anti-modernist and effectively conservative cultural restabilisation. We have equally seen that this attempt at cultural restabil-isation has largely misfired. The unintended consequences of the postmodernists' attempts described above have not been the humanist Utopia of a *sittlich*, balanced and harmonic polis but something closer to the dystopic landscapes and mediascapes of Jean Baudrillard's nightmare commentaries. The unintended consequences of the postmodernists have not been the resurrection of Italian Renaissance or neo-Classical urban space but the chaotic imbalance and chronic instabilitity of Ed Koch's New York. It has been the world of the profane juxtaposition of a home for the homeless framed in a Ridley Scott's *Blade Runner* urban wasteland with the glitzy spectacle of Donald Trump's towers and the *arriviste* downtown silicon networks of Tom Wolfe's *Bonfire of the Vanities*.

Is there, then, in postmodernist culture, no radical potential to match the disruptive possibilities and ethos of change in modernist experimentation? Must its vision, if not neo-conservative, be fully one of cultural pessi-mism? Here again, I should like to propose a response in the negative. The modernist challenge to the cultural status quo lay in its experimentation with the *signifier*, with its destabilisation of representation. Postmodernism's putative *restabilization* of the signifier, in its consequences, winds up, *destabilizing* the *referent*, be it in Lichtenstein's comic-book figuration or Philip Johnson's recent buildings. Thus the logic of modernism inheres in its problematisation of the representation, while the logic of postmod-ernism inheres in its problematisation of the reality. In other words, the postmodernists, whether intentionally or not, can direct our attention to a changing social reality of consumption increasingly comprised by the proliferation of images. And to a social reality of production which is, to an ever greater degree, semiotic in content. This problematisation of the real through art, through cultural forms, could indeed have considerable disruptive and radical potential.

III

On balance I am pessimistic, however, about any radical potential in postmodernism, because in the end it does not reverse the process of modernisation. Instead it exacerbates it. The postmodernist critique of modernism *looks like* de-differentiation or dis-autonomisation in the sense that real is imploded into representation, high culture into popular culture and literature itself into literary criticism. But this seeming *dis*-autonomisation is in fact *hyper*-autonomisation, this apparent de-differentiation instead hyper-differentiation. Postmodernism is thus not at all any sort of critique of modernity in the name of the particular or the local. It is no critique of modernist abstraction. It is instead an exercise in *hyper*abstraction.

Let me clarify this. The Enlightenment was already criticised by Hegel and many others for its excess of abstraction; for its abstract reason, abstract (Kantian) ethics, abstract aesthetics. This was already the reproach of *too* much autonomy from the social, from nature and so on. Now modernism further radicalised this autonomy. In turn-of-the-twentieth-century modernism, as I mentioned above, the cultural spheres took on an even fuller autonomy, a complete *Eigengesetzlichkeit*. Now the individual spheres construct their own criteria of validity. This is the Weberian model that Habermas developed in which each type of statement or utterance – theoretical, ethical, aesthetic – gains its validity from a discourse which inheres only in the same sphere as the statement it lends validity to. Thus Kantian, categorical ethics become the even-more-abstract discursively justified ethics; and realist epistemologies are replaced by theoretical statements backed up by reasoned argument. Art too takes on an even further abstraction than even realism had from meaning and social symbolism, as the new aesthetic features 'truth' not to reality but 'to the materials'. In this sense Habermas's position (which is modern*ist* in the sense of being characteristic of a very mature and late modernity) *is* a question of the process of completion of modernity's and the Enlightenment's *unvollendete Projekt*. His is a project of the ever-further sweeping away of more and more foundations, a process of exacerbating the already problematic abstraction of the Enlightenment (Habermas, 1985).

Now postmodernism in its canonical version, as exemplified by the French theorists and the American architects, does not *reverse* this process. Instead it drives it effectively to its furthest extreme. To reverse this process, postmodernisation would need somehow to re-insert the autonomised modernist spheres into the social. Instead, postmodernism does just the opposite. It destroys the integument of the spheres themselves, so that the practices within them lose even the minimalist foundations of any self-legislation that they once had. If pre-modernism featured heteronomous *Gesetzlichkeit*; and modernism *Eigengesetzlichkeit*; then canonical postmodernism entails no *Gesetzlichkeit* whatsoever. What replaces such self-legislation is the hyperabstraction of 'anything goes' (Feyerabend, 1975).

This is *not*, I repeat, de-differentiation, particularisation or localisation in any sense of these words. Modernist, already overdone autonomisation is instead only made worse. The practices in the spheres become *so* autonomous that they destroy the integument of the spheres themselves; so autonomous that even *self*-legislation, by standards developed in relatively autonomous practices, becomes insufficient. The upshot is that the standards and the very spheres themselves are destroyed and autonomy becomes so radical that it no longer has any meaning at all. Postmodernism in its canonical, neo-Nietzschean sense becomes radical anarchism. And this is not the critical and collectivist anarcho-syndicalism of autonomous tradespeople, skilled in the practice of their particular craft, who come to replace the central state in a highly localist manner. It is its antipode: the anti-collectivist, 'anything goes' anarchism of the Faustian individualist bourgeois.

In such postmodernisation, then, ethics float free even from Weberian self-legislation and possible discursive grounding. The ethical sphere is ripped asunder and all that is left is (absence of) grounding in the will to power. Theoretical statements as well float free from the theoretical sphere, and even discursive justification is replaced by Feyerabend's world of full epistemological contingency. Modernist 'truth to the materials' is forgotten as the aesthetic sphere is eclipsed, leaving only a meaningless playfulness, an energising aesthetics of desire and sensation, even an aesthetics of the ugly.

This process of postmodernisation gives meaning to Nietzsche's rejection of critique for a theoretics of *affirmation*. This is why postmodernism and post-structuralism can never, by any stretch of the imagination, be a *critical* theory. Critical theory entails a critique of the particular via the universal which preserves the rational moment of the universal *in* the particular. Thus can be understood the beginnings, as Nietzsche was aware, of particularisation of the abstract Cartesian ego in the Kantian categories. Critical theory is also exemplified in Hegel's notions of

Sittlichkeit and nature. In these Hegel replaces abstract Kantian terms with their counterparts in the particular, all the while saving what was rational in the abstract in the particular itself. It is eminently manifest in Adorno's (1973) preservation of the Utopian moment in non-identity thinking. But the neo-Nietzcheans – Deleuze, Baudrillard, Derrida and much of Foucault – do not criticise via the particular. Instead they *affirm* the abstract and giddily drive its logic even further.

It is curious that the post-structuralists (postmodernists) are usually read in terms of a particularist critique of generality, of totality, when, to the contrary, each of the canonical theorists is aware, indeed highly self-conscious of, his theoretical hyperabstraction (hence hypermodernity). Thus Deleuze and Guattari (1977) say that modernist 'de-territorialization', through the commodity-form, has not gone far enough. They propose instead *full* de-territorialisation. Thus for Baudrillard, the modernist simulacrum of exchange-value is not abstract enough. He does not criticise, but *affirms* this abstraction and drives it even further into 'sign-value' which is 'a simulacrum of a simulacrum'. Thus finally, for Derrida the modernist novelist or poet who, as author (subject) works through the aesthetic materials to create a literary object, is not abstract enough. This modernist author is operating in experimentation with language, already abstracted from its connection with the real. Full Derridan affirmation of hyper- thus postmodernist) abstraction results in destruction of both subject and object in the even more radically autonomous *écriture*.

With Ronald Reagan, canonical postmodernism says to Habermas's efforts in modernity's radicalisation and completion, through his self-legislating doctrine of discursive justification, 'you ain't seen nothing yet'. Deleuze, Baudrillard and their colleagues have *really* completed modernity's *unvollendete Projekt*. And in doing so they have partly caused it to self-destruct. What is left is Lyotard's (1973) free-floating desire which has 'cast adrift' both from Marx and Freud. What is left is an even more abstract '*Ich*' than Descartes' *cogito*. Only that '*Ich*' is the '*Es*' of desire.

10 Cultural Theory, Philosophy and the Study of Human Affairs: Hot Heads and Cold Feet[1]

John Haldane

INTRODUCTION

'Modernism in the technical sense of the word is pretty well dead.'

So wrote Hilaire Belloc in a volume entitled *Survivals and New Arrivals* published in 1929. On this account, the period of 'postmodernism' – assuming that to be an historical term – began well before the Second World War. Matters are not so simple, however, for in Belloc's 'technical sense', 'modernism' had a limited and unambiguous connotation and an equally determinate reference. It indicated a body of ideas developed within Roman Catholic thought by writers such as Baron von Hügel; ideas which came under ecclesiastical condemnation in the Papal Decree *Lamentabili*, and against which the so-titled 'anti-Modernist Oath' was directed. Once one departs from Belloc's use of the term, however, it is unclear that 'modernism' has any single determinate sense, and it is absolutely certain that the term 'postmodernism' does not.

Reading some of the remarkably varied recent literature which features in its titles, or otherwise makes great play with, the words 'postmodernism' and 'postmodernity' (not to mention phrases such as 'problematising multitemporality') it is difficult to resist the conclusion that these are terms in desperate – and unpromising – search of a unified theory. The role of a *mantra* or pious phrase in the spiritual life of devout members of a faith is to turn the mind to the deity by eliminating other mental noise. In reflective elucidation, however, the recurrence of terms and phrases of art is usually a substitute for thought, not a concentration of it. Yet all too often it now seems that literature in which the vocabulary of 'postmodernity' features repetitively is like a devotional litany in both form and purpose.

179

As regards the form, try substituting one of the favoured terms from the French or French-inspired end of the 'discourse' or 'poetics' of 'postmodernity' for the names of the blessed in, for example, a late nineteenth-century Catholic prayer book, that is, a book contemporary with the writings of the 'modernists', in Belloc's strict and technical sense of the term. The result might read as follows:

> Postmodernity I give you my heart and my soul.
> Postmodernity assist me in my agony.
> Postmodernity may I breathe forth my soul in peace with you.[2]

It is surprising, and disturbing, just how authentic this appears. Anyone who thinks my parody suffers from exaggeration might consider postmodernity-in-practice in the work of the 'human sculptures' Gilbert and George (1970: 3, 7), from one of whose text-pieces I draw the following litany:

> ART, what are you? You are so strong and powerful,
> so beautiful and moving . . .
> Art, where did you come from who mothered such a strange being?
> [Art] we ask always for your help, for we need much
> strength in this modern time, to be only artists of a life-time.

Of course, this sort of thing is flotsam, fragments of ideas gathered together only by the currents that underlie the tide of fashion, and there is a more serious and better integrated body of critical literature which characterises itself (or is characterised by others) as 'postmodernist'. Even among this, however, the virtues of clarity, precision and self-discipline are often conspicuously lacking, and the resulting confusions vitiate the attempts of the authors to say something true, significant and useful about the general character of western thought and culture in the contemporary period and in the centuries preceding this. Greater scholarship and improved critical skills – including those involved in self-criticism – would do much to assist the chroniclers of 'modernism' and the prophets of 'postmodernity' in their efforts; but there are, I believe, different kinds of difficulties that may not be overcome, and the intractability of which would help to explain the often poor standard of literature of these sorts. The present essay is concerned to identify and articulate these difficulties.

POSTMODERN ANALYSIS AND CULTURAL HISTORICISM

The problems in question concern the presuppositions of postmodernism (or, more accurately, of some postmodernisms – remembering the ambiguity and vagueness of the term). One such assumption is that of philosophical anti-realism in respect of knowledge, ontology and value; that is to say, the rejection of any view of reality as constituted independently of our conception of it – as being 'there' to be discovered by the exercise of reliable cognitive powers of conception and detection – and of values as forming part of this belief-independent reality. I shall return to this assumption later. A second common but problematic presupposition is that of a broad historicism, which regards the history of thought and culture as dividing into distinct periods, each unified by a set of dominant ideas and social forces and related one to another in significant ways, thereby composing a pattern of development into which the histories of philosophy, art, economics, science, psychology, religion and so on can be fitted. Inasmuch as this sort of cultural historicism is associated with the idea of laws of development, it belongs to a philosophy of history which some postmodernists reject as part and parcel of modernism, but which others accept as being the only enduring insight of modernist theory. What therefore distinguishes these latter from their modernist predecessors is a view about the current stage of historical development and about the future.

The idea, familiar from Hegel and Marx and indeed from Judaeo-Christian sacred history, that the course of human affairs is in some sense intrinsically intelligible, or is rationally ordered, or exhibits a narrative structure, is a controversial one and not just, or even for the most part, because of the difficulty of providing empirical evidence in support of it. The deepest difficulty is posed by the philosophical question: how is this possible? But setting that metaphysical puzzle to one side, large-scale historical claims about the development of thought and culture – such as are made by, for example, Scott Lash (Chapter 9) – *are* challenged by the empirical facts. I do not want to say that the historical assumptions of much postmodernist literature are false. They may be true; I simply do not know. But I do want to insist that they are unwarranted *assumptions*, and to suggest that as our knowledge of the history and internal structure of the various branches of thought and culture grows there is more reason to doubt than to accept the now familiar historicist theses. I say this notwith-standing that in philosophy, for example, there is a growing fashion among practitioners for the sort of synoptic vision offered by writers such as Rorty and MacIntyre. Indeed, my doubts are not so much allayed by these authors as encouraged by them. This said, however, I also believe that students of philosophy, art, religion, politics, economics and so on, can learn something from the attempt to set phases and aspects of these subjects into historical and logical relationships, and that part of what may be learnt in doing so is that the direction of progress need not be co-incident with that of time. To this extent, therefore, I am not altogether unsympathetic to the sort of broad-sweeping cultural characterisation undertaken by Lash in his chapter, though I remain doubtful about its accuracy and value.

What this cautions, then, is great care and attention to detail in the development of cultural analyses and of theories in the history of ideas, especially where these are employed in the service of philosophical arguments, be they in epistemology, metaphysics, aesthetics or social theory. Indeed, my first thesis arises from what has been said so far: it is that the vocabulary of 'modernism' and of 'postmodernism' is of little worthwhile service to serious enquiries and would be better resorted to rarely, if at all.[3] It encourages reckless generalisation and limits the possibilities of genuine understanding by discouraging independent enquiry in accord with heterodox intuitions: it heats heads and cools feet. In due course I shall discuss something of what has come to be described as 'postmodernist epistemology' as this is associated with Goodman, Putnam and Rorty, but at this point it may also be worth citing the latter's much-celebrated and -cited book *Philosophy and the Mirror of Nature* (1980) by way of illustrating the dangers of historicising philosophy.

RORTY AND THE HISTORY OF THE PHILOSOPHY OF MIND

Rorty's central and highly influential theses are that philosophy, as traditionally conceived of and practised, is in a state of terminal crisis and that the origins of its final phase lie in the modern invention of the mind by philosophers of the seventeenth century, most especially Descartes.[4] According to Rorty, the Cartesian philosophical creation was a conception of the mind as the locus of self-intimating states possessed by an enduring 'I', which is only contingently associated with the human figure it inhabits and through which it interacts with the empirical world; that is to say, a view of the mind as a distinct thing known directly to itself, a conscious subject resident within the frame of the physical body: in short, *mind–body dualism*. On Rorty's account, the idea of the self as the occupant of a logically private viewpoint and the associated epistemology of mental representations (ideas and images) concerning whose existence and character the subject is an incorrigible authority, provided the foundations for philosophy in the modern period. The various aspects of the 'philosophical project of modernity' are thus projected back to the invention of the Cartesian mind. And, of course, it is essential to Rorty's historicist account of past thought, and to the argument for his 'postmodernist' sequel (in which epistemology gives way to edification within the historically conditioned 'conversation of mankind'), that there should be this point of origination of classical dualism. Without this history, the 'problematic of modernity' and the 'postmodernist critique' lose their significance – we are just back into largely ahistorical philosophical debate.

Consider, then, the following statements of dualist theory of mind and epistemology – and of their rejection:

We ... have images that closely resemble [external] physical objects, but they are not material. They live in our minds where we use them in thinking ... But it is without any deceptive play of my imagination with its real or unreal visions that I am quite certain that I am, that I know that I am, and that I love this being and this knowing. Where these truths are concerned I need not quail when [it is said]: 'What if you should be mistaken?' If I am mistaken then I exist. For whoever does not exist can surely not be mistaken either, and if I am mistaken, therefore I exist. .... It follows also that in saying that I know that I know, I am not mistaken. For just as I know that I am, so it holds too that I know that I know. And when I love these two things, I add this same love as a third particular of no smaller value to these things that I know. Nor is my statement, that I love, a mistake, since I am not mistaken in the things that I love; [for] even if they were illusions, it would still be true that I love illusions.[5]

Some have held that our cognitive faculties know [directly] only what is experienced within them, for example, that the senses perceive only impressions. According to this opinion the intellect thinks only of what is experienced within it, i.e. ideas [*species*] ... The opinion, however, is obviously false ... we must say, therefore, that ideas stand in relation to the intellect not as that *of which* it thinks but as that *by which* it thinks [of things].[6]

Nobody knows that he is knowing save in knowing something else and consequently knowledge of an [external] object precedes intellectual self-consciousness.[7]

Each is conscious that it is he himself that thinks ... [but] one and the same man perceives himself both to think and to have sensations. Yet sensation involves the body, so that the body must be said to be part of man ... therefore the intellect whereby [one] thinks is a part of one in such a way that it is somehow united to the body.[8]

It was because [some] held that sensation belonged to the soul that [they] could speak of man [dualistically] as a soul using a body.[9]

The first passage, which offers a very clear statement of epistemological representationalism, of the *Cogito ergo sum* argument and of the doctrine of first-person incorrigibility (each identified by Rorty as central components of the Cartesian theory of mind), comes from St Augustine's *De Civitate Dei* (The City of God) written about 1200 years before Descartes' *Meditations*. The subsequent passages, opposing representationalism and dualism with currently fashionable 'post-Cartesian' doctrines of direct realism and psychophysical monism, are from works written by St Thomas Aquinas 700 years before Rorty's *Mirror of Nature* and the emergence of post-analytic philosophy.

Clearly something is amiss in the intellectual narrative. I have chosen for criticism just one example of an influential thesis flourished by a fashionable writer. Another suitable case for inspection is the set of claims made by Alasdair MacIntyre about the history of moral thought from the Greeks to the Enlightenment and beyond into the supposed crisis of modernity.[10] MacIntyre is a very much better informed writer than Rorty but as one examines the evidence, the general claims, in this case about the development of moral and political thought, again become increasingly doubtful and this, of course, undermines the characterisation of the contemporary period and *ipso facto* the philosophical theses to which the historicism is related. Let me say again that I am not denying the possibility of insight arising from thinking in an historical mode, from doing philosophy or social theory historically. But I am questioning the notion that there is a general tale to be told about the passage of western thought and culture through certain stages identifiable by period-specific sets of ideas and doctrines. In part my resistance to this way of thinking is methodological: it encourages prejudgements of uniformity and inattention to differences. But I am also resistant to the attempt to have historicism do the work of argument. For there is in this a liability to commit two fallacies, the first being simply that of supposing that, if sets of ideas or attitudes have come to be dominant in succession to others, the former are more likely to be true or appropriate. The second is related but runs deeper: it is the thought that the actual is somehow an indicator of the necessary; that is to say, that the current state of things, being part of an historical movement, points in the direction of what must be – of true reality (notwithstanding that this may be a condition of Heraclitean flux). I characterised this as a fallacy; but, of course, there is a tradition of thought in which it is an axiom: Hegelianism. It is not difficult to read some of the literature in which talk of the 'failure of the project of modernity' and the 'emergency of postmodernity' feature prominently in neo-Hegelian terms – nor, I think, is it implausible to do so given the influences on much of this sort of writing.

CULTURAL HISTORY IN THE APPROVED STYLE

An appropriate reaction to what I have been saying would be to observe that while it might be a suitable warning against prejudgement and perhaps an effective illustration, in connection with Rorty, of the dangers of historicising philosophical and other forms of thought, it does nothing to show that the content of any major claims associated with postmodernist writers is mistaken. Furthermore, I have not yet said anything, save by way of abstract generality, of relevance to the social sciences. Let me now address these points by first rehearsing the sort of historico-philosophical analysis about which I have been expressing reservations.

The senses of 'postmodernism' are many, disparate and possibly incompatible. None the less, some are predominant. These can be classified roughly as either *analytic-cum-descriptive* or *critical-cum-prescriptive* (or, in some uses, as a blend of the two). That is to say, the term 'postmodernism' is most often used either to characterise an historical period, a cultural condition or a set of attitudes and practices; or it serves to abbreviate a form of criticism of widely held assumptions, and a class of proposals as to how matters should be conceived of and dealt with. By and large these different senses of the word are related to a common use of the term 'modernism', and it may be useful, therefore, to give a rough account of this (admittedly vague) common usage before proceeding to assess certain 'postmodernist' theses and to consider their bearing on the social sciences. Here, then, is a quick guide to western culture presented in the approved style.

Pre-modernism

The ancient world was the site of the birth of two great forces – monotheism and philosophical rationalism. For a variety of reasons, in part to do with historical contingencies and in part due to the intrinsic character of these forces, there was a union of them in Christianity; most significantly, for what follows, in its western branch. Following well-known difficulties during the fourth, fifth and sixth centuries, the Holy Roman Empire came into its own and by the eleventh century the Papacy gained supremacy over the Emperor. The succeeding few hundred years saw the rise and domination of scholasticism as the intellectual elaboration of the theological, philosophical and political structure of (Catholic) Christendom.[11] But then things began to change.

Modernism – Phase 1

In religion, the idea of Church as a mystical union bestowing spiritual identity upon persons, as a body bestowing organic identity upon its parts, and of sacraments as the media of communion between God and man, came to be replaced by an individualist theology in which each has access to God (via His directly revealed word) without the mediation of a priesthood. In philosophy, the presumption of knowledge of the structure of reality, and confidence in the general reliability of the cognitive powers, came to be questioned and means were sought to establish the possession and security of knowledge by locating it in a certain and permanent foundation – self-evident principles (as in *rationalism*) or immediate experience (as in *empiricism*). In politics, the religious wars unsettled the doctrine of a social magisterium and the version of natural law which supported it, and gave rise to new attempts to provide generally compelling reasons to regulate one's behaviour in accord with principles of civil society. In art, meanwhile, the mediaeval conception of painting, sculpture and architecture as practical activities directed towards broadly utilitarian ends, and of artists as craftsmen co-operating with others in the production of works useful to man and glorifying God, came to be replaced by the renaissance idea of the artist as an original and autonomous creator of objects of contemplation.

Modernism – Phase 2

The transition in religion from Church to individual, from sacramental liturgy to private prayer and from scholastic theology to self-authenticating religious experience, proceeded towards greater fragmentation of Christendom, with each new denomination establishing itself in a preferred interpretation of scripture and in associated lifestyles. In connection with this, the eighteenth century attacks on natural theology led to a preference for historically warranted practices over transcendentally derived doctrine.

In philosophy, the efforts to provide a secure foundation for knowledge in either *a prioristically* determinable, metaphysical necessities or in indubitable experience, came to be abandoned and with them went epistemological and metaphysical realism. In place of these came Kant's 'Copernican Revolution', re-establishing the conformity of mind and world by treating the latter as, in some sense, 'made by' the former. In this way philosophical enquiry could again regard itself as discovering the structure of reality and the terms of the moral law – but the investigation was conducted within the domain of thought itself. The implication of this for politics was to restore optimism about the possibility of justifying principles of social organisation by appealing to a perspective beyond the contingent viewpoints of individuals but immanent within human reason itself and hence, in principle, attainable by each. In art, the ancient tradition of *mimesis* or representation grew steadily weaker as the idea of the artist as a creator of self-contained worlds developed into a full-blown theory, *romanticism*, and the corresponding aesthetics of disengaged contemplation came to dominate the culture.

Relative to this three-stage history, some of the overlapping features of the various uses of the term 'postmodernism' can now be brought into focus. None the less, it will be a point of contention whether what I mention next belongs to a late stage of 'modernism' or to an early phase of its suc-cessor. Indeed the prospect of such contention is more or less guaranteed by the uncritical methodology characteristic of the sort of historico-cultural analysis which favours this vocabulary.[12] To the extent that I consider there to be any value in thinking in these terms, I incline to the former view.

Modernism – Phase 3 / Postmodernism – Phase 1

Following upon the rise and continuing success of the physical sciences as explanatory and predictive theories (and the accompanying development of technology), earlier preoccupations with *justifying* the content of beliefs and the principles of conduct gave way to the attempt to explain them *non-rationalistically* by reference to the causal efficacy of underlying forces. Religion, art and human relationships came to be accounted for in terms analogous to those employed in the physical sciences – to which witness the writings of Mill, Marx, Durkheim and Freud. In short, human thought and action were taken to be more amenable to empirical investi-gation and explanation than to non-empirical rational justification.

Postmodernism – Phase 1 / Postmodernism – Phase 2

The previous departure from the ambitions of modernism, in its first and second phases, to provide reassurance about the powers of the mind to attain metaphysical and moral knowledge – be it through philosophy or art – did not go so far as to question its own reliance upon realist and rationalist assumptions. The emergent social sciences presumed the legitimacy of their methods of enquiry, the independence of their objects of study and the fixity of meaning and truth so far at least as these are required for a conception of human studies as genuinely scientific, that is, as apt to yield objective knowledge. But once reflexivity is added to scepticism the result is the corrosion of the residual elements of rationalism. Social observation can no longer be informed by presumptions of objectivity, universality and rationality. The naïve acceptance of the world and of thought as secure *givens* (which characterised the pre-modern world) and the belief in at least the possibility of re-establishing them by means of reflection (which was the conviction of modernism) are no longer available in the post-modern condition. All that remains, therefore, is to celebrate, lament or be indifferent to, the plurality of incommensurable, uncodifiable and radically contingent social worlds.

One could, of course, elaborate upon the features depicted in this re-presentation of the 'postmodern (western) world' as these take shape in the various areas of life: self-reference in visual imagery, the promotion of paradox and reflexivity in writing, the attempt (be it self-refuting) to employ *reductio ad absurdum* on the assumptions of realism and rationalism in philosophy, the attack upon the transcendental aspirations of neo-Kantian moral and political theory, the eclectic combination of culturally diverse elements, and so on. The pattern is familiar, notwithstanding that, as I argued previously, the method of design may be facile and suspect.

THE PHILOSOPHY OF POSTMODERNISM

I shall not be concerned further with the weaker versions of postmodern cultural analysis; those, that is, which simply claim that something such as I have set out above describes the course of western intellectual and social history. I have already observed that such analysis is liable to reckless generalisation and of its nature encourages rhapsodies of association.[13] One can only hope that in due course it will be replaced by a return to serious and disciplined scholarship. My interest now is in those other much more ambitious accounts in which this pattern of development – particularly in its latest elements – is treated as disclosing the ultimate facts of the human condition: what might be described as the 'philosophy of postmodernity'. Before turning to evaluate it, however, it will be as well to consider further the content of this philosophy.

There are, I think, three main routes into this: the *aesthetic*, the *socio-political* and the *epistemological*. Earlier I remarked upon the romanticist idea that the artist can be said to imitate nature not by mimetically repro-ducing its forms but rather by paralleling its world-making activity. This favours a conception of *art* as expressive rather than as representational, and of *content* as non-referential but self-contained. Works of art are then conceived of as symbols constituting their own significance. This is clearly a move away from the kind of aesthetic realism which regards the *world* as the source of meaning and art as a method of selectively representing this and thereby communicating it to an audience; that is, a view which regards art as only derivatively significant. None the less, the romanticism so far described is realist inasmuch as it implies standards of correct and incorrect interpretation fixed by reference to the independently constituted content of a given work. There is, on this view, a *fact* of the matter about what a work *means* which it is the task of interpretation to *discover* and to which a *true* account will *correspond*. In 'postmodernist' aesthetics, however, realism about art is abandoned in favour of a kind of subjectivism which focuses upon the interpretative activity of the spectator. In the official view this is part of a rejection of Romanticist theory (see Culler, 1982; Eagleton, 1983), though in fact it remains close to romanticism in treating the creative exercise of the imagination as the essence of art. None the less, it is anti-realist in spirit and in formulation. There is no interpretation-independent *fact* of the matter about the content of an image or the meaning of a text; which is to say there are no visual or literary *meanings* to be *discovered* as opposed to constructed, there is neither *truth* nor *correspondence*. Talk of the artist's 'creative imagination' is, in some versions of this account, a deceptive figment of bourgeois humanism, an illusion sustained by the impersonal language of the ruling art criticism. On the other hand, the interpretative activity of the spectator is unconstrained save by the social force of competing interpretations, and hence can claim no special status. As one commentator, drawing upon Derrida for style and substance, expresses it:

Disseminated into the absolute immanence of sign-play, the imagination ceases to function as a creative centre of meaning. It becomes instead a floating signifier without reference or reason . . .

... Post-modern culture jibes at all talk of original creations. It exclaims the omnipresence of self-destructing images which mime each other in a labyrinth of interreflecting mirrors.[14]

The idea that where previously it was supposed that reason shapes thought, the occupant of that role is in fact social force or power, is a familiar feature of continuing debates in social and political theory. Setting aside classical Marxist analysis (as retaining presumptions of a supposedly discredited rationalism) postmodern social theory treats the terms of political discourse as elements in a rhetorical fiction: 'truth', 'meaning', 'reason', 'knowledge' and so on are all represented as instruments of oppression (or of some other power relationship) operating under, in Foucault's phrase, the 'illusion of autonomous discourse'. Thus, political and social thought are themselves subjected to a sociological analysis which must either deny itself the resources of rationalistic theorising or else use the traditional terminology with ironic disingenuity. (I shall return to this dilemma shortly.) For Saussure, rational thought is possible, be it that it is not taken (as in Cartesian or Kantian theories) as prior to and more secure than language: 'Without language, thought is a vague uncharted nebula. There are no pre-existing ideas, and nothing is distinct before the appearance of language' (Saussure, 1974: 112). Likewise for Lévi-Strauss language constitutes an objective rationally structured phenomenon which (somehow) influences human conduct and thereby makes it intelligible (Lévi-Strauss, 1966). But for Foucault the idea that there is such a thing as human nature which expresses itself in intrinsically intelligible, and hence rationally explicable, activity is part of the fiction of modernist universalism. The reality, such as it is, is a plurality of distinct (and competing) historically determined 'discursive practices' involving the exercise of power not reason. What this implies, then, is the final rejection of a theory of human nature and *ipso facto* of the human sciences – an implication captured by the hyperbolical phrase 'the end of man' (Foucault, 1983).

The role of reflections on the nature of language in shaping the development of European social theory is obvious enough, as is the route by which such reflections have led to the radical relativism of Foucault and Derrida. A similar concern, leading to only slightly less extravagantly stated conclusions, has been a characteristic of recent analytic philosophy of language and epistemology. Here the argument runs roughly as follows. Pre-Cartesian philosophy was unreflective about the nature of knowledge itself. It presumed man was the measure of reality, *not* by constituting it but by being a reliable indicator of its condition – a fact explicable in terms of the mind as an undistorting receiver. Descartes put paid to this naïve realism and instituted a conception of the mind according to which knowledge could only be accounted for as involving adequate mental representations: the imagery *within* accurately depicting the world *without*. In Kant, the representational character of thought is formulated non-imagistically in terms of concepts, that is, rules of interpretation, which organise sensory input. These differences apart, the implication is the same: traditional realism is an unwarranted or, worse, an unintelligible assumption. The notion of an adequate representation involves the idea of fit or correspondence between one set of (mental) items and another set of (non-mental) items. But to make sense of this we need to have an account of the non-mental side of things – that is, an account of the world. However any attempt to formulate that (even to give content to the idea of the world) must, on the given epistemological assumptions, involve the formation and deployment of representations. In short, all we do, or can, have are our ways of thinking.

What emerges, then, is as before a form of relativism which cannot even speak its name.[15] For the realist, thought and language take their content from the world. For the contemporary anti-realists, however, content, meaning, truth and knowledge are determined from within the human realm and cannot be held constant as measures by which to assess thought and action wherever, whenever and by whomsoever they are engaged in. The attack by Quine (1961) on analyticity and necessity is taken to have undermined the possibility of providing secure foundations for knowledge by *a priori* reflection, in the style favoured by the rationalists. The parallel challenge presented by Wilfred Sellars (1963) to the idea of experiential 'givens' is presumed to have had the same effect on the empiricist effort at foundationalism. And, to repeat, the quite general considerations concerning the nature of concepts as representations or mental rules is taken to demonstrate the general incoherence of realism in anything other than an internal (that is, roughly coherentist) sort.

THE SELF-REFUTING CHARACTER OF 'POSTMODERN SOCIAL SCIENCE'

So much, then, for the considered verdict of postmodern and contemporary analytic philosophy on realism and reason. The foregoing sketch has been rough and ready, but it includes all the elements that I need to proceed to my conclusions. These can be stated as follows. First, if what I earlier titled 'the philosophy of postmodernism' is true, then social science – in the sense of the systematic study of human affairs within and across cultures (and over time) – is impossible, and likewise if analytical anti-realism, in the style of Rorty, Putnam and Goodman, is the case. But secondly, it is premature to suppose that the conditions necessary for the possibility of social science do not obtain. That is to say, it is not obvious, to me at least, that realism is excluded. On the contrary, I think there is reason to presume it to be true and to try to show how it can be and that it is so.

The considerations gathered together in the first conclusion can be articulated around the following briefer conditional proposition: *if relativism is true then social science is impossible*. Setting aside indifference or bemusement, there are two attitudes one can take to this conditional: to reject it or to accept it. Since acceptance is formally compatible with each of two further conflicting attitudes, let me first indicate why it should be accepted. Relativism of the extensive (indeed global) sort under discussion holds that the idea of an object or of a state of affairs or, at the highest level, of the world, or again such ideas as those of truth, knowledge, reason and meaning, lack the fixity given them by the realist. Rather, they are defined within and restricted to particular cultures, 'language games', 'discourses' or 'conversations'. But if that were so, then there are no objective criteria by which to assign meaning to the activities of those outside one's own 'conversation', or to assess their rationality, truth or value. It is obvious enough how this implication bears upon anthropology and history: without the possibility of deciding between rival interpretative claims made in respect of culturally distant peoples there can be no such studies. But the erosion of social science runs further: human geography, economic theory, social psychology, linguistics and so on, all presuppose the objectivity of the phenomena under investigation, the rationality of the methods of enquiry, the determinacy of assignments of meaning and of explanations by reference to agents' reasons, and the culture-indifferent existence of non-human objects and states of affairs implicated in such explanations. But these presuppositions are just what the postmodern and analytical relativists are concerned to reject. Hence, if that rejection is warranted then social science is an impossibility.

Suppose one takes these considerations to establish the conditional – *if relativism is true then social science is impossible* – how should one respond? There are two options: affirm the antecedent (*relativism is true*) and detach the consequent (therefore *social science is impossible*); or contrapose, that is, deny the consequent and *ipso facto* the antecedent (*social science is possible*, hence *it is not the case that relativism is true*). I said there are two options, but immediately a difficulty suggests itself. In the minds of some authors, and of many readers, postmodernism of the sort described is a social scientific theory standing in opposition to, say, varieties of rationalist, empiricist and realist conceptions of the social sciences. But this precludes anyone who takes this view from moving in either direction through the conditional. He or she cannot affirm that postmodernist social science is true and that social science is impossible; or that social science is possible and hence that the philosophy of postmodernism is false. In short, I am claiming that the idea of *postmodernist* (in the sense described) *social science* (in the sense described) is incoherent and that the attempt to articulate it is self-refuting.

What now? One could try to reconceive that which cannot, on its own terms, be a set of social scientific theories or methods of enquiry, as a 'discourse', and hold, consistent with this, that social science is indeed impossible. But the first part of this is either a polite or a self-deceiving way of failing to observe that it is *just* talk – part of the ungrounded, non-truth-bearing, group-specific conversation of some very small sub-set of mankind. As regards the second part, it is contrary to abundant evidence that there are operative and effective social sciences and also far less plausible than the claims of postmodern philosophy. Indeed, it is not difficult to see how the argument might be extended (along familiar anti-relativist lines) to show that these claims are incoherent and hence have a plausibility measure of zero.

What this suggests, then, is that the earlier conditional should be contraposed and that the central tenets of postmodern and analytical anti-realism must be rejected. It is not a requirement of doing this that one give a positive alternative account of truth, knowledge, reason and so on – jumping out of the frying pan isn't always jumping into the fire. This said, however, I think it is a proper challenge to show what the presuppositions of social science are and how they can coherently be conceived to obtain. In analytical philosophy this challenge is too rarely pressed and by and large the responses to it seem, to me at least, to be quite inadequate. Here again, I think, there are many cold feet (if fewer hot heads). Those who believe that history, psychology, economics and other studies of human affairs are forms of objective enquiry, with the potential to disclose important truths about people and their relation to the social and natural environment, ought not to lack the courage of their convictions and should push against current orthodoxies. I should add, however, that in my own estimate the account of how things must be in order to satisfy such an apparent truism as that there are rational agents with the power to discover facts about the world and their place in it, is now likely to seem rather strange and to belong to what, in the terms I do not much favour, was previously characterised as pre-modernism. But the explanation of this estimate is a task for other occasions.[16]

NOTES

1. This is the text of a paper given to a conference on *Postmodernism in the Social Sciences*, held in the University of St Andrews in Autumn 1989. I am grateful to my colleague Hugh Upton for discussion of material presented here. The paper was written during the period of a Fellowship at the Institute for Advanced Studies in the Humanities, University of Edinburgh. I am indebted to the Institute and to the Carnegie Trust for the Universities of Scotland for providing me with this opportunity for research.

2. The substitution has been worked upon the prayers of commendation listed in *A Simple Prayer Book* (Catholic Truth Society, 1979), first published in 1886. See p. 9 of the 1979 edition.

3. This is not to deny that, suitably defined, a term such as 'modernism' may be useful in characterising certain patterns of thought or practice. Belloc's discussion offers one such case; and in another context I have myself found occasion to follow common practice in describing certain ideas about the nature of art as belonging to 'modernist' theory (see Haldane, 1988b).

4. See Rorty (1980); especially Part One, ch. 1, and Part Two, chs 3 and 4.

5. Augustine (1968: 533–5).

6. Aquinas (1967–75: 1a, q. 85, art. 2).

7. Aquinas (1946: i, 3).

8. Aquinas (1967–75: 1a, q. 75, art. 1).

9. Ibid.: 1a, q. 75, art. 4.

10. MacIntyre (1981; 1988). For relevant commentary on the former see Larmore (1987: ch. 2). One example, from the more recent of MacIntyre's books, of likely misrepresentation resulting from the wish to fit the arguments and patterns of thought of historical writers into a preconceived pattern, is the discussion of Aquinas (see MacIntyre, 1988: chs 10 and 11, esp. 203–8). In making this point, however, let me also record my admiration for the breadth (and depth) of MacIntyre's scholarship and for the interest of his discussions.

11. For some account of the development of moral theology and ethics during this and the following period, see Haldane (1990).

12. For an example of this sort of contention, see Lash (ch. 9 in this volume) in which he is concerned to argue that: '[M]uch of what is usually regarded as postmodern culture is in fact really part and parcel of modernism ... what is characteristically understood in terms of a cultural paradigm (postmodernism) becoming pervasive in the past one or two decades is in fact much more characteristic of the set of modernist movements of the last century.'

13. As witness to which, consider the following passage from Kearney (1988: 115–16):

Meanings multiply themselves indefinitely. There is no identifiable origin or end to the Postal network of communications: 'In the beginning was the Post' [Derrida, 1980: 154–5]. The 'post' of post-modernity would thus seem to suggest that the human imagination has now become a postman disseminating images and signs which he himself has not created and over which he has no real control.

14. Kearney (1988: 115, 118). See also Lyotard (1984a). The latter is a highly regarded and widely cited source of commentary on contemporary thought and culture. From it comes the phrase, now much quoted: 'eclecticism is the degree zero of contemporary general culture'.

15. This, I think, is all that the argument given in Davidson (1984) actually establishes. Later writings, however, suggest a more ambitious line of reasoning in opposition to relativism. See, in particular, Davidson (1986). See also the following essays relevant to the themes of the present discussion: Root (1986), and Rorty (1986). For an interesting discussion related to issues of truth and interpretation as these feature in the work of Davidson, Rorty and contemporary continental writers, see Norris (1989).

16. This task is taken up in several places. For anyone who may be interested, the following items are relevant: Haldane (1985; 1988a, b, c; 1989a, b, c; 1990; and forthcoming).

Postmodern Horizons

Elspeth Graham and Joe Doherty

If there is a common message emanating from the contributions to this book, it is that there is, at present at least, no overall assessment or conclusion (in the sense of 'judgement', 'inference' or 'decision') that can usefully be made about postmodernism and the social sciences. Indeed, given the fact that the relationship between postmodernism and the social sciences is still under negotiation, that postmodernism's position is still fluid and unresolved, any attempt to come to such judgemental conclusions would appear to be foolhardy. Most of the social sciences still retain a modernist mainstream which is likely to prove more or less resistant to the encroachment of postmodernism. As we suggest in the introduction, the debate – or, more properly, debates – has hardly begun. The challenges of postmodernism are being interpreted differently in the different modernist disciplines according to the perceived advantages or novelties of particular postmodernist ideas. Perhaps the greatest challenge of postmodernism is that it threatens to redefine well-entrenched boundaries within the social sciences and thus to change the landscape of the modernist disciplines and undermine established interest groups within institutions of higher education. For this reason there is a danger of the postmodern challenge being rejected out of hand. Further, because the difficulties of grasping the nature of this challenge, especially in relation to *doing* social science, there must be a constant temptation amongst social scientists to leave the debate to others. This we think is a mistake, which is not to say that we are convinced of the future of 'postmodern social science'. It is not yet clear what might lie on the postmodern horizon in the social sciences.

Thus we offer these two papers as a conclusion purely in the sense of an 'end' or 'termination' of this particular book and not as the conclusion of the discussion. By taking up two issues which have been variously touched on, but not elaborated, by several of the book's authors – namely the questions of 'paradox' and 'postmodern politics' – we hope to focus attention on questions of common concern. These are the sort of questions which often lie behind the more particular debates within the various social sciences. The two topics we have chosen reflect personal interests and are not meant to convey any sense of privileging these issues over others. There are many facets to the impact of postmodernism on the social sciences. Further, the following coverage of 'paradox' and 'politics', by Graham and Doherty respectively, is not intended to be comprehensive in relation to either topic. We do not aim to present a definitive discussion. Rather, our objective is to draw together and elaborate on points which are covered diffusely elsewhere in this volume in order to raise questions and draw attention to issues which will continue the debate about postmodernism and the social sciences.

POSTMODERNISM AND PARADOX

Elspeth Graham

Postmodernism as an intellectual style entertains inconsistency, ambiguity and paradox. If we are to make sense of postmodernism we must come to some accommodation of its ambiguities and paradoxes. For those social scientists well imbued with modernist ways of thinking this accommodation is likely to prove difficult. It is the purpose of this endpiece to investigate these difficulties through an examination of three of the many puzzles or paradoxes which haunt the postmodern literature. For ease of reference I shall call these the fragmentation paradox, the paradox of periodisation and the grand narrative paradox. These paradoxes arise not from challenges to received opinion (though postmodernism certainly challenges many 'received' aspects of modernism), but from the apparently contradictory claims that are made in the name of postmodernism. It should be noted that it is not my intention to resolve the three paradoxes but rather to use them to highlight some common themes of the preceding chapters and to illustrate some of the things that are at stake in the debate between the advocates and the detractors of postmodernist ways of thinking.

The publicity for a recent book on *Modernity and Ambivalence* by Zigmunt Bauman (1990b) speaks of postmodernity as the time of learning how to live in an incurably ambivalent world. A too-easy acceptance of ambivalence can, however, make all choices impossible and render all questions pointless. It is thus something to be avoided. In reflecting on the ten chapters of this book I am left with the sense that many of the authors are themselves ambivalent *towards* postmodernism, at least in so far as it relates to the social sciences. Rather than simply accepting that ambivalence, I want to question its sources and ask about the implications for a wider understanding of postmodernism and of the social sciences.

The ambivalence arises, I think, from two main sources. First, the uncertainties surrounding the meaning of the term 'postmodernism', especially when it is applied to the social sciences. With Lash (Chapter 9) challenging what many others take to be major defining characteristics of postmodernism, it is evident that the constituents of postmodernism are still open to negotiation. The second source of ambivalence is closely connected with the first and arises from the difficulties involved in conceptualising 'postmodern social science'. Most of the authors in this volume offer some comment on the potential of postmodernism for a particular social science, but they are far more reticent about elaborating the nature of the postmodern discipline. Several mention a crisis in their modernist discipline and see potential in certain so-called 'postmodernist' approaches for dislodging the certainties and perhaps the intellectual imperialisms of recent mainstreams. This is particularly notable in the papers on social and developmental psychology. In Chapter 4, for example, Parker displays an ambivalence about the role of postmodernism which is shared by other contributors. He concludes that the ideas of postmodernism could be useful within social psychology, not as a solution to the methodological shortcomings of the mainstream but as a way of continuing what he sees as the current crisis. His appeal to the reader not to lose sight of the oppressive ways in which social psychology operates on people leaves the unanswered question of how much Parker himself is convinced by the postmodern turn and how far he regards it simply as useful for other purposes. Perhaps a clearer picture of the repercussions of that postmodern turn is needed before we could fairly demand an answer.

In looking to postmodern horizons, I have to admit to a personal ambivalence which arises from trying to make sense of certain apparent paradoxes which are thrown up by postmodernism in general and by the papers in this volume in particular. With many different voices now to be heard it is inevitable that some will talk against, rather than with, each other. This is no more than one of the more radical assertions of deconstruction which accepts unresolvable antinomies. And for some social scientists the simultaneous acceptance of multiple and conflicting readings appears to cause no difficulties (see, for example, Folch-Serra, 1989). Yet to the modern mind the very proposition must cause alarm for surely it is a logical truth that we cannot hold 'P' and 'not P' at one and the same time. This would be a straightforward contradiction which transgresses the tenets of rationality. The postmodern rejoinder might cut to the heart of the matter by challenging the exclusive nature of this 'modernist' notion of rationality and raising the spectre of alternative logics. That particular argument, though fundamental, is outside the scope of this endpiece. I mention it mainly to clarify the basis on which the following discussion proceeds and to illustrate the depth of the postmodern challenge. I want to start by assuming that there are some limits to acceptance of different readings or other logics. At a minimum, they must be recognisably 'readings' or 'logics'. If our study is of narrative then multiple interpretations must in some clear sense be of the *same* narrative. If this were not so there would be no problem of conflict in interpretation and hence no problem of acceptance.

The paradoxes of postmodernism, however, arise once such identifications are made when postmodernism embraces the claim that there are multiple meanings, multiple truths *and* conflicting truths in the text. There are three ways to respond to such paradoxes. The first is to celebrate their existence and put a stop to enquiry by the simple expedient of denying its possibility. This may well be what the postmodern turn requires but it would be a defeatist stance to take at this juncture for it seems evident to me that there are other questions to be asked when we are confronted by paradox. That the questions have no answer is a conclusion I wish to resist, at least for the moment. The second course is to dispel the paradox by demonstrating that the apparently paradoxical claims do not in fact lead us to a contradiction, that they are not in conflict, that all we are being asked to accept is 'P' and 'not P^1'. If we move in this direction we do not need to entertain talk of accepting contradictions or of alternative logics. However, it is not always possible to explain away a paradox. The third response provides an alternative strategy. This is to shift the paradox backwards, as it were, to the more fundamental level of logical principles by distilling the paradox into a more formal contradiction. We could then take one of two paths. Where we recognise that our paradoxical claims are indeed contradictory, we can either abandon one or both of those claims and accept the stricture of traditional logic that we cannot rationally hold a contradiction, or we can dispense with traditional logic and embrace some alternative which allows contradiction. If we take the first path, this removes the paradox but only by accepting the contradiction and then rejecting at least one of its propositions. If we take the second path and refuse to recognise the irrationality of accepting a straightforward contradiction, then we change the whole conception of dialogue and argument. The important point here is that any appeal to 'other logics' leaves both the contradiction and thus the paradox intact. As I have suggested, it may be that an important message of postmodernism is that we should open our minds to paradox without resolution. The grounds upon which we do this may vary, however, and we should at least be clear about our own reasoning. Further, even if we are tempted by this message, it gives us no grounds for failing to recognise the paradox and sketch its dimensions. Clarity is still to be valued whatever our treatment of the paradoxical turns out to be.

Paradox 1: The Fragmentation Paradox

The first paradox I want to discuss is perhaps more of a puzzle than a full-blown paradox. It is, at any rate, an area in which further clarification is needed before we can begin to speculate about postmodern horizons. The puzzle generally stated is the one that concerns Lash (Chapter 9), namely, that certain characteristics commonly held to be distinctively postmodern are actually (or also) characteristics of modernism. The puzzle has several dimensions and raises several questions. Why have certain characteristics come to be identified as postmodern? What challenge does this present to modernism if it is the latter and not the former that has these character-istics? And where does this leave our understanding of postmodernism? By way of illustration of the issues involved, let me select one such characteristic – that of fragmentation.

Nearly all the contributors to this volume take fragmentation to be part of the postmodern condition. Burman (Chapter 5) talks of 'fragmented and contradictory subjectivity'. Fardon (Chapter 1), whilst protesting the impossibility of defining postmodernism, quotes Zavala's (1988) lengthy inventory of its features which includes fragmentation. Dow (Chapter 8) takes postmodernism in economics to be pluralism at the level of theory, allowing a range of possible methodologies with mutual tolerance being of advantage to all. When compared with the 'unitary choice of technique' presented by modernist economics, this postmodern pluralism promises a fragmentation alien to late-modern economics. Smith (Chapter 3) paints a picture of moving from a monolithic modernism into a postmodern world in which 'that which was previously conflated as a whole explodes into fragments'. Shields (Chapter 2) describes Jameson's (1984) article on postmodernism as celebrating, amongst other things, fragmentation in the culture of urban America. And Parker (Chapter 4) notes that, in the postmodern, personal meanings of each citizen of the modern state have given way to fragmented, contested and situation-dependent experiences. Pluralism, fragmentation and many truths go hand in hand under conditions of postmodernity.

In contrast lies what Smith (Chapter 3) calls the 'heavy-metal' unity and dominance of modernism, characterised by the methods and techniques associated with logical positivism. Firm epistemological foundations allow a search for universals, an ability to predict and a confidence in progress which are all threatened by the postmodern. Under such circumstances it is hardly surprising that even those most sympathetic to postmodern projects find it necessary to defend themselves against charges of 'waffling eclecticism' (Thiher, 1984). Yet if postmodernism is properly characterised by fragmentation and an antipathy to universals this creates a puzzle, for neither is fragmentation a novelty nor can the postmodern be consistently contrasted with the universal. Fragmentation, and indeed progressive fragmentation, is a feature of modernism. Within the social sciences the dominance of positivism has led to increasing specialisation and division between the various 'disciplines'. Economics, sociology and psychology have all evolved more or less independently of each other. Their crises have been local crises, albeit that they share certain common elements. Their aims, topics and interests are different and their social networks overlap only to a limited extent. This is evident in the current volume. But the fragmentation of modernist social sciences has been taken much further. Disciplinary labels often shelter a multitude of sub-specialisms as, for example, in geography. Rengger and Hoffman (Chapter 7) make the same comment about international relations, suggesting that this fragmentation is unavoidable arising as it does from the comprehensiveness of a social science which 'literally considers the fate of the world'. Fragmentation cannot be *introduced* by postmodernism because it is already inherent in the definition of international relations.

So here we have our paradox: fragmentation is a characteristic of modernist social science yet also a defining characteristic of postmodernist social science. As I have suggested, there are two possible responses to this if we wish to advance our understanding and not simply admire the paradoxical. Either we deny that it is a paradox by showing, for example, that we are talking about different kinds of fragmentation so that a defining characteristic of postmodernism is not already present in modernism in quite that form. (This may seem the obvious answer in this case but is nevertheless a good illustration of the way in which the apparently paradoxical may be shown not to be so.) Or we recognise the contradiction inherent in the paradox and either reject one of the contradictory claims or embrace the more fundamental philosophical debate about other forms of logic and rationality. Whichever route we choose, it is important to note that there is something more to be said beyond a celebration of paradox. Any complacent acceptance of paradox as a fact of life simply misses this point. One of the great dangers of postmodernist ideas in the social sciences is that they encourage intellectual cold feet with a failure to push argument to a conclusion. The more reflective writers on postmodernism are well aware of this danger. Huyssen (1988: 220), for example, concludes his discussion of mass culture by noting the importance of 'resistance to that easy postmodernism of the "anything goes" variety'. The problem for the social sciences lies in the possibility that the messages of postmodernism are imported in a simplistic form with 'many voices' becoming 'any voices' and critical analysis forgotten. This would not only be politically disenabling, as several authors in this volume point out, but also intellectually disenabling, a point to which I shall return below.

Paradox 2: The Paradox of Periodisation

By outlining a paradox and pointing out the dangers of complacency in the face of it I have not, of course, faced up to it myself. My own inclination would be to demonstrate that the paradox does not contain a formal contradiction and that the fragmentation of postmodernism is different from that of modernism, just as the universals of modernism differ from the universals of the postmodern world. However, a prerequisite for such a demonstration would be some independent indication of what is to count as 'modern' and what is to count as 'postmodern'. It is here we meet a further problem because a reading of the literature, including the discussions in this book, makes it abundantly clear that our use of these terms cannot be taken for granted and that their meanings remain to some degree indeterminate. For example, Hudson (1989) lists fourteen identifiably different characterisations of 'postmodernity', from 'myth' to 'project'. My second paradox concerns only one of these – postmodernity as an historical periodisation. It is worth bearing in mind that this is not the only available characterisation.

The paradox here is evident in the chapter by Lash (Chapter 9) and highlighted in the chapter by Haldane (Chapter 10). It is encapsulated in the idea that postmodernism is both part of modernism and beyond modernism, where both -isms are taken to be historical referents. Shields (Chapter 2) captures this ambiguity well in his emphasis on postmodernism as a complex moment of change which none the less continues and extends a modernist inheritance. It was Toynbee (1956) who first spoke of the 'post-modern age of western history' but others who have developed the conception of the relationship between the modern and the postmodern. Lyotard (1984a) defines postmodernism as a recurring stage within the modern itself. Foucault (1980a), reviewing the 'relentless theorisation of writing' in the 1960s of which his own past concerns with language were part, describes them as 'doubtless only a swansong', with writers fighting to preserve their political privilege. Huyssen (1986: 216) then provides us with a more subtle expression of our paradox when, in commenting on Foucault, he declares, 'Swansong of modernism indeed; but as such already a moment of the postmodern'. While Jameson (1990) now sees the postmodern as the fulfilment of the modern. So what can we make of the paradox? Can we accept that postmodernism is both part of and after (that is, not part of) modernism?

Again there are two main strategies if we want to continue the discussion. One is to recognise the contradiction. This will lead us either to abandon one or more of the contradictory propositions (and with it much of what passes for postmodernism) or to join the debate about other rationalities. The alternative is to suggest that the paradox is only apparent. One problem with this second strategy is that the literature is far from helpful. Some writers, in some of their writings, deny the first part of our contradiction, namely, that postmodernism is part of modernism. Take, for example, the following passage from Jameson written in the 1970s:

> All the straws in the wind seem to confirm the widespread feeling that 'modern times are now over' and that some fundamental divide, some basic *coupure*, or qualitative leap, now separates us decisively from what used to be the new world of the early or mid-twentieth century, of triumphant modernism and the revolt against positivism and Victorian or Third Republic bourgeois culture. (Jameson, 1988d: 17)

This undermines the paradox by implicitly denying its first clause. Postmodernism is not, in any sense, part of modernism. It is the other side of a fundamental divide. Thus *post*modernism represents a break with modernism and, according to Huyssen (1988), this break is nowhere more obvious than in recent American architecture. The differences between the cubic forms of the modern multi-storey and the self-conscious decoration of the pseudo-vernacular is easily perceptible. It would be equally easy, however, to identify common factors in the type of materials used and the engineering principles followed. The basic 'coupure', if there is one, does not extend to all aspects of architecture. Nor is our contemporary experience of architecture in the built environment one of exclusive postmodernism. As was pointed out in the Introduction, any contemporary urban landscape displays a mixture of the modern and the postmodern, where these are understood as the products of different conceptions of architecture.

A similar story can be told in the social sciences. The identification of modernism with positivism in the passage from Jameson makes any non-positivist methodology a candidate for the label 'postmodern'. Yet we would be hard pressed to find any coherent methodology which had nothing in common with positivism. Our experience in the social sciences may be one of multiple methodologies but it is not exclusively postmodern (however we might define that) for it includes the intellectual products of that representative of triumphant modernism – positivism. My point here is that talk of basic 'coupures' must be tempered by a recognition of the constituents of contemporary experience and the difficulties of disentangling these. And talk of divides and leaps is not a valid escape from the paradox of periodisation, for the divides are blurred in experience and the origins and destinations of the leaps can only be made distinct through some deft defining of terms.

If the paradox cannot be undermined by denying its first proposition, then perhaps there is another way of following my second strategy and showing that it is not a paradox at all. Remember that we are talking about postmodernism as an historical referent, postmodernity as a periodisation. To escape the paradox it would be imperative to show that what we call postmodernism is, *in some sense*, present in the modern era yet also that the postmodern era (characterised by postmodernism) comes after, *in some other sense*, and is distinct from what we call modernism. The complication here is that there are many varieties of modernism and versions of postmodernism. Not only have phases of modernism been identified in the literature, each with different characteristics, but strong and weak versions of postmodernism throw up different assumptions and hold different implications. In one sense the literature is also replete with attempts to dispel this paradox of periodisation for Foucault, Lyotard and even Jameson all sketch, at different times, ways in which postmodernism might be conceived of as both part of and after modernism. The detail of these sketches is complex and is, anyway, not central to the present discussion. No valid judgement as to whether the paradox is dispelled by these writings can be made without a careful consideration of them. However, my primary concern in the present context is not to reach a conclusion about what that judgement ought to be but to point out the necessity of making such a judgement. If we seek answers to the questions which the paradox provokes then we cannot escape from this necessity. And should we conclude that the paradox cannot be dissolved by taking the sting out of its apparent contradiction then we are left with that contradiction and the implication that all use of postmodernism as an historical referent is contradictory and should thus be abandoned.

This is a conclusion with which Haldane (Chapter 10) might well concur for one of his concerns is to demonstrate the confusion which abounds in the literature over historical periodisations. Even as the loosest of historical referents, postmodernism seems to run into trouble for many of the major features which are characteristics of the post-1960s have historical precedents. And this trouble is compounded when the characteristics in question are philosophical ideas. Here, I think, we have a conflict between what might be called the sociological and the philosophical imagination. To the sociological imagination the social context of ideas is always important and increasingly involves placing the abstract in its local and historical setting. To the philosophical imagination the ideas are paramount, the 'who' and the 'why' and the 'where' merely of additional interest. If a denial of 'Cartesian' dualism predates Descartes this raises many questions for the sociologist about the basis of Descartes' influence on the course of western philosophy. But for the philosopher it is of minor interest. The philosophical imagination deals only in ideas in its search for philosophical 'truths'. If ideas are in conflict then the arguments on both sides have to be pursued. That these arguments were first formulated hundreds of years ago or yesterday is not of central interest. It is the ability of the arguments to support one or other of the conflicting ideas which matters to the philosopher. To ask whether the arguments are good arguments or bad arguments is the mark of a philosophical imagination. To ask when and under what conditions the arguments were formulated marks a sociological imagination. These imaginations are not mutually exclusive but the failure to recognise the distinction between them can be a source of confusion.

I have, of course, simplified the characterisation of the philosophical and the sociological in order to heighten the contrast between them. In practice many sociologists are interested in philosophical argument and ideas and many philosophers attend to the wider social context of their discipline, though it must be added that some philosophers would deny the relevance of social context just as some sociologists would resist argument abstracted from such a context. In these simplistic terms, however, postmodernism as an historical referent is the product of a sociological imagination which sees diverse cultural traits as coming together to give a distinctive character to an epoch or age. I have to admit to some scepticism about this use of 'postmodern' as an historical referent. At the very least, more is placed on its shoulders than its currently vague conception can support. Whether or not we can make sense of this historical dimension and resolve our paradox of periodisation, however, there are other interpretations of postmodernism which survive. We can, for example, treat the ideas of postmodernism in the terms of a philosophical imagination to which their 'when' and their 'where' is largely irrelevant. The problem, then, is that we again come face to face with the paradoxical.

Paradox 3: The Grand Narrative Paradox

The last paradox of postmodernism I wish to discuss is also, I think, the most important, for although postmodernist ideas can survive a successful onslaught against periodisation, no periodisation can survive the denial of those ideas. The architectural analogy is apt here, for it is evident that architectural schools can in some sense be timeless if their proponents live at different historical times and there is never any one time with which they are uniquely identified. This rarely happens of course, for most major architectural movements have their heyday, albeit within a restricted cultural setting. Nevertheless, we do not need to be able to divide these movements into historical 'ages' in order to appreciate the differences in architectural thinking between the schools. Descriptions like 'neo-Gothic' suggest that some architectural styles repeat themselves over time, and we can learn to identify a Gothic building without knowing when it was constructed. In the same way we can treat many of the central ideas of postmodernism as 'timeless', as challenges to the ideas of modernism, and simply ask, 'Which makes the most sense?' The answer, however, is far from simple.

Again I shall take only one of the many ideas of the postmodernist challenge to illustrate my point. The idea is represented in many commentaries on postmodernism as a rejection by major sectors of contemporary culture of the 'universalising and totalising gesture' of the historical avant-garde of modernity (Huyssen, 1986: 175). It is central to Lyotard's oft-quoted mistrust of metanarratives (Lyotard, 1984a: xxiv) and is taken as a major characteristic of postmodernism by several of the contributors to this volume. The idea is that postmodernism lays down a major challenge to the universalising grand narratives of modernism. This challenge can be expressed in different ways. Shields (Chapter 2), for example, talks of the postmodern attention to spatiality allowing 'the many voices to break through the metanarrative of the total'. Bowers (Chapter 6) picks up the same image when he talks of postmodernism in the social sciences 'raising a multitude of local, hitherto silenced voices', and Rengger and Hoffman (Chapter 7) link this multiplicity of voices to the recognition of the 'nonexistence of ultimately objective discourse'. The full flavour of the challenge is, however, captured in the preface to a collection of essays on *The Unspeakable*:

They speak a language of resistance to all totalising ideologies that justify the repression of the common-sense world in the name of utopia, or seek to legitimize practice and judgement as the expression of theory. They deny that theory is the enabling condition for rational life, and they overturn the notion that knowing is the necessary means and precondition of doing, saying and feeling. They express the mood of postmodern sentiment.   (Tyler, 1987: Preface)

I quote this not for any deeper illumination but merely to illustrate that there are other aspects to the challenge than the one I am about to consider.

The challenge is to the *meta-*, the grand, the imperialist pretensions of modernism and it attacks the foundations of modernist intellectual life by denying those very foundations. Where the Enlightenment project gave modern conceptions of knowledge and truth a firm grounding in rationality, postmodernism aims to remove this grounding and to change these conceptions by denying a single truth, a single rationality. This is the kernel of Derrida's view of intertextuality. According to Derrida there is no transcendent logos which could privilege a particular reading of a text. Thus multiple readings become multiple truths in the absence of any overarching criteria to distinguish between them. This, like the radical deconstructionism in international relations mentioned by Rengger and Hoffman (Chapter 7), dispenses with foundationalism and embraces a reflexivity and self-referentiality which are alien to modernist thinking. (I say this *pace* Lash (Chapter 9) who introduces the spectre of another paradox much like that concerning fragmentation which I considered earlier.) The self-referentiality and the stand against metanarratives go hand in hand. The image of postmodernity so often presented in the literature is one of a whole series of inward-looking life-worlds or language-games with their local rationalities and truths.

At the same time proponents of postmodernism, like Jameson, wish to commend this image to other social scientists as a way of coming to understand what is happening in the world. The message that they convey goes something like this: Forget the scientistic monopolies of modernist social science – they were wrong, misguided; look at the world in all its cultural spheres and you will appreciate not only that it is changing, but that social scientists need new ways of seeing and understanding it. It is this message which, in itself, constitutes a paradox for it is a metanarrative warning against metanarratives, an attempt to remove the foundations of truth whilst balancing precariously upon them. This is rather like trying to remove the carpet from under your feet while you are still standing on it. Perhaps it can be done, but just how is not at all obvious at the present time.

In case the paradox is not yet clear, let me sharpen the focus a little. There are two closely related facets to the apparently contradictory claims that form the paradox. The first concerns metanarratives. Postmodernism rejects metanarratives like those which underpin modernism. Yet postmodernism, whether the term is used as an historical referent or to refer to a set of ideas, also appears to rely upon metanarrative. As Rée (1990) points out, it is a remarkable feature of writings on the postmodern that, despite the strong anti-Hegelian character of Foucault's work, Lyotard (1984a) is content to sketch a period style where all aspects of an age are joined – a celebration of Hegelian historicism which must surely epitomise the very totalising discourse that the postmodern condition is supposed to reject. Further (and this is the second facet of the paradox), the rejection of metanarratives at the heart of postmodernism introduces the relativism of 'many voices' which in turn confronts a basic logical problem – it is self-defeating. Having removed the metanarratives of truth and rationality, the postmodernist has no ground or transcendent standpoint from which to convince the sceptic of the rightness or truth of any postmodern view. The self-referential quality of local language games denies any such broader foundations which could establish the truth of claims outside the rules of particular language games. The claim that there are a number of such language games (or a number of different and incommensurable voices) must, by its very nature, stand outside any one of these language games and thus requires just the kind of metanarrative that the postmodern relativist wishes to deny. Lyotard has been justly criticised for offering an account of postmodernity as the eclipse of the grand narrative which is itself a grand narrative. Again this highlights the problems of relativism, problems which arise not only in the context of postmodernism but are also frequently raised as criticisms of anti-realism more generally in philosophy. The real danger of this sort of relativism, if Haldane (Chapter 10) is right, is that it is intellectually paralysing.

This worry surfaces in different forms in several commentaries on postmodernism, including those in this volume. In the social sciences it is most frequently represented in the claim that postmodernism is politically disenabling (see Parker, Chapter 4; Burman, Chapter 5; Doherty, 'Postmodern Horizons'). If there are no truths of oppression or inequality but rather multiple interpretations of the plights of minorities, all of which must, in some sense, be accepted, it is not difficult to see how political causes evaporate. Even everyday politics would have to change, for the usual democratic strategy of trying to demonstrate that political opponents are *wrong* would have to be abandoned. Under the tenets of postmodernism, they could simply be playing another language-game. In this context,

Parker (Chapter 4) makes an important distinction between being reflexive and being reflective. Reflexivity, often taken as one of the defining characteristics of postmodernism, dissolves our experiences into a plurality of perspectives, a perpetual reminder of the impossibility of truth. Reflection, on the other hand, can be part of an understanding of the world which is grounded in the assumption that truth may be discovered. With reflection, the notion of progress towards the truth makes sense. Reflexivity, in contrast, is turned in upon itself in an infinite spiral of contemplation. If reflexivity is a hallmark of postmodernity and reflection a feature of modernity, then modern ways of thinking are indeed difficult to give up.

Early writers amongst the literary intellectuals, like Irvine Howe in an essay published in 1959, recognised the difficulties involved in rejecting modernism. Howe himself was aware of an anti-intellectual undercurrent in postmodern literature and both he and, later, Daniel Bell (1973) (writing on post-industrial society) ultimately rejected postmodernism mainly because of its anti-intellectual traits. The writings of the last two decades have hardly assuaged those fears. From the triumphs of pop culture to the uncomfortable undermining of all truth claims in the social sciences, the espousal of postmodernism can be portrayed as nothing short of intellectual suicide. Even if there is an escape from the horns of the dilemma posed by Haldane (Chapter 10) and from his conclusion that a postmodern social science is a logical impossibility, it would still be apposite to ask, 'Can the intellectual be anti-intellectual?' In case anyone is inclined to treat that question lightly, let me rephrase it: 'Can those dedicated to the pursuit of truth and the exercise of reason at the same time deny their possibility or, *a priori*, circumscribe their operation?' If the contradiction suggested by these questions sticks, as Haldane thinks it must, then the confirmed postmodernist is no longer the intellectual but the entertainer, toying with light or colours or words. And the superficiality of the postmodern world is overwhelming.

Living with Paradox ...

The notion of 'the postmodern' in the social sciences is still far from clear. It is ironic that, whilst some writers note the anti-intellectual character of postmodernism, Bauman (1988b) suggests that the concept of postmodernity has value only in so far as it stands for the 'coming out' of intellectuals. Bauman does not doubt that there has been an implosion of intellectual vision but he recognises that this can be interpreted as either a symptom of hopelessness or as a sign of maturation. A route out of the hopelessness might be to reverse the implosion and resist the changes in the status and role of intellectual work which Bauman sees as the heart of the matter. This essentially means resisting the encroachment of a postmodern relativism in the social sciences. On the other hand, if Bauman is right, it is the indifference of politicians which has forced the change in the role of intellectuals and we must draw the conclusion that intellectuals have only limited influence over their own role and status in the wider society. Whatever powers to shape its own future we may suppose the intellectual community to have, it is clear that an analysis of this sort is painted on a broad canvas drawing attention to some of the most general features of contemporary intellectual life. Thus the account is, in itself, something of a metanarrative, a theory of the postmodern which sits ill with many of the features of postmodernism. We have not yet escaped from the grand narrative paradox discussed above.

For the moment, it seems, the social sciences will have to live with paradox. Postmodernism introduces many paradoxes, inconsistencies and ambiguities. There is much that could be said about these and this reflection has necessarily been both selective and partial. I have touched upon only three of the paradoxes which have left their trail through the papers in this volume, three paradoxes which it seems to me are charac-teristic of postmodern thought. None of these paradoxes is yet resolved for that was not the purpose of this endpiece. Rather, I wanted to demonstrate what is, or will be, at stake in their various resolutions. Above all I have tried to illustrate the implications or repercussions of rejecting certain ideas which have become associated with modernism; in particular, the Enlightenment idea of grounded truth and a certain conception of rationality. Burman (Chapter 5) accuses modernism of stigmatising the non-rational, and with some cause in the area of social psychology. But postmodernism runs the risk of being *anti*-rational and rendering any attempt at understanding pointless.

Finally, in the mine-field of postmodernism it is easy both to misunder-stand and to be misunderstood. Both 'modernism' and 'postmodernism' are complex and poorly defined concepts, at least as they are used in the social sciences. In pointing out the paradoxes of the latter, I am not committed to a wholesale acceptance of the former. In finding certain metanarratives essential to intellectual pursuits, for example, I am emphatically *not* claiming that there can be universal truths of human behaviour or that positivism provides the only secure epistemological base for the social sciences. Multiple methodologies require negotiation and raise many complex issues. The potential for such negotiation in the social sciences is still unclear, although Rengger and Hoffman (Chapter 7) believe that it is possible to reconstruct and reformulate a postmodern theory of international relations which draws on various critiques of mainstream theory. However, it is too early to equate methodological diversity of this sort with *postmodern* social science, even if Dow (Chapter 8) and others find it convenient to do so. Further, to be postmodern at the level of epistemology, methodology or theory is rather different from the study of postmodernism as a series of cultural phenomena. The creation of a work of art such as an aleatory painting is not essentially a rational activity but it is difficult to conceive of the analysis of that creation – if analysis is possible at all – as anything else. Fardon (Chapter 1) declares his faith in the anthropology of postmodernism but is doubtful about postmodern anthropology. It may be that to *do* anthropology, or any other social science, elements of modernist methodologies are essential. Analysis requires a conception of what it is to be rational and, as social scientists concerned with the analysis of social and cultural phenomena, we must seek some coherent conception of our own rationality and role in that analysis. The recognition of paradox can and should be an intellectual stimulus and not the end of the discussion, not the provocation of a destructive self-doubt. That is why postmodernism is so important, for it issues a major challenge to what have become our natural presumptions. The dimensions of that challenge are not always clear and, despite the volume of recent literature on the topic, the mainstream debate has hardly started. Thus the future is uncertain, for much depends upon the social scientist's experience of postmodernity. Clear analytical thinking (constructive self-doubt) is needed to make sense of this experience and care must be taken not to duck the difficult questions by hiding behind a pretext of 'many voices'. We must be equally careful, however, not to succumb to the temptation, noted by Smith (Chapter 3), to dismiss postmodernism as an escape route for bored intellectuals. The horizons of postmodernism in the social sciences are still hazy but one task is clear. It behoves us as social scientists to look for an answer to Haldane's (Chapter 10) question: 'Can we redescribe a postmodern social science that is not "just talk"?' If we are successful, then the projects of postmodernism will flourish and change the face of the social sciences. If we are not, then 'postmodern social science' will be stillborn. Whatever our answer, postmodernism is unlikely to leave the social sciences of the future untouched.

POSTMODERN POLITICS

Joe Doherty

The politics of postmodernism are not naïvely given. Politically, as intellectually and culturally, postmodernism in its attempts to transcend modernism, welcomes diversity, celebrates difference and applauds fragmentation. 'Chameleon-like', says Elizabeth Wilson (1990), 'postmodernism appeals to a wide range of political positions.' Hebdige (1989) goes further denying 'theories of the "post" ', as he puts it, any 'intrinsic political belonging'; and Alex Callinicos (1990), reflecting rather differently but in a related manner on the same theme, characterises postmodernism as an ideology without referent in the real world. The ambivalent politics of postmodernism coincide with a topsy-turvy world in which 'liberal' has become a term of abuse, green has become a symbol of health, radicals have become conservatives and conservatives, radicals. This slippage in political language reflects the political condition of postmodernity in which, for some individuals and recently for some societies, old certainties and categorisations have been questioned, long-held political allegiances jettisoned and new philosophies enthusiastically embraced.

As in other arenas, there is room for much debate and disagreement about the politics of postmodernism, for while postmodernism is part of the intellectual backdrop to this ferment of political change its direct and overt political impact has been uneven and often equivocal. For some, especially on the left, it has provided a cerebral justification for shifts in political allegiance, permitting, in the words of Seldon's (1990) acute but politically loaded appraisal, a withdrawal from Marxism with 'the maximum of political dignity and the minimum of intellectual contrition'. The impact of postmodernism on the political right has been less overt and less marked, reflecting perhaps the current political, economic and innovatory ascendency of the right on the international and many national stages, and the confidence in established political philosophies that that brings. While postmodernism is embraced, with alacrity by some and more cautiously by others, it is also rejected out of hand and ignored, largely because it is perceived as of marginal political relevance or as a distraction from more immediate material concerns. As Hudson (1989: 158) notes:

> Much of the current discussion is an in-house dialogue between Anglo-American and Franco-German philosophy and literary cultures, a dialogue in which having read Derrida or Heidegger or Wittgenstein or

Adorno is much more important than understanding the world economy or having experience of famine in Africa.

The lack of apparent tangible links between postmodernism and immediate political and social concerns is a matter of regret for some (Forbes, 1990) but explicable given postmodernism's often noetic and obtuse quality, its base in western cultural experience and its in-house, privileged language of discourse. It is at the level of ideas and philosophy rather than at the level of political strategy that postmodernism has made its most overt political mark. But political theory, as all protagonists in the postmodernist debate (whether embracing or rejecting) recognise, has practical import. Indeed, it is the very logic of the practice that is judged to emanate from the political implications of postmodernism that not infrequently determines the position taken with regard to postmodernism at large.

Postmodernism – The Negation of Politics?

The anti-universalism and celebration of difference that are among the hallmarks of postmodernism offer a challenge to all established political positions. Politics, particularly in its modernist versions, is an arena of conflict, where the privileging of respective positions is alternately asserted and challenged. Modern political practice requires policy, planning and strategy on the one hand to ensure adherence and conformity on the other – the formulation and dissemination of a political 'metanarrative'. Political success is judged by the degree to which such a 'metanarrative' is 'universalised' and opposition silenced. Postmodernism, in challenging the desirability or even the possibility of privileging one political perspective over others, negates much modern political practice; by denying the validity of the existence of universal values and ethics to which all political positions lay claim in the privileging process, postmodernism undermines the entire basis on which political privileging is constructed.

In some respects such a challenge would seem to open the arena for 'other' voices, to offer support for political minorities and clear the way for their entry and impact. But postmodernism in this interpretation proves a frail champion, for while celebrating the diversity that many voices bring, it (in the last instance) undermines the attempt of these others to privilege their position *vis-à-vis* established and competing political perspectives. One conclusion of such reasoning is political silence; is, at least in the conventional modernist sense, no political activity at all.

Indeed, this seems to be the fate of some of the early adherents of postmodernism such as Derrida, whose political silences are now regarded as symptomatic (Harvey, 1989: 118).

The negation of much modern political practice, however, does not depoliticise postmodernism; it is still claimed by both right and left (albeit often with equivocation and in apparently contradictory ways) variously as a support for enunciated positions or as a weapon with which to belabour opponents.

Postmodernism and the New Right

The evacuation of the horizon of universal value leads in the end to an irrationalist embrace of the agnostics of opposition – to . . . the adoption of the universal principle that might is right; of the sunny complacency of pragmatism, in which it is assumed that we can never ground our activities in ethical principles which have more force than just saying 'this is the sort of thing we do because it suits us' . . . this cultural analysis always risks falling into complicity with the increasing globalised forms which seek to harness, exploit and administer and therefore violently curtail . . . diversity.   (Connor, 1989: 243–4)

Connor's characterisation is of an unprincipled, amoral postmodern politics easily (perhaps too easily) associated with the individualistic, hedonistic, 'anything goes' yuppies of the libertarian right; of the 'greed is good' school of thought encapsulated by Michael Douglas in his portrayal of the evangelising financial tycoon in the film *Wall Street*. Yet, despite such cinematic representations, the occasional flirtation with postmodernism by right-wing philosophers (Scruton, 1990) and the association of some postmodernists such as Paul de Mann with Fascistic and anti-Semitic views, the link between postmodernism and the political right is largely one of implication rather than demonstrable celebration and adoption; we look in vain for a clear articulation of that 'postmodernism of reaction' which Foster (1983: x) claims to have identified. More typically, politicians and political philosophers of the right selectively associate themselves with postmodernism, most notably by adopting its anti-modernist perspective in the assertion of the 'verities of tradition', in which, 'pre and postmodern elements are elided and the humanist tradition preserved' (Foster, 1983: x). Others on the right have voiced outright hostility recognising in postmodernism an attack on all metanarratives, of the right as well as the left, potentially undermining the universalism and totalising discourse of the market as much as those of Marxism (Bell, 1973).

The alliance between the political right and postmodernism is more circumspect and the benefits more indirect than some have suggested. The diversionary potential of postmodernism identified by Hudson (quoted earlier), which seems to be a particular problem for the left, can serve to distract opposition from real world issues by encouraging a disproportionate engagement with questions of referentiality and representation, leaving the locus of power effectively unchallenged. Benefits for the right are also, arguably, to be found in the fragmentation of the left opposition which has accelerated under the influence of postmodernism. The cultivation of autonomous political activity in opposition to collective, unified action which follows from the postmodern denial of universal value and ethical referents, leads, as Connor argues, to the emergence of an 'agnostics of opposition'; an 'agnostics' in which potential opponents of the status quo succumb to a fatalistic political paralysis (Lovibond, 1989: 114) and are rendered ineffective. In negating politics, postmodernism not only immobilises opposition but, contrary to its own dictates, also opens the door to the metanarrative of 'might', to domination by those who hold the reins of power. In the present historical conjuncture, when retaining walls are pulled down and a market tide floods the East, such negation facilitates the triumphalism of the West and encourages claims about the resolution of ideological battles and the 'end of history' (Fukuyama, 1989).

Postmodernism and the New Left

The political left has engaged more directly with postmodernism, consequently the ramifications are more pronounced than on the right. The continuing international dispute and debate over the postmodernist and Marxist credentials of Jean Baudrillard illustrate the equivocal and divisionary impact of postmodernism on the political left. While Baudrillard is celebrated by some as a, perhaps the, postmodernist 'reinvigorator of marxism' (Kroker, 1988), others stress his anti-Marxist leanings and even challenge his postmodernist attachments (Kellner, 1989; Gane, 1990). While some engage seriously with Baudrillard's ideas (Wakefield, 1990), others are entirely dismissive, characterising him variously, from a feminist perspective, as the 'pimp' of postmodernism (Moore, 1988) and, from a revolutionary Marxist position, as indulging in 'intellectual dandyism' (Callinicos, 1990). These by no means exhaust the range of positions but serve to illustrate the multifarious responses from the left, not only to Baudrillard's work, but also to that on postmodernism at large. Some observers, in celebration of postmodernism's relevance, have identified an *a priori* case for a close alliance between postmodernism and the left, others have been more selectively welcoming, while yet others have rejected postmodernism as an irrelevancy and a distraction. The political outcome is a kaleidoscope of action, reaction and deactivation; of invigorated political practice, of hard-nosed resistance to change and of political paralysis.

The politically disabling effect of postmodernism has already been referred to. It is an effect which can be exaggerated, but one which has been most pronounced on the left, particularly among some of the original adherents of postmodernism. Harvey, in this context, selects as examples such men of the left as Derrida and Lyotard, and Wakefield would place the late Baudrillard in this category. Following through the logic of their postmodernism, which replaces dialectics and ethics with rhetoric and aesthetics and universalises the concept of difference while denying legitimacy to universal concepts of justice and liberty, they have, observes Harvey (1989: 117), become 'obsessed with deconstructing and deligitimating every from of argument they encounter', which ends in a self-condemnation of 'their own validity claims to the point where nothing remains of any basis for reasoned action'. Valuing logical principle over social imperative, unable to make judgemental statements or decisions, they have been disabled politically, retreating to 'a celebration of meaninglessness and a despairing assessment of the uselessness of all political action' (Wakefield, 1990: 8).

In contrast to this political paralysis, by far the most positive reaction to postmodernism on the left has come from a group of political commentators and activists, the so-called 'new timers', gathered round the journals *Marxism Today* and *Economy and Society* (Woodiwiss, 1990: 19); a position which, though not identical to, has much in common with a revisionist European communist stance led by Ernesto Laclau and Chantal Mouffe. These latter, self-styled, '*post-Marxists*' summarise their position thus:

> The discourse of radical democracy is no longer the discourse of the universal; the epistemological niche from which 'universal' classes and subjects spoke has been eradicated and it has been replaced by a polyphony of voices, each of which constructs its own irreducible discursive identity.   (Laclau and Mouffe, 1985: 191)

The tense of this statement is significant. Laclau and Mouffe are not giving expression to a political ambition; rather, they are reporting what is in their view an already existing reality in which the classical (read modernist) Marxist privileging of the working class as the subject of history, as the agent of social change, has effectively been challenged and in the vacated spaces a plurality of political voices has been raised each with an equal (superior in some contexts) claim to agency. For Laclau and Mouffe things should always have been thus; their work casts a critical and dismissive eye over Marxist politics from the Second International, challenging key concepts and using the emergence of new social movements and the work of Derrida and Foucault to support their case for 'radical democracy' against the notions of 'proletarian socialism'. In the work of the 'new timers', however, these developments are linked more explicitly with late twentieth-century changes in the organisation of capitalism; changes for which there are several categorisations: post-Fordism (Murray, 1989), flexible specialisation (Piore and Sabel, 1984) and 'disorganised' capitalism (Lash and Urry, 1987). Notwithstanding varying nuances of meaning, each of these categories reflects broadly similar developments consequent on deindustrialisation and the global-isation of capital. The changing material reality of late capitalism, in which it is claimed that capital has emancipated itself from labour (Bauman, 1987), coincides with the attack of postmodernism on the outmoded essentialism seen as inherent in classical Marxism; for the 'new timers' postmodernism is in this sense the political as well as 'the cultural logic of late capitalism' (Jameson, 1984).

The left opposition to postmodernism comes from a variety of sources: from Marxist aesthetes such as P. Anderson (1983), from what Woodiwiss (1990: 19) graphically labels 'no bullshit marxists' (Cohen, 1978; Elster, 1985), and from revolutionary Marxists (Callinicos, 1990). While the basis for opposition varies in detail from one group to another, they all take issue with the postmodern political philosophy of the 'new timers', and are particularly concerned with the consequences of postmodernism for political practice.

The political fissility of postmodernism is not welcomed by the left opposition: its pluralism and eclecticism, its apparent privileging of the individual and the local over the social and the global, the support it lends to autonomous political activity and its negation of collective praxis are seen as politically counterproductive and undermining of an effective assault on capitalism. Further, the replacement of socialism by concepts such as 'radical democracy' is seen as indicative of a tendency in postmodern politics to elide distinctions between the left and the political centre; the recent obsession of some on the British left with concepts of 'citizenship' and constitutional reform associated with a bill of rights (Charter 88) can be seen as symtomatic (Hall and Held, 1989; Osborne, 1989). Postmodern political practice leads to the fragmentation of the left on the one hand, and, on the other, to the decentring of political objectives in which socialist visions blur and eventually evaporate. In a very real sense, for the left opposition postmodernism is the negation of politics: the rejection of Enlightenment perspectives denies the possibility of ever formulating a unitary understanding of the world and, even more pessi-mistically, of ever bringing about fundamental change in society; postmodernism negates the objectives and the Utopian visions which have traditionally sustained left political activity. But the left opposition to postmodernism is more than a restatement of socialist objectives and a blanket dismissal of the legitimacy of postmodern politics. From the barri-cades of classical Marxism a counterattack is launched on postmodernism and its adherents. Two lines of attack are paramount: first, that post-modernism, in many accounts, presents a distorting caricature of classical Marxism and in practice brings little that is new to Marxism's on-going autocritique, and, secondly, that postmodernism is an ideology formulated and latched on to by former revolutionaries disillusioned by the defeat of a wave of working-class struggles through the late 1960s and the 1970s; defeats which have been aggravated during the 1980s. The merits of the first of these lines of argument are clearly supportable: Marxism has never been a dead or even dormant political philosophy, its history is replete with argument and schisms in which debate has raged round many of the issues with which postmodernism has attempted to beat Marxism: the primacy of class, the relative autonomy (or otherwise) of the political and the role of the state. The *ad hominem* arguments, attributing particular motivations to individuals, make the legitimacy of the second line of argument more debatable. But, for whatever reasons, the observed shifts in political leanings have taken place and, for many, past attachments are now conveniently ignored or even denied. Among left opponents (such as Callinicos, 1990), postmodernism is regarded as a defeatist – even a panic – ideology which presents a distorted picture of history and a selective and partial understanding of the present, its appeal explained by the turbulence and resulting uncertainty caused by the changing political and economic circumstances of late twentieth-century capitalism. In claiming a causal link between the realm of ideas and the material base, the left opposition thus reasserts its attachment to the basic tenets of historical materialism as the basis for disputing many of the claims of the 'new timers' and, more generally, for negating the political challenge of postmodernism.

CONCLUSION

The foregoing reflections on postmodern politics have revealed an uneven and complex pattern of activity and influence: claimed as avant-garde, characterised as neo-conservative, condemned as anarchy, postmodernism truly seems to lack 'any intrinsic political belonging' (Hebdige, 1989). Like a rudderless ship, postmodernism has been buffeted every which way by countervailing political currents. The churning that results has created discomfort not just for those on board but for all afloat in the vicinity. The least discomforted appear to be the 'new timers' among whom postmodernism has come closest to finding a political niche. Here, arguably, it has made a positive contribution to the politics of the left by facilitating the expression of 'other' voices, in heightening the political profile of culture and raising consciousness of the importance of consumption alongside production. But the emergent, cosy relationship blinds some to the gathering storm clouds. As Rowbotham (1989) among others has argued, modern left thinking 'lacks a theory of how to combine different sections of workers, different subordinated groups and differing organisational forms'. Postmodernism, whether in conjunction with 'new timers' or not, does little to assist in this task (Jameson and Hall, 1990). Indeed, in giving expression only to selected 'other' voices (where are the representatives of the Third World, the homeless and the emergent 'underclass'?; see Roberts and Seabrook, 1989), and in encouraging 'positional' politics, in which political identity is based solely on individual oppressed status, postmodernism fragments and undermines the emergence of a united politics of resistance. Devoid of an effective steering mechanism postmodernism is in danger of becoming locked into a vortex which can only lead to political oblivion. Without a well-charted course or a clearly identifiable destination, the political horizons of postmodernism remain obscure.

The political ambivalence of postmodernism, its schizoid character, simultaneously appealing to 'conservatives' and 'radicals', is an issue commented upon by many of the contributors to this volume. Within their limited briefs, the meanings attributed by these authors to terms such as 'conservative' and 'radical' frequently relate more to the degree of attachment to the intellectual traditions of a specific social science discipline than to an assessment of political orientation or political practice. Thus Haldane's scepticism (Chapter 10) relates almost exclusively to the intellectual contribution that postmodernism might make to the social sciences, and even in Fardon's (Chapter 1) more grounded, though equally sceptical, treatment the political remains tangential; others consider the politics of postmodernism less obliquely, but nevertheless perfunctorily (for example, Chapters 2, 7, 8 and 9 by Shields, Rengger and Hoffman, Dow, and Lash respectively). The remaining contributors, however, take up the political theme more explicitly: Burman (Chapter 5) and Parker (Chapter 4) clearly interpret the issue of intellectual change as an inherently political problem and join Smith (Chapter 3) and Bowers (Chapter 6) in considering the question of appropriate political practice. While all the authors who consider the politics of postmodernism are cautious about making categorical judgements (and in this respect a spirit of 'critical postmodernism' is apparent throughout), differences in interpretations are clearly demonstrated, though the absence of a representative of the political right – perhaps itself a reflection of the lack of attachment, noted earlier, of the political ideologies of the right to postmodernism – restricts the potential breadth of this diversity. But while the differences between authors is apparent, there is a more general point to be made and one which embraces all the contributors to this volume. Whether confining themselves to the intellectual realm or encompassing the political, the current concern of social scientists with postmodernism reflects their continuing attempts to come to grips, albeit from within their own disciplinary perspectives, with the turbulent social, political and economic changes which have accompanied late twentieth-century capitalism. Just as the economic crises of the late 1960s and early 1970s, and the failure of established paradigms to anticipate or produce a useful understanding of those crises, opened the door for the revival of Marxism as a source of understanding and explanation, so, it can be argued, the political crises of the 1980s have revealed the deficiencies of at least some versions of Marxism, as well as the continuing inadequacies of the paradigms of yesteryear, and have encouraged the search for alternative approaches to provide explanation. Whether postmodernism, in whatever guise, can provide in the 1990s quite the insights that, some have claimed, Marxism produced in the 1970s is still far from clear; but, as the authors of this volume have demonstrated, at the very least postmodernism has invited and stimulated debate and controversy, forcing many to revise, refine and even reject long-held certainties.

Bibliography

Adair, G. (1989) 'The low-lit world of the lager-yuppies', *Weekend Guardian*, 16–17 December, p. 40.

Adorno, T. A. (1973) *Negative Dialektik, Jargon der Eigentlichkeit* (Frankfurt: Suhrkamp) vol. 6.

Agnew, J. (1989) 'Sameness and difference: Hartshorne's *The Nature of Geography* and geography as a real variation', in J. N. Entrikin and S. Brunn (eds), *Reflections on Richard Hartshorne's 'The Nature of Geography'*; Occasional Publications of the Association of American Geographers (Washington, D.C.: AAG) 121–39.

Alker, H. R. and T. Biersteker (1984) 'The dialectics of world order: notes for a future archaeologist of international savoir fair', *International Studies Quarterly*, 28:2.

Anderson, B. (1983) *Imagined Communities* (London: Verso).

Anderson, J. (1973) 'Ideology and geography: an introduction', *Antipode* 5(3): 1–6.

Anderson, P. (1983) *In the Tracks of Historical Materialism* (London: Verso).

Anderson, P. (1984) 'Modernity and revolution', *New Left Review*, 144: 96–113.

Antaki, C. (ed.) (1988) *Analysing Everyday Explanation: A Case Book of Methods* (London: Sage).

Appleyard, D., (1970) 'Notes on urban perception and knowledge', in J. Archea and C. Eastman (eds) *EDRA 2: Proceedings of the Second Annual Environmental Design Research Association Conference* (Strodsburg, Pa.: Dowden, Hutchison & Ross) pp. 97–101.

Aquinas, St T. (1946) *Super Boethium de Trinitate*, trans. and ed. R. Brennan (St Louis, Mo.: Herder).

―――― (1967–75) *Summa Theologiae* (London: Eyre & Spottiswoode).

Ardener, E. (1974) 'Social anthropology and population', reprinted in Ardener (1989: 107–26).

―――― (1985) 'Social anthropology and the decline of modernism', reprinted in Ardener (1989: 191–210).

―――― (1987) '"Remote areas" – some theoretical considerations', reprinted in Ardener (1989: 211–23).

―――― (1989) *The Voice of Prophecy and Other Essays*, ed. Malcolm Chapman (Oxford: Basil Blackwell).

Ardener, S. (1983) *Women and Space* (Cambridge: Cambridge University Press).

Ashley, R. K. (1981) 'Political realism and human interests', *International Studies Quarterly*, 25: 2.

―――― (1983) 'The eye of power: the politics of world modelling', *International Organization*, 37: 4.

―――― (1984) 'The poverty of neorealism', *International Organization*, 38: 2.

―――― (1986) 'The poverty of neorealism', in Keohane (1986).

―――― (1987a) 'The geopolitics of geopolitical space: towards a critical social theory of international politics', *Alternatives*, 12: 4.

―――― (1987b) 'Living on border lines: man, poststructuralism and war', in der Derian and Shapiro (1987).

_____ (1988a) 'Untying the sovereign state: a double reading of the anarchy problematique', *Millenium*, 17: 2.

_____ (1988b) 'Genealogy, supplementary, criticism: a reply to Professors Roy and Walker', *Alternatives*, 13: 1.

Augustine, St (1968) *The City of God (Against the Pagans)*, trans. D. S. Weisen (Cambridge, Mass.: Harvard University Press).

Bachelard, G. (1958) *La Poétique de l'espace* (Paris: Presses Universitaires françaises).

Bailey, F. (1969) *Stratagems and Spoils: A Social Anthropology of Politics* (Oxford: Basil Blackwell).

Bakhtin, M. (1984) *Rabelais and his World*, trans. H. Iwolsky (Bloomington, Ind.: Indiana University Press).

Bal, M. (1985) *Narratology: Introduction to the Theory of the Narrative* (Toronto: University of Toronto Press).

Bandura, A., Ross, D. and Ross, S. (1963) '"Vicarious" reinforcement and imitative learning', *Journal of Abnormal Psychology*, 67: 601–7.

Banham, R. (1977) *America Deserta* (Berkeley, Cal.: University of California Press).

Banks, M. (1985) 'The inter-paradigm debate', in Light and Groom (1985).

Barnes, B. (1989) *The Nature of Power* (London: Macmillan).

Barrett, M. (1987) 'The concept of "difference"', *Feminist Review*, 26: 29–41.

Barth, F. (1966) *Models of Social Organization* (London: Royal Anthropological Institute).

Barthes, R. (1984) 'From "Work to Text"', in B. Wallis (ed.), A*rt after Modernism: Rethinking Representation* (New York: New Museum of Contemporary Art).

Barton, A. (1989) 'Investigation into the attitudes of children towards comics with regard to the particular comics read and the sex of subject', undergraduate project, Manchester Polytechnic.

Baudrillard, J. (1983a) *The Procession of Simulacra* (New York: Semiotexte).

_____ (1983b) *Simulations* (New York: Semiotext[e]).

_____ (1989) *America* (London: Verso).

Bauman, Z. (1987) 'Fighting the wrong shadow', *New Statesman*, 27 September: 20–2.

_____ (1988a) 'Sociology and postmodernity', *Sociological Review*, 36 (4): 790–813.

_____ (1988b) 'Is there a postmodern sociology?', *Theory, Culture and Society*, 5 (2/3): 217–37.

_____ (1988c) 'Strangers: the social construction of universality and particularity', *Telos*, 78: 1–42.

_____ (1990a) 'Squaring social theory with the real world', *The Times Higher Educational Supplement*, 21 September: 24.

_____ (1990b) *Modernity and Ambivalence* (Cambridge: Polity).

Baynes, K. *et al.* (eds) (1987) *Philosophy: End of Transformation?* (New York: MIT Press).

Beauregard, R. (1988) 'In the absence of practice: the locality research debate', *Antipode*, 20: 52–9.

Bell, Daniel (1973) *The Coming of Post-Industrial Society: A Venture in Social Forecasting* (New York: Basic Books).

Belloc, H. (1929) *Survivals and New Arrivals* (London: Sheed & Ward).
Benjamin, W. (1975) 'The work of art: the age of mechanical reproduction', in W. Benjamin (ed.), *Illuminations* (London: Fontana).
_____ (1978) 'Passagenwerke', in R. Tiedemann (ed.), *Gessamelte Schriften* (Frankfurt: Suhrkamp).
Bennett, A. (1910) *Clayhanger* (London: Methuen).
_____ (1911) *Hilda Lessways* (London: Methuen).
Benveniste, E. (1966) *Problèmes de linquistique générale*, vol. 1 (Paris: Gallimard).
Berger, J. (1974) *The Look of Things* (New York: Viking Press).
Berman, M. (1982) *All that is Solid Melts into Air: The Experience of Modernity* (New York: Simon & Schuster).
_____ (1983) 'The signs, the streets', *New Left Review*, 144: 114–23.
Berque, A. (1982) *Vivre l'espace au Japon* (Paris: PUF).
Billig, M., Condor, S., Edwards, D., Gane, M., Middleton, D. and Radley, A. (1988) *Ideological Dilemmas: A Social Psychology of Everyday Thinking* (London: Sage).
Blaug, M. (1980) *The Methodology of Economics* (Cambridge: Cambridge University Press).
Boland, L. A. (1982) *The Foundations of Economic Method* (London: George Allen & Unwin).
Bondi, L. (1990) 'Feminism, postmodernism and geography: space for women?', *Antipode*, 22(2): 156–67.
Borges, J. L. (1972) *A Universal History of Infamy* (New York: Dutton).
Bourdieu, P. (1971) 'The Berber house or the world reversed', in M. Douglas (ed.), *Rules and Meanings* (Harmondsworth, Middx: Penguin) 98–110.
_____ (1977) *Outline of a Theory of Practice*, trans. R. Nice (Cambridge, Mass.: MIT Press).
_____ (1979) *La Distinction* (Paris: Gallimard).
_____ (1984) *Distinction: A Social Critique of the Judgement of Taste* (Cambridge, Mass.: Harvard University Press).
_____ (1988) *Homo Academicus* (Cambridge: Polity).
Bowers, J. M. (1988) 'Essay review of "Discourse and Social Psychology"', *British Journal of Social Psychology*, 27: 185–92.
_____ (1990) 'All hail the great abstraction: Star Wars and the politics of cognitive psychology', in J. Shotter and I. Parker (eds), *Deconstructing Social Psychology* (London: Routledge).
Braudel, F. (1975) *The Perspective of the World: 15th to 18th Century* (New York: Harper & Row; reprinted 1985).
British Film Institute (1989) *Children and Television: What's Going On*, conference brochure, 3 March.
Buckingham, D. (1987) 'Children and television: an overview of the research paper', presented at the BFI Summer School *In Front of the Children*.
Bulkeley, R. and Spinardi, G. (1986) *Space weapons* (Cambridge: Polity).
Burgin, V. (1986) *The End of Art Theory* (London: Macmillan).
Burman, E. (1990) 'Differing with deconstruction: a feminist critique', in I. Parker and J. Shotter (eds), *Deconstructing Social Psychology* (London: Routledge).
Caldwell, B. J. (1982) *Beyond Positivism: Economic Methodology in the Twentieth Century* (London: Allen & Unwin).

_____ (ed.) (1984) *Appraisal and Criticism in Economics* (London: Allen & Unwin).

_____ (1989) 'Post-Keynesian methodology: an assessment', *Review of Political Economy*, 1 (March): 43–64.

Callinicos, A. (1985) 'Anthony Giddens: a contemporary critique', *Theory and society*, 14: 133–66.

_____ (1985) 'Postmodernism, poststructuralism and post-marxism?', *Theory, Culture and Society*, 2(3): 85–102.

_____ (1990) *Against Postmodernism: A Marxist Critique* (Cambridge: Polity).

Callon, M. (1986) 'Some elements of a sociology of translation: domestication of the scallops and the fishermen of St Brieuc Bay', in J. Law (ed.), *Power, Action and Belief: A New Sociology of Knowledge?* (London: Routledge & Kegan Paul) *Sociological Review* monograph, no. 32.

Carabelli, A. (1988) *On Keynes's Method* (London: Macmillan).

Carr, E. H. (1939) *The Twenty Years' Crisis* (London: Macmillan).

Catholic Truth Society (1979) *A Simple Prayer Book* (London: Catholic Truth Society).

Clarke Stewart, A. (1983) *Day Care* (London: Fontana).

Clifford, J. (1988) *The Predicament of Culture: Twentieth-Century Ethnography, Literature, and Art* (Cambridge, Mass.: Harvard University Press).

Clifford, J. and Marcus, G. (eds) (1986) *Writing Culture: The Poetics and Politics of Ethnography* (Berkeley, Cal.: University of California Press).

Coddington, A. (1976) 'Keynesian economics: the search for first principles', *Journal of Economic Literature*, 14: 1258–73.

Cohen, A. P. (1986) *Symbolizing Boundaries* (Manchester: Manchester University Press).

Cohen, G. A. (1978) *Marx's Theory of History* (London: Verso).

Cohen, S. (1972) *Folk Devils and Moral Panics* (London: MacGibbon & Kee).

Colander, D. C. and Klamer, A. (1987) 'The making of an economist', *Journal of Economic Perspective*, 1: 95–112.

Coleman, J. S. (1990) *Foundations of Social Theory* (Cambridge, Mass.: Harvard University Press).

Collins, J. (1987) 'Postmodernism and cultural practice: redefining the parameters', *Postmodern Screen*, 2: 11–26.

Colquhoun, A. (1984) 'Three kinds of historicism', *Oppositions*, 27: 28–39.

Connolly, W. (1987) 'Identity and difference in global politics', in der Derian and Shapiro (1987).

Connor, S. (1989) *Postmodernist Culture: An Introduction to Theories of the Contemporary* (Oxford: Basil Blackwell).

Cooke, P. (1987) 'Clinical inference and geographic theory', *Antipode*, 19: 69–78.

_____ (ed.) (1989) *Localities: The Changing Urban and Regional Structures* (London: Unwin Hyman).

Cox, K. and Mair, A. (1989) 'Levels of abstraction in locality studies', *Antipode* 21: 121–32.

Cox, R. W. (1986) 'Social forces, states and world orders: beyond international relations theory', *Millenium*, 10: 2; reprinted with Postscript in Keohane (1986).

Creed, B. (1987) 'From here to modernity: feminism and postmodernism', *Postmodern Screen*, 2: 47–67.

Culler, J. (1982) *On Deconstruction: Theory and Criticism after Structuralism* (Ithaca, N.Y.: Cornell University Press).

Davidson, D. (1984) 'On the very idea of conceptual scheme', in D. Davidson (ed.), *Inquiries into Truth and Interpretation* (Oxford: Oxford University Press).

_____ (1986) 'A coherence theory of truth and knowledge', in LePore (1986).

Davis, M. (1985) 'Urban renaissance and the spirit of postmodernism', *New Left Review*, 151: 106–14.

Dear, M. (1985) 'Postmodernism and planning', *Environment and Planning: Society and Space*, 4: 367–84.

_____ (1988) 'The postmodern challenge: reconstructing human geography', *Transactions of the Institute of British Geographers*, 13: 262–74.

de Certeau, M. (1988) *The Practice of Everyday Life* (Berkeley Cal.: University of California Press).

de Landa, M. (undated) 'Policing the spectrum', *Zone*, 1/2: 176–87

Deleuze, G. (1972) *Differences et repetition* (Paris: Presses universitaires françaises).

_____ (1980) *Mille Plateaux* (Paris: Éditions de Minuit).

_____ (1988) *Foucault* (Minneapolis, Minn.: University of Minnesota Press).

_____ and Guattari, F. (1976) *The Anti-Oedipus* (Paris: Éditions de Minuit).

_____ and _____ (1977) *Anti-Oedipus: Capitalism and Schizophrenia* (London: Viking Press).

_____ and _____ (1987) *A Thousand Plateaus* (Minneapolis, Minn.: University of Minnesota Press).

der Derian, J. (1987a) *On Diplomacy: A Genealogy of Western Estrangement* (Oxford: Basil Blackwell).

_____ (1987b) 'Spy vs spy: the international power of international intrigue', in der Derian and Shapiro (1987).

_____ (1987c) 'The boundaries of knowledge and power in international relations', in der Derian and Shapiro (1987).

_____ and Shapiro, M. (eds) (1989) *International/Intertextual Relations: Postmodern Readings of World Politics* (Lexington, Mass.: Lexington Books).

Derrida, J. (1976) *Of Grammatology* (Baltimore, Md.: Johns Hopkins University Press).

_____ (1980) *La Carte postal* (Paris: Flammarion).

_____ (1984) 'Of an apocalyptic tone adopted in recent philosophy', *Oxford Literary Review* 6(2): 96–107.

Deutsche, R. (1988) 'Uneven development: public art in New York City' *October*, 47: 8–52.

_____ (1990) 'Men in space', *Artforum* 29: 12–21.

Dews, P. (1987) *Logics of Disintegration: Post-structuralist Thought and the Claims of Critical Theory* (London: Verso).

_____ (1989) 'The return of the subject in late Foucault', *Radical Philosophy*, 51: 37–41.

Dickens, P. (1988) *One Nation?* (London: Pion).

di Stefano, G. (1990) 'Dilemmas of difference: feminism, difference and postmodernism', in L. J. Nicholson (ed.), *Feminism/Postmodernism* (New York: Routledge) 63–82.

Dow, S. C. (1985) *Macroeconomic Thought: A Methodological Approach* (Oxford: Basil Blackwell).

Drakopoulos, S. (forthcoming) 'Modern physics and mainstream economics', in *Essays in Honour of Professor L. Humanidis* (Piraeus: Piraeus School of International Studies).

Duncan, S. S. (1985) 'What is locality?', University of Sussex Working Papers, Urban and Regional Studies (Brighton: University of Sussex).

———— and Savage, M. (1989) 'Space, scale and locality', *Antipode*, 21: 179–206.

Durkheim, E. (1984) *The Division of Labor in Society*, trans. W. D. Halls (London: Macmillan); first published 1893.

———— and Mauss, M. (1963) *Primitive Classifications* (Chicago, Ill.: University of Chicago Press).

Dyer, H. and Mangessarian, L. (eds) (1989) *Study of International Relations: The State of the Art* (London: Macmillan).

Eagleton, T. (1983) *Literary Theory: An Introduction* (Oxford: Basil Blackwell).

———— (1985) 'Capitalism, modernism and postmodernism', *New Left Review*, 152: 60–73.

Eco, U. (1976) *A Theory of Semiotics* (Bloomington, Ind.: University of Indiana Press).

Eliot, T. S. (1922) *The Waste Land* (London: Faber & Faber).

Elshtain, J. B. (1987) *Women and War* (New York: Basic Books).

———— (1989) 'Feminist themes and international relations discourse', paper presented at the Joint ISA/BISA Conference, London.

Elster, J. (1985) *Making Sense of Marx* (Cambridge: Cambridge University Press).

Entrikin, J. N. (1989) 'Introduction: "The Nature of Geography" in perspective', in J. N. Entrikin and S. Brunn (eds), *Reflections on Richard Hartshorne's 'The Nature of Geography'*, occasional publication of the Association of American Geographers (Washington, D.C.: AAG) 1–15.

Fabian, J. (1983) *Time and the Other: How Anthropology Makes its Object* (New York: Columbia University Press).

Fardon, R. (ed.) (1990a) *Localizing Strategies: Regional Traditions of Ethnographic Writing* (Edinburgh: Scottish Academic Press).

Fardon, R. (1990b) 'Malinowski's precedent: the imagination of equality', *Man*, 25(4): forthcoming.

Featherstone, M. (1988) 'In pursuit of the postmodern: an introduction', *Theory, Culture and Society*, 5: 195–215.

Ferguson, I. and Mansbach R. (1987) *The Elusive Quest: Theory and International Politics* (Columbia, S.C.: University of South Carolina Press).

Fernandez, J. (1986) *Persuasions and Performances: The Play of Tropes in Culture* (Bloomington, Ind.: Indiana University Press).

Feyerabend, P. (1975) *Against Method* (London: New Left Books).

Firth, R. (1989) 'Fact and fiction in ethnography', in E. Tonkin *et al.* (1989).

Fish, S. (1980) *Is There a Text in this Class? The Authority of Interpretive Communities* (Cambridge, Mass.: Harvard University Press).

———— (1988) *Change, Rhetoric, and the Practice of Theory in Literary and Legal Studies* (Durham, N.C.: University of North Carolina Press).

Fitch, R. (1989) 'What's left to write? Media mavericks lose their touch', *Village Voice Literary Supplement*, May: 19.

Fitzgibbons, A. (1988) *Keynes's Vision: A New Political Economy* (Oxford: Clarendon Press).

Fodor, J. (1981) *Representations* (Brighton, Sussex: Harvester Press).

Folch-Serra, M. (1989) 'Geography and postmodernism: linking humanism and development studies', *Canadian Geographer*, 33: 66–75.

Forbes, D. (1990) 'Geography and development practice: a postmodern challenge', *Society and Space*, 8(2): 131–3.

Foster, H. (1983) *The Anti-Aesthetic* (San Francisco, Cal.: Bay Press).

Foucault, M. (1964) 'Language de l'espace', *Critique*, 203: 378–82.

_____ (1966) *Les Mots et les choses* (Paris: Gallimard).

_____ (1970a) 'History discourse and discontinuity', *Salmagundi*, 20: 225–48.

_____ (1970b) *The Order of Things* (New York: Random House).

_____ (1972) *The Archaeology of Knowledge*, trans. A. M. Sheridan Smith (New York: Colophon).

_____ (1973a) *Discipline and Punish* (London: Allen Lane). (See also Foucault, 1977a.)

_____ (1973b) *Moi, Pierre Rivière, ayant égorgé ma mère, ma soeur et mon frère. Un cas de parricide dans le dix-neuvième siècle* (Paris: Gallimard).

_____ (1975) *The Birth of the Clinic: An Archaeology of Medical Perception* (New York: Vintage–Random House).

_____ (1977a) *Discipline and Punish* (Harmondsworth, Middx: Penguin). (See also Foucault, 1973a.)

_____ (1977b) 'What is an author?' in M. Foucault (ed.), *Language, Counter-Memory, Practice* (Oxford: Basil Blackwell).

_____ (1979) *History of Sexuality*, vol. 1: *An Introduction* (London: Allen Lane).

_____ (1980a) 'Questions on geography', in Foucault, 1980d: 63–77.

_____ (1980b) 'Two lectures', in Foucault, 1980d: 78–108.

_____ (1980c) 'Truth and power', in Foucault, 1980d: 109–127.

_____ (1980d) *Power/Knowledge: Selected Interviews and Other Writings, 1972–1977* (Brighton, Sussex: Harvester Press).

_____ (1982a) 'Space, knowledge and power', in Hoy (1986: 239–56).

_____ (1982b) 'The subject and power', Afterword to H. Dreyfus and P. Rainbow (eds), *Michel Foucault: Beyond Structuralism and Hermeneutics* (Brighton, Sussex: Harvester Press).

_____ (1983) 'The subject and power', in ,H. Dreyfus and P. Rabinow (eds), *Michel Foucault: Beyond Structuralism and Hermeneutics* (Chicago, Ill.: University of Chicago Press).

_____ (1986) 'Of other spaces', *Diacritics*, 16: 22–7.

Frampton, K. (1983) 'Towards a critical regionalism: six points for an architecture of resistance', in H. Forster (ed.), *Postmodern Culture* (London: Pluto) 16–30.

Friedman, M. (1953) 'The methodology of positive economics', in M. Friedman (ed.), *Essays in Positive Economics* (Chicago, Ill.: Chicago University Press) 3–43.

Frisby, D. (1985) *Fragments of Modernity: Theories of Modernity – the Work of Simmel, Kracauer and Benjamin* (Cambridge: Polity).

Frosh, S. (1989) 'Melting into air: psychoanalysis and social experience', *Free Associations*, 16: 7–30.

Frost, M. (1985) *Towards a Normative International Theory* (Cambridge: Cambridge University Press).

Fukuyama, F. (1989) 'The End: Not with a Bang but a ?', *Guardian*, 4 November.

Gane, M. (1990) 'Ironies of postmodernism: fate of Baudrillard's fatalism', *Economy and Society*, 19(3): 314–33.

Gauld, A. O. and Shotter, J. (1977) *Human Action and its Psychological Investigation* (London: Routledge & Kegan Paul).

Geertz, C. (1966) *Person, Time, and Conduct Bali: An Essay of Cultural Analysis* (Detroit, Mich.: Yale University Press) Southeast Asia Studies, Cultural Report series no. 14.

_____ (1973) *The Interpretation of Cultures* (New York: Basic Books).

_____ (1980) 'Blurred genres: the refiguration of social thought', reprinted in Geertz (1983: 19–34).

_____ (1983) *Local Knowledge: Further Essays in Interpretive Anthropology* (New York: Basic Books).

_____ (1988) *Works and Lives: The Anthropologist as Author* (Cambridge: Polity).

Genette, G. (1980) *Narrative Discourse: An Essay in Method* (Ithaca, N.M.: Cornell University Press).

Giddens, A. (ed.) (1974) *Positivism and Sociology* (London: Heinemann).

_____ (1979) *Central Problems in Social Theory* (London: Macmillan).

_____ (1984) *The Constitution of Society* (London: Harper & Row).

Gilbert and George (1970) *To Be With is All We Ask* (London: Art for All).

Gilbert, G. N. and Mulkay, M. (1984) *Opening Pandora's Box: A Sociological Analysis of Scientists' Discourse* (Cambridge: Cambridge University Press).

Gilligan, C. (1982) *In a Different Voice: Psychological Theory and Women's Development* (Cambridge, Mass.: Harvard University Press).

Gittins, D. (1985) *The Family in Question: Changing Households and Familiar Ideologies* (London: Macmillan).

Gluckman, M. (1940) *Analysis of a Social Situation in Modern Zululand*, Rhodes-Livingstone Papers no. 8 (Cape Town: University of Cape Town).

Goffman, E. (1963) *Behaviour Public Places* (Glencoe, Ill.: Free Press).

_____ (1970) *Strategic Interaction* (Oxford: Basil Blackwell).

Gould, J. and White, R. (1974) *Mental Maps* (London: Penguin).

Graham, J. (1988) 'Post-modernism and Marxism', *Antipode*, 20: 60–6.

Grant, R. (1989) 'Feminist criteria in international relations theory: a survey of co-operation and critical thinking', paper presented at the Joint ISA/BISA Conference, London.

Gregory, D. (1984) 'Space, time and politics social theory: an interview with Anthony Giddens', *Environment and Planning. D: Society and Space*, 2: 123–32.

_____ and Urry, J. (1985) *Social Relations and Spatial Structures* (London: Macmillan).

Gregson, N. (1987) 'The CURS initiative: some further comments', *Antipode*, 19: 364–70.

Gross, D. (1981–2) 'Time, space and modern culture', *Telos*, 59–78.

Grunberg, I. (1991) 'The inter-text of international political economy', in Rengger and Hoffman (1991).

Guelke, L. (1978) 'Geography and logical positivism', in D. T. Herbert and R. J. Johnston (eds), *Geography and the Urban Environment. Progress Research and Applications*, vol. 1 (New York: John Wiley) 35–61.

Gunn, G. (1987) 'The semiotics of culture and the diagnosis of criticism: Clifford Geertz and the moral imagination', in G. Gunn (ed.), *The Culture of Criticism and the Criticism of Culture* (New York: Oxford University Press).

Habermas, J. (1981a) *Theorie des kommunikativen Handels*, vol. 1 (Frankfurt: Suhrkamp).
_____ (1981b) 'Modernity vs postmodernity', *New German Critique*, 22: 3–14.
_____ (1983) 'Modernity – an incomplete project', in H. Foster (ed.), *The Anti-Aesthetic. Essays on Postmodern Culture* (Port Towsend, Wash.: Bay Press) 3–15.
_____ (1985) *Der philosophische Diskurs der Moderne* (Frankfurt: Suhrkamp).
Hagihara, N. *et al.* (eds) (1985) *Experiencing the Twentieth Century* (London: University of Tokyo Press).
Hahn, F. H. (1983) *Money and Inflation* (Cambridge, Mass.: MIT Press).
Halbwachs, M. (1964) *Esquisse d'une psychgologie des classes sociales* (Paris: M. Rivière).
Haldane, J. (1985) 'Individuals and the theory of justice', *Ratio*, 27: 178–84.
_____ (1988a) 'Psychoanalysis, cognitive psychology and self-consciousness', in P. Clark and C. Wright (eds), *Mind, Psychoanalysis and Science* (Oxford: Basil Blackwell) 113–39.
_____ (1988b) 'The modernist fallacy: philosophy as art's undoing', *Journal of Applied Philosophy*, 5: 227–37.
_____ (1988c) 'Folk psychology and the explanation of human behaviour', *Proceedings of the Aristotelian Society*, Supplementary 62: 223–54.
_____ (1989a) 'Naturalism and the problem of intentionality', *Inquiry*, 32: 305–22.
_____ (1989b) 'Brentano's problem', *Grazer Philosophische Studien*, 34: 1–28.
_____ (1989c) 'Metaphysics in the philosophy of education', *Journal of Philosophy of Education*, 64: 161–83.
_____ (1990) 'Medieval and Renaissance ethics', in P. Singer (ed.), *A Companion to Ethics* (Oxford: Basil Blackwell).
_____ (forthcoming) 'Mind-world identity theory and the anti-realist challenge', in J. Haldane and C. Wright (eds), *Realism and Reason* (Oxford: Oxford University Press).
Hall, S. and Held, D. (1989) 'Citizens and citizenship', in S. Hall and M. Jacques (eds) *New Times* (London: Lawrence & Wishart) 173–90.
Hamelin, L.-E. (1980) *Nordicite Canadienne* (Montreal: Hurtubise HRH).
Hare-Mustin, R. T. and Marecek, J. (1988) 'The meaning of difference: gender theory, postmodernism and psychology', *American Psychologist*, 43(6): 455–64.
Harré, R. and Secord, P. F. (1972) *The Explanation of Social Behaviour* (Oxford: Basil Blackwell).
Hartshorne, R. (1961) *The Nature of Geography: A Critical Survey of Current Thought in the Light of the Past* (Lancaster, Pa: Association of American Geographers); first published 1939.
Harvey, D. (1973) *Social Justice and the City* (London: Edward Arnold).
_____ (1982) *Limits of Capital* (Baltimore, Md: Johns Hopkins University Press).
_____ (1987) 'Flexible accumulation through urbanisation: reflections on "postmodernism" in the American city', *Antipode* 19: 260–86.
_____ (1989) *The Condition of Postmodernity: An Enquiry into the Origins of Cultural Change* (Oxford: Basil Blackwell).
Hassan, I. (1985) 'The culture of postmodernism', *Theory, Culture and Society*, 2 (3): 119–31.
Heath, S. (1981) *Questions of Cinema* (London: Macmillan).

Hebdige, D. (1989) 'After the masses', *Marxism Today*, 33(1): 48–53
Heidegger, M. (1951) 'Building, dwelling, thinking', in M. Heidegger (ed.), *Poetry, Language, Thought* (London: Harper & Row) 143–62.
_____ (1962a) *Being and Time*, trans. J. Macquarrie and E. Robinson (New York: Harper & Row).
_____ (1962b) 'Appendix on Hegel's time and space', in Heidegger (1962a: 479–86).
Hennessy, J. M. (1989) 'Restructuring capitalism: the world catches takeover fever', *New York Times*, 21 May.
Henriques, J., Holloway, W., Urwin, C., Venn, C. and Walkerdine, V. (1984) *Changing the Subject: Psychology, Social Regulation and Subjectivity* (London: Methuen).
Herbert, A. P. (1934) *Holy Deadlock* (London: Methuen).
Hertel, A. (1971) *Baroque and Pictorial Imagery* (New York: Dover).
Hesse, M. (1980) *Revolutions and Reconstructions in the Philosophy of Science* (Brighton, Sussex: Harvester Press).
Hirst, P. (1982) 'The social theory of Anthony Giddens: a new syncretism?', *Theory, Culture and Society*, 1(2): 78–82.
Hobart, M. (1990) 'Who do you think we are? The authorized Balinese', in Fardon (1990a: 303–28).
Hodge, B. and Tripp, D. (1986) *Children and Television: A Semiotic Approach* (Cambridge: Polity).
Hoffman, M. (1987) 'Critical theory and the inter-paradigm debate', *Millenium*, 16: 2.
Hoffman, S. (1977) 'An American social science: international relations', *Daedalus*, 106: 3.
Hollis, M. and Smith, S. (1989) 'Roles and reason in foreign policy decision making', *British Journal of Political Science*, 16: 2.
_____ and _____ (1990) *Explaining and Understanding International Relations* (Oxford: Clarendon Press).
Holsti, J. K. (1985) *The Dividing Discipline* (London: Allen & Unwin).
Horvath, R. and Gibson, K. (1984) 'Abstraction in Marx's method', *Antipode*, 16: 12–25.
Howe, I. (1959) 'Mass society and postmodern fiction', *Partisan Review*, 26: 420–36; reprinted in I. Howe (1970), *The Decline of the New* (New York: Harcourt, Brace and World) 190–207.
Hoy, D. C. (ed.) (1986) *The Foucault Reader* (Oxford: Blackwell).
Hudnut, J. (1949) *Architecture and Spirit of Man* (Cambridge, Mass.: Harvard University Press).
Hudson, W. (1989) 'Postmodernity and contemporary social thought', in P. Lassan (ed.), *Politics and Social Theory* (London: Routledge) 142–60.
Hughes, T. (1979) 'The electrification of America: the system builder', *Technology and Culture*, 20(1): 124–62.
Huyssen, A. (1988) *After the Great Divide: Modernism, Mass Culture and Postmodernism* (London: Macmillan).
Ian, M. (1990) 'Two's company, three's a construction: psychoanalysis and the failure of identity', paper presented at the Rutgers University Center for Historical Analysis, 6 February.
Inden, R. B. (undated) 'Social scientific thinking or four (and more) ideas of human nature', mimeo.

Jameson, F. (1983) 'Postmodernism and consumer society', in H. Forster (ed.), *Postmodern Culture* (London: Pluto) 111–15.

_____ (1984) 'Postmodernism, or the cultural logic of late capitalism', *New Left Review*, 146: 53–92.

_____ (1986) 'Third-World literature in the era of multinational capitalism', *Social Text*, 15: 65–88.

_____ (1988a) 'The ideology of the text', in Jameson (1988d: 16–71).

_____ (1988b) 'Architecture and the critique of ideology', in his *The Ideologies of Theory*, vol. 2 (London: Routledge) 35–60.

_____ (1988C) 'Postmodernism and consumer society', in E. Ann Kaplan (ed.), *Postmodernism and its Discontents, Theories, Practices* (London: Verso) 13–29.

_____ (1988d) *The Ideologies of Theory*, vol. 1 (Minneapolis, Minn.: University of Minnesota Press).

_____ (1988e) 'Cognitive mapping', in C. Nelson and L. Grossberg, *Marxism and the Interpretation of Culture* (London: Macmillan).

_____ (1989) 'Marxism and postmodernism', *New Left Review*, 176: 31–45.

_____ and Hall, S. (1990) 'Clinging to the wreckage', *Marxism Today*, 34(9): 28–31.

Jencks, C. (1986) *What is post-modernism?* (New York: St Martin's Press).

Johnson-Laird, P. (1985) *Mental Models* (Cambridge: Cambridge University Press).

Kahn, J. (1989) 'Culture: demise or resurrection?', *Critique of Anthropology*, 9(2): 5–25.

Kant, E. (1968) 'Concerning the ultimate foundations of the differentiation of regions space', in *Selected Pre-Critical Writings*, selected by G. H. R. Parkinson; trans G. B. Kerferd and D. E. Walford; G. R. Lucas, contributor (Manchester: University of Manchester Press) xii–xvii.

Kaplan, E. A. (ed.) (1987) *Rocking Around the Clock: Music, Television, Postmodernism and Consumer Culture* (London: Methuen).

Karnoouh, C. (1986) 'The lost paradise of regionalism: the crisis of postmodernity in France', *Telos*, 67: 11–26.

Kearney, R. (1988) 'The crisis of the post-modern image', in A. Phillips Griffiths (ed.), *Contemporary French Philosophy* (Cambridge: Cambridge University Press).

Keely, J. F. (1990) 'Toward a Foucauldian analysis of regimes', *International Organisation*, 44: 1.

Kellner, D. (1989) *Jean Baudrillard, From Marxism to Postmodernism and Beyond* (Cambridge: Polity).

Kent, R. C. and Nielsson, G. P. (eds) (1980) *The Study and Teaching of International Relations* (London: Frances Pinter).

Keohane, R. O. (ed.) (1986) *Neorealism and its Critics* (New York: Columbia University Press).

Kern, S. (1983) *The Culture of Time and Space* (London: Weidenfeld & Nicolson).

King, A. (1983) 'Culture and the political economy of building form', *Habitat*, 7(5–6): 237–48.

Kirby, A. (1982) *The Politics of Location* (London: Methuen).

Klamer, A. (1987a) 'The advent of modernism', University of Iowa, mimeo.

_____ (1987b) 'New classical economics: a manifestation of late-modernism', University of Iowa, mimeo.

Knorr, K. and Rosenau, J. N. (eds) (1969) *Contending Approaches to International Politics* (Princeton, N.J.: Princeton University Press).

Kolaja, J. (1969) *Social System and Time and Space* (Pittsburgh, Pa: Duquesne University Press, and Louvain: editions E. Nauwlaerts).

Krier, L. (1978) 'The consumption of culture', *Oppositions*, 14: 54–9.

Kroeber, A. L. and Kluckhon, C. (1952) *Culture: A Critical Review of Concepts and Definitions* (Harvard, Mass.: Peabody Museum).

Kroker, A. (1988) 'Baudrillard's Marx', in Kroker and Cook (1988).

_____ and Cook, D. (1988) *The Postmodern Scene, Excremental Culture in an Age of Hyper-aesthetics* (Toronto: New World Perspectives, and London: Macmillan).

Kuhn, T. S. (1962) *The Structure of Scientific Revolutions* (Chicago, Ill.: Chicago University Press).

_____ (1970) 'Reflections on my critics', in I. Lakatos and A. Musgrave (eds), *Criticism and the Growth of Knowledge* (Cambridge: Cambridge University Press) 231–78.

Laclau, E. (1989) 'Politics and the limits of modernity', in A. Ross (ed.), *Universal Abandon: The Politics of Postmodernism* (Edinburgh: Edinburgh University Press) 63–82.

Laclau, E. and Mouffe, C. (1985) *Hegemony and Socialist Strategy* (London: Verso).

Lacoff, G. and Johnson, M. (1979) *Metaphors We Live By* (Chicago, Ill.: University of Chicago Press).

Lacoue Labarthes, P. (1986) 'On the sublime', in *Postmodernism* (London: Institute for Contemporary Arts) ICA documents no. 4.

Larmore, C. (1987) *Patterns of Moral Complexity* (Cambridge: Cambridge University Press).

Lash, S. (1988) 'Discourse of figure? Postmodernism as "regime of significance"', *Theory, Culture and Society*, 5 (2/3): 311–36.

_____ (1990) *Sociology of Postmodernism* (London: Routledge).

_____ (forthcoming) *Urban Imagery* (London: Routledge, Chapman, Hall).

_____ and Urry, J. (1987) *The End of Organized Capitalism* (Cambridge: Polity).

Latour, B. (1986) 'The powers of association', in J. Law (ed.), *Power, Action and Belief: A New Sociology of Knowledge?* (London: Routledge & Kegan Paul) Sociological Review monograph no. 32.

_____ (1987) *Science in Action: How to Follow Scientists and Engineers through Society* (Milton Keynes, Bucks: Open University Press).

Lavoie, D. (1990) 'Hermeneutics, subjectivity and the Lester/Machip debate', in W. J. Samuels (ed.) *Economics as Discourse* (Boston, Mass.: Kluwer) pp. 167–84.

Law, J. (1986) 'On the methods of long-distance control: vessels, navigation and the Portuguese route to India', in J. Law (ed.), *Power, Action and Belief: A New Sociology of Knowledge?* (London: Routledge & Kegan Paul), *Sociological Review* monograph no. 32.

Lawson, H. (1984) *Reflexivity: The Postmodern Predicament* (London: Hutchinson).

Leach, E. R. (1989) 'Tribal ethnography: past, present, future', in Tonkin *et al.* (1989: 34–47).

LeFaivre, M. (1987) 'Representing the city: Daniel Hudson Burnam and the making of an urban strategy', PhD dissertation, Department of Geography and Environmental Engineering, Johns Hopkins University.

Lefebvre, H. (1974) 'La production de l'espace', *Homme et la société*, 18: 15–32.
_____ (1976) *The Survival of Capitalism* (London: Allison & Busby).
_____ (1979) 'Space: social product and use value', in J. Freiberg (ed.), *Critical Sociology: European Perspectives* (New York: Irvington) 285–95.
_____ (1981) *La Production de l'espace*, 2nd edn (Paris: Anthropos).
_____ (forthcoming) *The Production of Space* (Oxford: Basil Blackwell).
Lehman, J. P. (1982) *Roots of Modern Japan* (London: Macmillan).
LePore, E. (ed.) (1986) *Truth and Interpretation: Perspectives on the Philosophy of Donald Davidson* (Oxford: Basil Blackwell).
Lévi-Strauss, C. (1966) *The Savage Mind* (London: Weidenfeld & Nicolson).
_____ (1969) *The Elementary Structures of Kinship*, trans. James Hawk Bell, John Richard von Strummer and Rodney Needham (Boston, Mass.: Beacon Books).
Ley, D. (1977) 'Social geography and the taken-for-granted world', *Transactions of the Institute of British Geographers*, N.S. 2(4): 498–512.
Light, M. and Groom, A. J. R. (eds) (1985) *International Relations: A Handbook of Current Theory* (London: Frances Printer).
Linklater, A. (1986) 'Realism, Marxism and critical international theory', *Review of International Studies*, 12: 3.
_____ (1990a) *Beyond Realism and Marxism: Critical Theory and International Relations* (London: Macmillan).
_____ (1990b) *Postscript: Men and Citizens in International Relations,* 2nd edn (London: Macmillan).
Little, R. (1980) 'The evolution of international relations as a social science', in Kent and Nielsson (1980).
Lovering, J. (1989) 'Postmodernism, Marxism and locality research: the contribution of critical realism to the debate', *Antipode*, 21: 1–12.
Livibond, S. (1989) 'Feminism and postmodernism', *New Left Review*, 178: 5–28.
Lowe, D. M. (1982) *History of Bourgeois Perception* (Chicago, Ill.: University of Chicago Press).
Luhmann, N. (1984) *The Differentiation of Society* (New York: Columbia University Press).
Lukács, G. (1971) *History and Class Consciousness*, trans. R. Livingstone (Cambridge, Mass: Harvard University Press).
Lumnis, T. (1982) 'The historical dimension of fatherhood: a case study, 1890–1914', in L. McKee and M. O'Brian (eds), *The Father Figure* (London: Tavistock).
Lynch, K. (1956) *The Image of the City* (Cambridge, Mass: MIT Press).
Lyotard, J.-F. (1973) *Derive à partir de Marx et Freud* (Paris: UGE).
_____ (1979a) *La Condition postmoderne* (Paris: Éditions de Minuit).
_____ (1979b) *The Postmodern Condition: A Report on Knowledge*, trans. G. Bennington and B. Massumi (Manchester: Manchester University Press).
_____ (1984a) *The Postmodern Condition: A Report on Knowledge* (Minneapolis, Minn.: University of Minnesota Press).
_____ (1984b) 'The differend, the referent and the proper name', *Diacritics*, special issue on Lyotard (Minneapolis, Minn.: University of Minnesota Press).
_____ (1989) 'Defining the postmodern', in L. Appignanesi (ed.), *Postmodernism: ICA Documents* (London: Free Association Books) 7–10.
McCloskey, D. N. (1983) 'The rhetoric of economics', *Journal of Economic Literature*, 21: 481–517.

_____ (1986) The *Rhetoric of Economics* (Brighton, Sussex: Wheatsheaf).

_____ (1989) 'The very idea of epistemology: a comment on "Standards"', *Economics and Philosophy*, 5: 1–6.

MacIntyre, A. (1981) *After Virtue* (London: Duckworth).

_____ (1988) *Whose Justice? Which Rationality?* (London: Duckworth).

McKee, L. (1982) 'Father's participation in infant care: a critique', in L. McKee and M. O'Brian (eds), *The Father Figure* (London: Tavistock).

McNamara, T. (1986) 'Mental representations of spatial relations', *Cognitive Psychology*, 18: 87–121.

Maffesoli, M. (1988) *Le Temps de tribus* (Paris: Meridiens-Klinksieck).

Mair, A., Florida, R. and Kenney, M. (forthcoming) 'The new geography of automobile production: Japanese transplants in North America', *Economic Geography*.

Malkan, J. (1987) 'Against theory, pragmatism and deconstruction', *Telos*, 71: 129–54.

Margolis, J. (1989) 'Postscript on modernism and postmodernism, both', *Theory, Culture and Society*, 6: 5–30.

Martin, G. (1989) *Journey through the Labyrinth: Latin American Fiction in the Twentieth Century* (London: Verso).

Marx, K. (1973) *Grundrisse* (Harmondsworth, Middx: Penguin).

Massey, D. (1984) *Spatial Divisions of Labour: Social Structures and the Geography of Production* (New York: Methuen).

_____ (1985) 'New directions in space', in D. Gregory and J. Urry (eds), *Social Relations and Spatial Structures* (London: Macmillan) 10–19.

Mercer, K. (1988) 'The boy who fell to earth', *Marxism Today*, July: 35–7.

Merquior, J. G. (1986) *From Prague to Paris: A Critique of Structuralist and Post-Structuralist Thought* (London: Verso).

Messenger Davies, M. (1989) *Television is Good for Your Kids* (London: Hilary).

Meyer, J. (1988) 'Mies van der Rohe', in F. Zimmermann (ed.), *Der Schrei nach dem Turmhaus* (Berlin: Bauhaus-Archiv) 106–11.

Meyrowitz, J. (1985) *No Sense of Place* (London: Oxford University Press).

Miller, D. (1987) *Material Culture and Mass Consumption* (Oxford: Basil Blackwell).

Mills, C. (1988) 'Life on the upslope: the postmodern landscape of gentrification', *Environment and Planning. D: Society and Space*, 6: 169–89.

Mintz, S. W. and Wolf, E. R. (1989) 'Reply to Michael Taussig', *Critique of Anthropology*, 9(1): 25–31.

Mirowski, P. (1984) 'Physics and the marginalist revolution', *Cambridge Journal of Economics*, 8: 361–80.

Montag, W. (1988) 'What is at stake in the debate on postmodernism?' in E. A. Kaplan (ed.), *Postmodernism and its Discontents: Theories, Practices* (London: Verso) 88–104.

Moore, S. (1988) 'Getting a bit of the other – the pimps of postmodernism', in R. Chapman and J. Rutherford (eds), *Male Order: Unwrapping Masculinity* (London: Lawrence & Wishart).

Morgenthau, H. (1973) *Politics among Nations* (New York: Alfred Knopf).

Mulkay, M. (1985) *The Word and the World: Explorations in the Form of Sociological Analysis* (London: George Allen & Unwin).

Murphy, J. W. (1988) 'Making sense of postmodern sociology', *British Journal of Sociology*, 39(4): 600–14.

Murray, R. (1989) 'Fordism and Post-Fordism', in S. Hall and M. Jacques (eds), *New Times: The Changing Face of Politics in the 1990s* (London: Lawrence & Wishart) 38–53.

Nash, D. and Wintrob, R. (1972) 'The emergence of self-consciousness in ethnography', *Current Anthropology*, 13(5): 527–42.

Nash, N. (1986) 'Mending financial safety net', *New York Times*, 7 October.

Needham, R. (1971) 'Introduction', in R. Needham (ed.), *Rethinking Kinship and Marriage* (London: Tavistock) xiii–cxvii.

_____ (1973) *Right and Left: Essays on Dual Symbolic Classification* (Chicago, Ill.: University of Chicago Press).

_____ (1981) *Circumstantial Deliveries* (Berkeley, Cal.: University of California Press).

Nicolaides, P. (1988) 'Limits to the expansion of neoclassical economics', *Cambridge Journal of Economics*, 12: 312–28.

Norris, C. (1989) 'Reading Donald Davidson: truth, meaning and right interpretation', in R. Schusterman (ed.), *Analytic Aesthetics* (Oxford: Basil Blackwell).

Onuf, N. (1990) *World of our Making: Rules and Rule in Social Theory and International Relations* (Durham, S.C.: University of South Carolina Press).

Osborne, P. (1989) 'Extension of liberty: what Charter 88 leaves out', *Interlink*, Feb/March: 22–3.

Owens, C. (1985) 'The discourse of others: feminists and postmodernism', in H. Foster (ed.), *Postmodern Culture* (London: Pluto Press).

Pace, D. (1983) *Claude Lévi-Strauss: The Bearer of Ashes* (London: Routledge).

Panofsky, E. (1960) *Renaissance and Renascences in Western Art* (Stockholm: Almqvist & Wiksell).

Parke, R. (1981) *Fathering* (London: Fontana).

Parker, I. (1988) 'Deconstructing accounts', in C. Antaki (ed.), *Analyzing Everyday explanation: A Casebook of Methods* (London: Sage).

_____ (1989a) *The Crisis of Modern Social Psychology, and How to End It* (London: Routledge).

_____ (1989b) 'Discourse and power', in J. Shotter and K. J. Gergen (eds), *Texts of Identity* (London: Sage).

_____ (1990) 'Discourse: definitions and contradictions', *Philosophical Psychology*, 3(2): 189–204.

_____ and Shotter, J. (eds) (1990) *Deconstructing Social Psychology* (London: Routledge).

Parkin, D. (ed.) (1982) *Semantic Anthropology* (London: Academic Press).

Parnas, D. (1985) *Software Aspects of Strategic Defense Systems* (University of Victoria, British Columbia, Canada) Department of Computer Science research report DCS-47-IR.

Peacock, J. (1986) 'Barchester Towers in Appalachia: negotiated meaning', in P. P. Chock and J. R. Wyman (eds), *Discourse and the Social Life of Meaning* (Washington, D.C.: Smithsonian Institution Press) 127–45.

Phoenix, A. (1987) 'Developmental psychology: children and television', paper presented at the British Film Institute Summer School *In Front of the Children*, May

Piaget, J. (1933) 'Social evolution and the new education', *Education Tomorrow*, 4: 3–25.

_____ (1957) 'The child and modern physics', *Scientific American*, 197: 46–51.

_____ (1969) *The Child's Conception of Time* (London: Routledge & Kegan Paul); first published 1946.

_____ (1977) 'Biology and war', in H. Gruber and J. Voneche (eds), *The Essential Piaget: An Interpretive Reference and Guide* (London: Routledge & Kegan Paul); first published 1918.

_____ (1982) *The Child's Conception of the World* (London: Paladin); first published 1929.

Piore, M. and Sabel C., (1984) *The Second Industrial Divide* (New York: Basic Books).

Pocock, D. and Hudson, R. (1978) *Images of the Urban Environment* (London: Macmillan).

Podgorecki, A. (1975) *Practical Social Sciences* (London: Routledge & Kegan Paul).

Polan, D. (1988) 'Postmodernism and critical analysis today', in E. Ann Kaplan (ed.), *Postmodernism and its Discontents. Theories, Practices* (London: Verso) 45–58.

Popper, K. (1970) 'Normal science and its dangers', in I. Lakatos and A. Musgrave (eds) *Criticisms and the Growth of Knowledge* (Cambridge: Cambridge University Press) 51–8.

Potter, J. (1987) 'Reading repertoires: a preliminary study of some techniques that scientists use to construct readings', *Science and Technology Studies*, 15 (3/4): 112–21.

_____ (1988a) 'What is reflexive about discourse analysis? The case of reading readings', in S. Woolgar (ed.), *Knowledge and Reflexivity: New Frontiers in the Sociology of Knowledge* (London: Sage).

_____ (1988b) 'Cutting cakes: a study of physiologists' social categorizations', *Philosophical Psychology*, 1: 17–33.

_____ and Wetherell, M. (1987) *Discourse and Social Psychology: Beyond Attitudes and Behaviour* (London: Sage).

Probyn, E. (1989) 'Travels in the postmodern: making sense of the local', in L.J. Nicholson (ed.), *Feminism/Postmodernism* (New York: Routledge) 176–89.

Quine, W. V. O. (1961) 'Two dogmas of empiricism', in Quine, *From a Logical Point of View* (New York: Harper & Row).

Radhakrishnan, R. (1989) 'Poststructuralist politics: towards a theory of coalition', in D. Kellner (ed.), *Postmodernism: Jameson Critique* (Washington, D.C.: Maisonneuve Press) 301–32.

Rée, J. (1990) 'Dedicated followers of fashion', *The Times Higher Education Supplement*, 25 May: 15, 17.

Reichlin, B. (1988) 'L'Esprit de Paris', *Archt*, 90/91: 47–58.

Reiss, T. J. (1982) *The Discourse of Modernism* (Ithaca. N.Y.: Cornell University Press).

Rengger, N. J. (1988) 'Serpents and doves in classical international theory', *Millenium*, 17: 2.

_____ and Hoffman, M. (eds) (1991) *Beyond Inter-Paradigm Debate: Critical Theory and International Relations* (Brighton, Sussex: Wheatsheaf).

_____ and _____ (forthcoming) *International Relations Theory: A Re-interpretation and Restructuring* (Aldershot: Edward Elgar).

Rich, A. (1986) *Blood, Bread and Poetry: Selected Prose, 1979–1985* (New York: W. M. Norton).

Ricoeur, P. (1973) 'The task of hermeneutics', *Philosophy Today*, 17(2–4): 112–28.

Riley, D. (1983) *War in the Nursery: Theories of Child and Mother* (London: Virago).

Roberts, Y. and Seabrook, J. (1989) 'Meet the new times', *New Statesman and Society*, 27 October: 14–15.

Robinson, R. and Lechiner, F. (1983) 'Modernisation, globalisation and the problem of culture world systems theory', *Theory, Culture and Society*, 2(3): 103–17.

Root, M. (1986) 'Davidson and social science', in LePore (1986).

Rorty, R. (1980) *Philosophy and the Mirror of Nature* (Oxford: Basil Blackwell).

————— (1986) 'Pragmatism, Davidson and truth', in LePore (1986).

————— (1989) *Contingency, Irony and Solidarity* (Cambridge: Cambridge University Press).

Rose, N. (1985) *The Psychological Complex* (London: Routledge & Kegan Paul).

Rosenau, J. (1990) *Turbulence in World Politics* (Brighton, Sussex: Wheatsheaf).

Ross, K. (1988) *The Emergence of Social Space: Rimbaud and the Paris Commune* (Minneapolis, Minn.: University of Minnesota Press).

Rotman, B. (1977) *Piaget: Psychologist of the Real* (Brighton, Sussex: Harvester Press).

Rowbotham, S. (1989) Editorial, *Interlink*, 11: 5–6.

Russell, G. (1987) 'Problems in role-reversed families', in C. Lewis and M. O'Brian (eds), *Reassessing Fatherhood* (London: Sage).

Rustin, M. (1989) 'Post-Kleinian psychoanalysis and the postmodern', *New Left Review*, 173: 109–28.

Sack, R. D. (1980) *Conceptions of Space Social Thought* (Minneapolis, Minn.: University of Minnesota Press).

————— (1989) '*The Nature* in light of the present', in J. N. Entrikin and S. Brunn (eds), *Reflections on Richard Hartshorne's 'The Nature of Geography'*, Occasional Publication of the Association of American Geographers (Washington D.C.: AAG) 141–62.

Saïd, E. (1978) *Orientalism* (New York: Viking).

Sampson, E. E. (1978) 'The deconstruction of the self', in J. Shotter and K. J. Gergen (eds), *Texts of Identity* (London: Sage).

Sandler, S. and Kelly, J. (1988) *The Woman who Works, the Parent who Cares* (New York: Bantam Press).

Saunders, P. (1985) *Social Theory and the Urban Question*, 2nd edn (London: Hutchinson).

Saussure, F. de (1974) *Course in General Linguistics* (London: Fontana).

Savage, M., Barlow, J., Duncan, S. and Saunders, P. (1987) 'Locality research: the Sussex programme on economic restructuring, social change and locality', *Quarterly Journal of Social Affairs*, 3(1): 27–51.

Sayer, A. (1985) 'The difference that space makes', in Gregory and Urry (1985): 49–66).

————— (1989) 'The new regional geography and problems of narrative', *Environment and Planning. D: Society and Space*, 7: 253–76.

Sayers, J. (1986) *Sexual Contradiction* (London: Tavistock).

Scholte, J. (forthcoming) *International Relations on World Historical Sociology* (Milton Keynes, Bucks: Open University Press).

Schön, D. A. (1983) *The Reflective Practitioner* (New York: Basic Books).

Schorske, C. (1981) *Fin-de-siècle Vienna* (New York: Vintage).

Schulte-Sasse, J. (1987) 'Introduction: Modernity and modernism, post-modernity and postmodernism: facing the issues', *Cultural Critique* (special issue): 5–12.

Scott, A. (1986) 'High technology industry and territorial development: the rise of the Orange County complex, 1955–1984', *Urban Geography*, 7: 3–43.

_____ (1988) 'Flexible accumulation and regional development: the rise of new industrial spaces in North America and Western Europe', *International Journal of Urban and Regional Research*, 12: 171–86.

Scruton, R. (1990) *The Philosopher on the Dover Beach* (London: Carcanet).

Seamon, D. (1979) *A Geography of the Lifeworld* (New York: St Martin's Press).

Seddon, D. (ed.) (1978) *Relations of Production: Marxist Approaches to Economic Anthropology* (London: Frank Cass).

Seldon, A. (1990) *Capitalism* (Oxford: Basil Blackwell).

Sellars, W. (1963) 'Empiricism and the philosophy of mind', in Sellars, *Science Perception and Reality* (London: Routledge & Kegan Paul).

Sennett, R. (1976) *The Fall of a Public Man* (Cambridge: Cambridge University Press).

Shallice, T. (1984) 'Psychology and social control', *Cognition*, 17: 29–48.

Shapiro, M. (1987) 'Representing world politics: the sport/war inter-text', in der Derian and Shapiro (1987).

Shields, R. (1986) *Towards a Theory of Social Spatialisation: Henri Lefebvre, the Question of Space and the Postmodern Hypothesis'*, MA Thesis, Department of Sociology and Anthropology, Carleton University, Ottawa, Canada.

_____ (1989) 'Social spatialisation and the built environment: the case of the West Edmonton mall', *Society and Space*, 7(2): 147–64.

_____ (1990) *Places on the Margin: Alternative Geographies of Modernity* (London: Routledge, Chapman, Hall).

Shotter, J. (1987a) 'The ephemeral "I": transitory personalities in an era of postmodernism', paper for American Psychological Association conference, New York.

_____ (1987b) 'Cognitive psychology, "Taylorism", and the manufacture of unemployment', in A. Costall and A. Still (eds), *Cognitive Psychology in Question* (Brighton, Sussex: Harvester Press).

_____ and Gergen, K. J. (eds) (1989) *Texts of Identity* (London: Sage).

_____ and Parker, I. (eds) (1990) *Deconstructing Social Psychology* (London: Routledge).

Simon, H. (1981) 'What computers mean for man and society', in T. Forrester (ed.), *The Microelectronics Revolution* (Cambridge, Mass.: MIT Press).

Sivanandan, A. (1989) 'All that melts into air is solid: the hokum of New Times', *Race and Class*, 31(3): 1–30.

Smith, N. (1987) 'Dangers of the empirical turn', *Antipode*, 19: 59–68.

_____ (1989) 'Geography as museum: private history and conservative idealism in *The Nature of Geography*', in J. N. Entrikin and S. Brunn (eds), *Reflections on Richard Hartshorne's 'The Nature of Geography'*, Occasional Publication of the Association of American Geographers (Washington D.C.: AAG) 89–120.

_____ (1990) *Uneven Development: Nature, Capital and the Production of Space*, 2nd edn (Oxford: Basil Blackwell).

———— and Dennis Ward (1987) 'The restructuring of geographical scale: coalescence and fragmentation of the northern core region', *Economic Geography*, 63: 160–82.

Sohn-Rethel, A. (1978) *Intellectual and Manual Labour: A Critique of Epistemology* (London: Macmillan).

Soja, E. (1980) 'The socio-spatial dialectic', *Annals of the American Association of Geographers*, 70(2): 207–25.

———— (1988) 'Postmodern geographies: the three restructurings', paper presented at Rutgers University, February.

———— (1989) *Postmodern Geographies: The Reassertion of Space in Critical Social Theory* (London: Verso).

Sorokin, P. A. (1943) *Sociocultural Casaulity, Space, Time* (Durham N.C.: Duke University Press).

Southwold, M. (1978) 'Buddhism and the definition of religion', *Man*, 13: 362–79.

Spivak, G. C. (1988) 'Can the subaltern speak?', in C. Nelson and L. Grossberg (eds), *Marxism and the Interpretation of Culture* (Urbana, Ill.: University of Illinois Press) 271–313.

Stallybrass, P. and White, A. (1986) *The Poetics and Politics of Transformation* (Brighton, Sussex: Harvester Press).

Steiner, G. (1989) *Real Presences* (London: Faber & Faber).

Stern, R. (1980) 'The double of postmodernism', *Harvard Architectural Review*, 1: 75–88.

Stoller, P. (1986) 'The reconstruction of ethnography', in P. P. Chock and J. R. Wyman (eds) *Discourse and the Social Life of Meaning* (Washington, D.C.: Smithsonian Institution Press) 51–74.

———— and Olkes, C. (1987) *In Sorcery's Shadow: A Memoir of Apprenticeship among the Songhay of Niger* (Chicago, Ill.: Chicago University Press).

Strathern, M. (1987) 'Out of context: the persuasive fictions of anthropology', *Current Anthropology*, 28(3): 251–81.

———— (1988) *The Gender of the Gift: Problems with Women and Problems with Society in Melanesia* (Berkeley, Cal.: University of California Press).

Suganami, H. (1977) 'The peace through law approach', in Taylor (1977).

———— (1989) *The Domestic Analogy and World Order Proposals* (Cambridge: Cambridge University Press).

———— (1990) 'Bringing order to the causes of war debates', *Millennium: Journal of International Studies*, 19: 1.

Sullivan, E. (1977) 'A study of Kohlberg's structural theory of moral development: a critique of liberal social science ideology', *Human Development*, 20: 352–75.

Sylvester, C. (forthcoming) *Feminist Theory and International Relations in Postmodern Era* (Cambridge: Cambridge University Press).

Taylor, T. (ed.). (1977) *Approaches and Theory in International Relations* (London: Longmans).

Therborn, G. (1971) 'Jürgen Habermas: "A New Eclecticism"', *New Left Review*, 67: 69–83.

Thiher, A. (1984) *Words in Reflection: Modern Language Theory and Postmodern Fiction* (London: University of Chicago Press).

Thompson, E. P. (1967) 'Time, work-discipline and industrial capitalism', *Past and Present*, 38: 56–96.

_____ and Thompson, B. (1985) *Star Wars: Self-destruct Incorporated* (London: Merlin).

Thompson, G. (1955) *The First Philosophers* (London: Lawrence & Wishart).

Tolman, E. C. (1948) 'Cognitive maps in rats and men', *Psychological Review*, 55: 189–208.

Tonkin, E., McDonald, M. and Chapman M. (eds) (1989) *History and Ethnicity* (London: Routledge).

Toynbee, A. (1956) *Historians Approach to Religion* (New York: Oxford University Press).

Tuan, Y.–F. (1974) *Topophilia: A Study of Environmental Perception, Attitudes and Values* (Englewood Cliffs, N.J.: Prentice-Hall).

Turing, A. M. (1950) 'Computing machinery and intelligence', *Mind*, 59: 433–60.

Turner, V. W. (1968) *The Drums of Affliction: A Study of Religious Processes among the Ndembu of Zambia* (London: International African Institute).

_____ (1979) *Process, Performance and Pilgrimage* (New Delhi: Concept).

Tyler, S. A. (1987) *The Unspeakable: Discourse, Dialogue and Rhetoric in the Postmodern World* (Madison, Wis.: University of Wisconsin Press).

Unger, R. (1987a) *Social Theory: Its Situation and its Tasks* (Cambridge: Cambridge University Press).

_____ (1987b) *False Necessity* (Cambridge: Cambridge University Press).

_____ (1987c) *Plasticity into Power* (Cambridge: Cambridge University Press).

Urry, J. (1982) 'Duality of structure: some critical issues', *Theory, Culture and Society*, 1(2): 101–6.

_____ (1988) 'Cultural change and contemporary holiday-making', *Theory, Culture and Society*, 5: 35–55.

Urwin, C. (1986) 'Developmental psychology and psychoanalysis: splitting the difference', in M. Richards and P. Light (eds), *Children of Social Worlds* (Cambridge: Polity Press).

Valsiner, J. (1988) *Culture and the Theory of Human Action* (Chichester: John Wiley).

van Paassen, C. (1957) *The Classical Tradition of Geography* (Groningen: J. B. Wolters).

van Gennep, A. (1960) *The Rites of Passage*, trans. M. B. Vizedom and G. L. Caffee (Chicago, Ill.: University of Chicago Press).

Venn, C. and Walkerdine, V. (1978) 'The acquisition and production of knowledge: Piaget's theory reconsidered', *Ideology and Consciousness*, 3: 67–94.

Venturi, R. and Scott-Brown, D. (1980) Interview, *Harvard Architectural Review*, 1: 228–39.

Voice Literary Supplement (1989) 12 December.

Wakefield, N. (1990) *Postmodernism: The Twilight of the Real* (London: Pluto).

Walker, R. B. J. (1984a) 'World politics and western reason: universalism, pluralism, hegemony', in Walker (1984b).

_____ (ed.) (1984b) *Culture, Identity and World Order* (Boulder, Col. Westview Press).

_____ (1987a) 'Realism, change and international political theory', *International Studies Quarterly*, 31: 1.

_____ (1987b) 'The prince and the pauper', in der Derian and Shapiro (1987).

_____ (1988) *One World/Many Worlds* (Boulder, Col.: Lynne Reinner).

_____ (1990) 'Rationalisation processes and international history: a critical theory, post-structuralism and international relations', in Rengger and Hoffman (1990).

Walkerdine, V. (1984) 'Developmental psychology and the child-centred pedagogy: the insertion of Piaget into early education', in Henriques *et al.* (1984).

Waltz, K. (1979) *Theory of International Politics* (Reading, MA: Addison-Wesley).

Weaver, O. (1989) 'Beyond the beyond of critical theory', paper presented at Joint ISA/BISA Conference, London.

Wendt, A. (1987) 'The agent–structure problem in international relation theory', *International Organization*, 41: 3.

Williams, R. (1989) 'When was modernism?', *New Left Review*, 175: 48–52.

Wilson, E. (1990) 'The postmodern chameleon', *New Left Review*, 180: 187–90.

Windsor, P. (1985) 'The twentieth century on self-conscious history', in Hagihara *et al.* (1985).

_____ (1987) Introduction, *Millenium: Journal of International Studies*, special issue on the Study of International Relations, 16(2); reprinted in Dyer and Mangessarian (1989).

Winn, M. (1977) *The Plug-in Drug* (New York: Viking).

Wittgenstein, L. (1953) *Philosophical Investigations* (Oxford: Basil Blackwell).

Woodiwiss, A. (1990) *Social Theory after Postmodernism: Rethinking Production, Law and Class* (London: Pluto).

Woolgar, S. (1988) *Science: The Very Idea* (Chichester, Sussex: Ellis Horwood, and London: Tavistock).

Wright, J. K. (1947) 'Terrae incognitae: the place of imagination geography', *Annals of the American Association of Geographers*, 37: 1–15.

Wright, P. (1985) *On Living in an Old Country: The National Past in Contemporary Britain* (London: Verso).

Zavala, I. M. (1988) 'On the (mis-)uses of post-modern: Hispanic modernism revisited', in C.O. D'haen and H. Bertens (eds), *Postmodern Fiction in Europe and the Americas* (Amsterdam: Rodopi) 83–113.

Zukin, S. (1988) *Loft Living* (London: Radius).

_____ (1990) *American Market/Place: Landscapes of Economic Power* (Berkeley, Cal.: University of California Press).

Index